A Calf In The Kitchen

Echoes from a Ranch Woman

by Elizabeth Gumbel Vorenberg

*To Bob Kelley
with best wishes!
Elizabeth G. Vorenberg*

Edited by Bonnie L. Vorenberg
Book Design by Julie Meyer
Cover Design by Patrick Burke

ArtAge
Publications
∞

ArtAge Publications
Portland, Oregon

10   9   8   7   6   5   4   3

Published in the United States of America by ArtAge Publications, P.O. Box 12271, Portland OR 97212-0271.

Printed in the United States of America

Library of Congress Card Number: 00-192134

Library of Congress Cataloging-in-Publication Data
Vorenberg, Elizabeth Gumbel
        A Calf in the Kitchen: Echoes from a Ranch Women / Elizabeth Gumbel Vorenberg--
        1st ed.
        ISBN 0-9669412-1-7
        1. Ranch life--Colorado
        2. Biography
        3. Title
978.8   B-V   2000

DEDICATION

This book is dedicated to my wonderful family, without whom there would have been no story to tell.

My husband, Fred, was my teacher, my constant source of support while our children, Tom, Bonnie, Susan and Jack proved to be the kind of people of whom anyone would be proud.

Were it not for my family's enthusiastic mantra, these accounts would never have found their way into print.

The names mentioned within the various chapters are in part correct while others are fictitious. I appreciate the Ranchland News, the Gazette Telegraph and other newspapers for use of their clippings in this book. The individual stories are all truthful, candid, and sincere.

TABLE OF CONTENTS

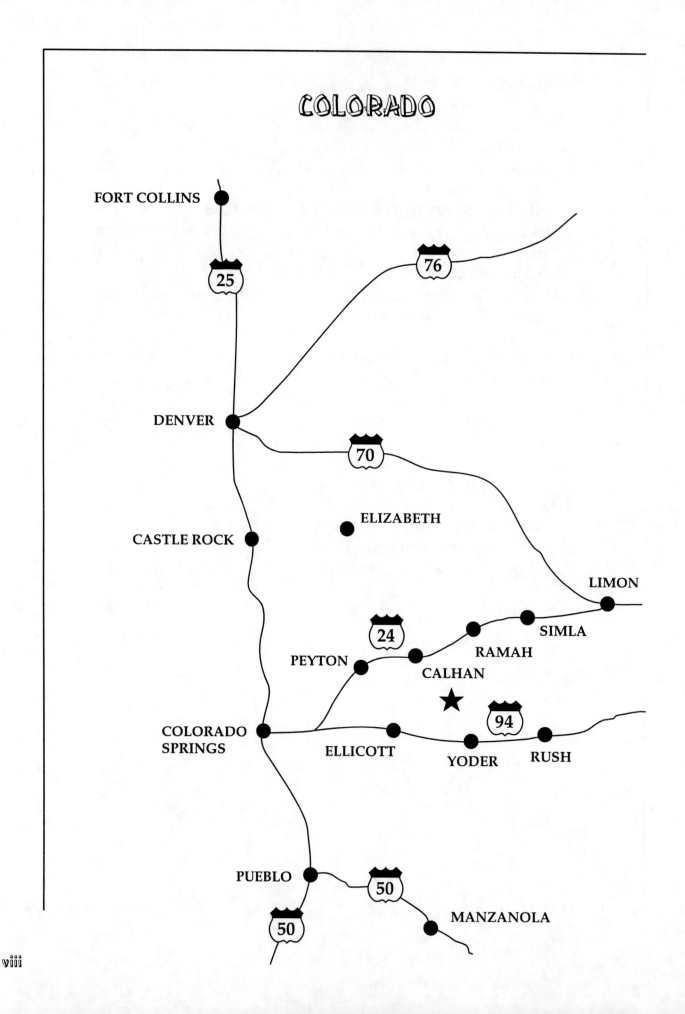

COLORADO

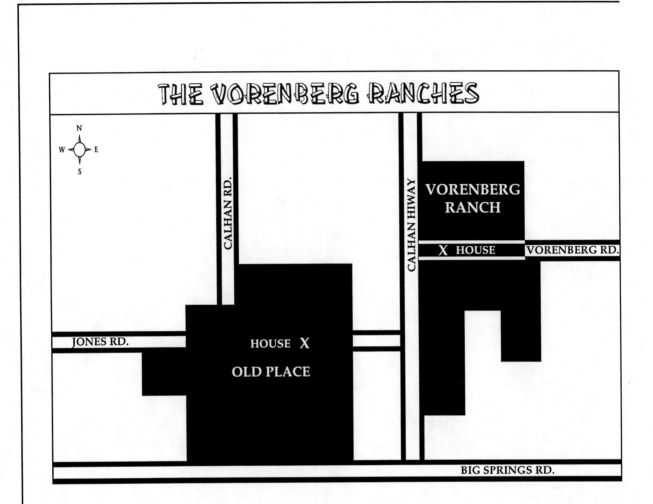

INTRODUCTION

Every day for thirty-seven years, my husband and I wrote in diaries, recording experiences, both expected and unexpected on our cattle ranch. They remain indelible in our mind, never to be blotted out. For me, a transplanted city girl and a former immigrant, living on a ranch was a complete turnabout. Of course, I always loved animals but that was not enough. Country living is so much more. There was so much to learn, so much to do, and so much TO DO WITHOUT. But for me, the transition to a rural life-style became a completely fulfilling experience.

This book will hopefully touch those who have lived on a ranch, those who dream of living on one, and for city-slickers who have never even seen a cow! To protect the privacy of many people mentioned in the book, I changed some of the names, but it was impossible to dilute the color of their character.

Fred and I chose a lifetime occupation in which we were efficient and one which we also enjoyed but, unfortunately, one which did not produce considerable financial rewards. Yet, though our lifestyle was relatively simple, we never considered ourselves poor. Indeed we felt rich—we appreciated our children whom we adored, we loved our relatives and friends, and respected our colorful neighbors. More importantly, ranching was in our blood and we were able to fulfill our dream.

For me, added satisfaction came from the many animals, not only the dogs I loved, but all the creatures who became my special friends. There is nothing better than a little gosling looking up to you as a 'Mother Goose' or lambs wanting to snuggle close just to be near you. Even chickens would beg to sit on my lap and crowd together making soft, contented music, their eyes closed, their bodies completely relaxed.

Caring for newborn calves in the warm kitchen was nothing extraordinary when a blizzard was howling outdoors. Their survival depended on being warm and dry, along with many bottles of warm milk guzzled when they stayed with us 'overnight'. It all gave them an extra boost along with plenty of comfort. We were a highly recommended motel by the bovine community!

Most city folks believe that ranch life must be wonderful, filled with fresh air, beautiful scenery, contented cows and peaceful living. In fact, there are many disappointments such as money problems, miserable weather conditions, uncooperative bureaucracy, and the many near disasters created when humans and animals come into close contact. To contrast, we had the strength, cheerfulness and optimism of the entire family who joined in the adventure and helped us achieve our goals.

We learned from experience and just when we thought we knew it all, Mother Nature would throw us another curve. And it was time to tackle the latest problem. "Accept what cannot be changed, and nurture it", has always been my motto.

Ranching is an adventure. The bulls didn't always think of us as 'neat' people, the cows with new calves didn't appreciate us being too close to their babies, and the hens enjoyed pecking at our hands while we were trying to retrieve their newly laid eggs. The geese became our watchdogs, honking whenever someone would drive up and finding delight in chasing anyone on foot. So, I ask, "Who's the boss on the ranch?" Certainly, not the rancher!

Our family looks back upon these years on the ranch with love and fondness. It was priceless.

Chapter 1

THE EARLY YEARS

Who I Am

In 1933 when Hitler came into power in Germany, the lives of Jewish people began to change drastically. A different, cool attitude was displayed toward anyone who was Jewish. The atmosphere quickly became so harsh and severe that we felt concerned about our future in our country. For most families, money became a problem because any kind of work or profession became extremely restricted. Wealthy families were suddenly forced to live a different lifestyle. Unfortunately, large numbers of non-Jewish people throughout the country started to believe the hateful propaganda constantly emitted by the Nazi regime. Many Jewish families began thinking that they might have to leave the land where their ancestors had been content for generations.

My parents, Joseph and Melanie Gumbel, lived in Worms, a small town in Germany, where my father founded and operated a large flour mill. There were four children: Max, Anne, Martin and I, Elizabeth, the youngest. I was born on April 6, 1920. Two years later, the family moved to Bad Homburg, a picturesque town filled with spas, near the beautiful Taunus mountains, just north of Frankfurt. It was to these woods where my father took the children on daylong excursions, often on Sundays. Other times, we would go to the valleys where farmers planted their grain in the rich, black soil. Dad would then explain the difference between rye, wheat, and other grains and all about flour and how it is processed.

My education went smoothly. Foreign languages were my best subjects while math and sewing were my least. Though swimming and ice skating were some of my favorite activities, I spent a great deal of time being the goalie for the neighborhood boys who asked me to be on their land hockey team. The only girl! Besides sports, I already had a special feeling for any kind of animal. My mother, who was afraid of dogs, never allowed us to own one but all the mutts in town, who would run at will, knew me and we were the best of friends!

Suddenly, I felt Hitler's influence when all the other Jewish students and I were expelled from their schools. So at age 15, in 1935, we moved to Frankfurt where I entered a Jewish Home Economics School. Later, in 1938, after spending a couple of years working as a maid in Duesseldorf, the Nazis ordered what became known as Kristallnacht, the 'Night of the Broken Glass.' At 11 PM, storm troopers entered, uninvitedly, almost every Jewish home and destroyed whatever they could. They went into the streets and set fires to synagogues throughout Germany. To add insult to injury, the local firemen were ordered to stand watch so the fires only burned the intended religious buildings. In one short night, the political climate had exploded beyond our wildest imagination.

We knew we had to act. Our survival depended on us leaving Germany as soon as

3

possible. Overnight, we found out that in order to immigrate to another country we needed to secure a quota number. My father was alert enough to get one in the 9,000 range for all of us. We were lucky because within a day or two the numbers had jumped to 40,000-50,000. We hoped to leave Germany relatively soon.

It was a worrisome time. Each of us left the country immediately after our passports were issued. Max left in 1933; Anne in 1937; my parents, Martin and I in 1939. Max travelled to Switzerland, France, Spanish and French Morocco and, eventually to New Orleans in 1940. Anne went straight to New York where she found employment. My parents, Martin and I ended up in London, England where we awaited our visa to the U.S.A. Just four weeks after our arrival, the war started between Germany and England.

During my nine months in London, I worked in a nursery and home for unwed mothers. The Matron took a liking to me and spoiled me. I needed that because I was extremely timid and shy. It was with relief, and a lot of luck, that we boarded a Cunard White Star Line Ship, the "Brittanic" for America—the last ship to leave England before the Blitzkrieg over London started. In order to avoid torpedoes, we spent the first days zig-zagging across the ocean. Though dangerous, we felt safer than we did in either Germany or England.

We landed in New York and distant cousins, one of whom was Dr. W. Levy, helped us settle in New Orleans. He secured for me a 3-year Nursing scholarship at the 350-bed hospital, Touro Infirmary. Indeed, a new world was opening up to me, so fast, so sweet and I was ready to absorb it all.

My New World

My parents and I were settling down in the interesting city of New Orleans surrounded by warm-hearted and easy-going neighbors. I answered an ad for a nanny and was employed there until I entered Toro Infirmary, School of Nursing on September 23, 1943—a day I will never forget. Thirty-five 'preliminaries' were assigned, two to a room, in the basement of the Nurses Dorm. The accommodations were very stark with only two beds, a table, a couple of chairs, and two closets with locks. We were told to come for a physical examination that afternoon at 1 PM, dressed in only a bra and panties under our robes. But I owned no robe. Frantically, I raced to the streetcar on St. Charles Avenue, paid my seven-cent fare, and headed for Maison Blanche, a major department store on Canal Street. I bought a blue and white seersucker robe with short sleeves for $3 and was back in time for the physical.

After two or three weeks, a girl approached me asking whether I was from Mississippi because I reminded her of someone. She was a beautiful, bright 18-year old, with

Rosalind

strawberry blond hair, freckles on her fair skin, an inch taller than I was and full of ideas, many of which seemed a bit weird to me. It was the beginning of my friendship with Rosalind.

In no time at all, Rosalind and I became roommates. She was as neat as a pin and we even received a first place 'Tidiest and Prettiest Room' Award. When she was a senior in high school she had gone to Mexico and bought many articles such as vases, a colorful tablecloth, and a ceramic chili with which she used to decorate our room. In addition, her mother gave us a sweet potato plant which, as it grew, delighted our senses. Not owning many clothes, she offered me hers and it was the green corduroy dress that quickly became my favorite—wearing it on many occasions. She took me under her wing and even corrected my poor English, for which I was immensely grateful. Rosalind taught me the American way of life which included shaving my legs and under my arms as well as how to do my hair. I was so fortunate to have found her—rather, that she found me!

One day she told me excitedly how she met a boy whom she thought I would like and she had even made a date for me. This was how I met my first love, Walt.

Walt and I had wonderful times together. We went to many concerts in City Park and played records, all classical music. After he discovered that I had never eaten a steak, he began introducing me to many new foods and took me to all sorts of restaurants, including Laffite's in the French Quarter. But, it was wartime and Walt was going to be shipped out. Before he left, he confided in me that he was engaged which, of course, put a damper on our relationship. Even so, I missed him terribly. I never heard from him again.

Later, Rosalind and I worked on the same hospital wing, A-2, an area reserved for Norwegian sailors. There were two big wards, one with six beds, the other with four. The sailors were a happy bunch who seemed to enjoy being sick and surrounded by young nurses. All the beds had curtains which could be drawn for privacy. Years later, Rosalind confided in me that one time after smoothly and carefully pulling the curtain, she kissed one of the sailors! It was on A-2 where she taught me how to flirt. She was a good teacher and...I excelled!

Once, Rosalind and I enticed the two most handsome sailors, Anders and Soderland, to leave the hospital to see what the French Quarter was like after dark. She borrowed her father's car and we picked up our sailor friends around 8 PM, unbeknownst to the head nurse on duty. The French Quarter was alive and noisy. We went into several bars, lured in by trumpet music and loud laughter, and ended the evening at the 'Puppy House'. There, we enjoyed a Rum and Coca-Cola and danced close together on an area no larger than 12 X 12 feet.

Suddenly a roaring, laughing and applauding noise erupted from behind us as a scantily dressed lady appeared. I judged her to be about forty-ish. Her shoulder length hair was straight and as black as coal. She was a bit on the plump side but oh—could she wiggle! And then it happened...Urged on by the music, she started to disrobe, one item at a time which she carelessly flung onto the floor in front of her.

This proved to be too much for our young sailors. Anders, Rosalind's date, blushed so severely I was afraid he would pass out. It came as no surprise when he suggested that we should leave.

It was time to start watching the clock anyway as we had to have the guys back in bed before the night shift made their rounds and found them missing. By 11 PM we pulled up in front of Touro, let the happy-go-lucky Norwegians out of the car to make their way to the ward on their own. Luckily, they had not been missed. Though the hospital was lenient and gave them freedom to meander around the grounds, they certainly never expected patients to leave the building and go dancing! Their broken bones mended and illnesses cured, Anders and Soderland returned to their duties on the high seas while a new bunch of patients appeared with the usual variety of problems and the same willingness to share our charms. I would have given anything to hear those guys telling their friends about all those wild American nurses!

Rosalind had many boyfriends. She dated a lot but there was one special boy, a medical student named Joffe. One day during our senior year, they sneaked off and 'tied the knot'——breaking the rule that no student nurse could be married while in training. We kept it a secret so the Director of Nursing, Miss Ingram, would not expel Rosalind for the violation.

Time went on. Rosalind and I graduated, passed State Board Exams, and worked as R.N.s in different hospitals. It was years before we saw each other again. Rosalind came to our ranch two times, once with her father and another time with her husband, Joffe, and three of her children. Those were special and delightful times. We went sightseeing to the Garden of the Gods and the Royal Gorge. But most of the time we reminisced while the children got along famously. They were special days indeed, remembering the 'old' days, our many laughs, and the daring escapades we shared. Both visits were much too short and we promised to do it more often.

But it was not to be. It was years before I visited her in New Orleans. Things had changed. Joffe and two of her children had died and she was living in a small apartment in a senior complex. But I was pleased that my good friend was content and happy.

I never had an easy time making friends, but Rosalind made it comfortable for me. Her friendliness reached out and I was able to accept and appreciate her thoughtfulness and hopefully, return her kindness in full. Most importantly, she introduced me to the true 'American spirit.' Indeed, she was a class act! I felt like I was the luckiest person on earth. I doubted if people born in the U.S.A. were as deeply aware of their good fortune as I was. As an immigrant, I appreciated my new life, every day, to the fullest! 🐎

Public Health Class. Front row in uniform: 2nd is Me, Elizabeth, and 3rd is Rosalind.

The Operating Room

The operating room was always my favorite department in the hospital. Every day would bring with it new experiences and I would undergo new emotions. It seemed like a whole new world was evolving around me. It was not always tense in those six rooms at Touro. There was one surgeon, for example, who used to sing arias from the opera Carmen while operating on tonsils! Another one sent a brand new student nurse for a 'sterile Fallopian tube,' an often-used trick on a novice! The very strict supervisor never failed to mention that instruments cannot be 'a little sterile', just like a student nurse couldn't be a 'little pregnant'.

I especially enjoyed working with a group of doctors one of whom was a famous chest surgeon. He had been to Frankfurt, Germany and he used to tease, calling me 'Schnickelfritz!' One time during an operation, I happened to look outside and noticed something strange on top of the building across the street. "Yes indeed, those are monkeys. They are Rhesus and we are studying the RH factor", was the doctor's explanation. We all went back to work!

Meanwhile, World War II had broken out and Tulane University had sent a group of doctors to North Africa. I was in charge of Minor Surgery, which was located on the first floor of the hospital. Another nurse and I were heading towards the cafeteria when I noticed Dr. DeBakey with whom I had worked often when I was a student. Since I hadn't seen him in a while I exclaimed loud enough for him to hear, "There's Dr. DeBakey!"

"You are the only person who knows me around here!" He immediately walked towards me and kissed me on the cheek. I felt flattered. Dr. DeBakey has since become known worldwide as The heart surgeon. He still works at Baylor College in Houston, Texas. I felt immensely privileged and honored to have known and worked with this great man.

So, went my first few years in a new country—one I had never planned to see or live in.

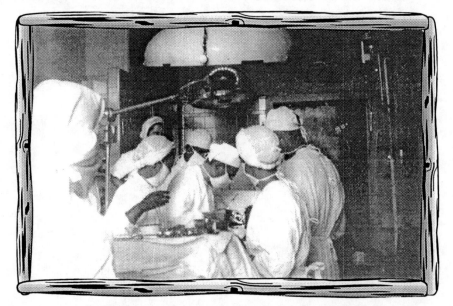

In my element, the operating room, with Dr. Oschsner.

Colorado, My New State

My family and I moved to Denver in 1946 and lived on Gaylord Street in a nice garden-like neighborhood. We loved our apartment and enjoyed the lush greenery of its trees and lawns. You could see the snow-capped Rocky Mountains from Colfax Avenue, or from anywhere else for that matter. I longed to someday find myself in those gorgeous mountains.

The day after I arrived in Denver, I took a trolley downtown to see what the city looked like. I was waiting at the bus stop and people were coming and going. Each one said a few pleasantries to me. How nice these Coloradans were! On the trolley, a lady who must have been around 50, sat next to me and started a conversation, "There are so many people moving here from all over the States. I wish they'd pack up and leave. It's getting so crowded here and we don't want them, Denver is already too big. Don't you agree?"

Keeping my newness a secret, I said, "Oh yes, I fully agree with you. I don't want all these people coming here either." I must have been convincing because she dropped the subject and proceeded to tell me about the big white sale at the Denver Dry Goods Company. But, I couldn't do any shopping that day. I merely walked around and marvelled at the cleanliness of the streets and the delightful, pure, fresh air. What a country! This was going to be 'my' state and, I said to myself, "I will never leave Colorado!"

Me, Elizabeth Gumbel,
finally a Registered Nurse.

The next day, my sister Anne and I walked to Presbyterian Hospital to see if we could get jobs as R.N.s. Immediately, she was hired to work on the 2nd floor-medical and I was placed on the 1st floor with both medical and surgical patients. I appeared for work the next day and couldn't believe my first assignment which was to "clean the linen closet." I was amazed. In New Orleans, we had maids do that kind of work. They also washed and boiled used articles, wiped down every bed, and prepared it for new patients. All of a sudden, here in Denver, nurses, supposedly professionals, were assigned to do these menial tasks. Anne, who had trained in New Jersey, continually teased me, "You Southerners are so spoiled!"

One night, Anne and I were working the 3-11 shift when a sudden snowstorm blew in. It was early in the season and the blizzard was not in the weather forecast. It was such a bad storm that the evening supervisor told us not go home but to stay overnight in the hospital. Along with two other nurses, we chose an empty 4-bed ward on my floor and, thus had our first American slumber party. Early next day, we got up quickly and made up the beds for the incoming patients while still laughing at some of the jokes we heard long into the night!

Years later, we found out that this same storm caused much damage to the ranches. It

Behind Fred and me; Uncle Sam, my Mother, Aunt Blanche, Uncle Herman. In back: My Brother Martin. My Brother Max took this photograph.

even broke trees in half. People still remembered this storm and how cattle from many neighbors were mixed up for miles around. It took days to sort them out and get them returned to their home pastures.

Though work took a lot of my time, I longed for companionship. The social department of the synagogue formed an organization for Jewish newcomers, the '46 Club.' My current boyfriend, Fred (to whom I was introduced by my mother's doctor saying, "Have I got a boy for you!") and I decided to go to the first meeting. Here is was where he introduced me to another Fred. Since the first Fred was ignoring me, the new Fred moved in. We began dating a short month later, he proposed to me. I answered, "I think that would be nice!" I have been teased about that remark ever since! We planned to be married in the fall.

Fred was born to a middle class Jewish family on May 1, 1922 in a Kassel hospital, just ten miles from his village of 600, Meimbressen Germany. His parents, Adolf and Bina, owned a big farmhouse with living quarters upstairs and a stable downstairs. Adolph owned some pasture at the edge of town where he raised and traded cattle. He also grew a few crops. Fred's grandmother, a strong-willed woman, lived with them and she and Bina took care of a big garden by their house. The family practiced the Jewish Orthodox religion.

Fred was an inquisitive, bright child who got in trouble often. Once as a youngster, he and an older boy set fire to a house and, luckily, both were rescued before harm could come to them. Fred excelled in school, especially in mathematics. Feeling the fear of a very uncertain future, Fred's family made plans for him to emigrate from Germany. Two uncles in Colorado were willing to supply an affidavit for him in 1936. Soon, he said goodbye to his parents and younger sister, Hannelore, and found himself on the high seas heading towards the United States.

The happy couple after the wedding.

In 1941, Fred's parents wrote him what would be their last desperate note, saying they were "going to be deported the next day—address unknown." We found out years later that they were shipped to a concentration camp in Minsk, Russia, and eventually killed.

Meanwhile in Denver, Uncle Herman and his wife, Blanche, took care of Fred, sending him to public schools in Denver and having him work and learn the cattle business on their ranch near Castle Rock, south of Denver. It instilled in him an intense love of ranching. Fred's education continued as he entered Colorado 'Aggies' in Fort Collins, later known as Colorado State University.

Fred and I on his graduation day.

Before Fred could finish college, World War II began and he was drafted into the Army. His tour took him to Hawaii, Okinawa, and Korea. Upon concluding his 38-month stint, he re-entered CSU. It was in 1947 when we met and were married nine months later.

My good friend Josie, who worked with me in surgery in New Orleans, came for a visit in August of 1947. We decided to go to a dude ranch for a few days. What fun we had...the food, the horseback riding, the flirting with the rangers. Wow!

When we returned to Denver, Fred decided that he, Josie, and I should drive to Fort Collins. He had one year remaining until he would receive his Animal Husbandry degree from Colorado State University and we had heard that finding housing was difficult. The college had only enough Quonset huts for a few married couples and they were assigned a year earlier. We looked and looked. It was unusually competitive because of all the veterans, many financed by the GI Bill.

Finally, we found a corner house with a basement apartment—one room with a bed. In a corner was the 'john' partitioned off with plywood boards—for privacy! The cooking

The 'Old Green International" Truck with a 'fine second gear".

corner in the washroom had an electric 2-burner hot plate and when we put a board across the deep tubs, they became a sink. There was no refrigerator. The heating 'system' was an 'Electric Sun'. All this 'luxury' for $25 a month plus the chore of shoveling snow off the sidewalk. We rented it immediately!

Once again, I went searching for work. This time it was to Larimer County Hospital. The Supervisor, Miss Low, was overjoyed and asked me, "Can you start tomorrow?" I told her that I was first going to get married and go on a honeymoon. We agreed on a date when I would start. The hiring took less than 7 minutes!

The Rabbi married us on September 10, 1947 and my mother served homemade pastries and drinks at the Gaylord Street apartment. I always dreamed that the man I would marry would like classical music, love dogs the way I did, and always have clean fingernails. None of this came true. Instead, I got a rancher with manure-soaked boots, the hands of a working man, and a head full of dreams.

Me, and My Beloved, Fred
on our Wedding Day.

As a wedding present Aunt Blanche offered us a rental car for our honeymoon in Rocky Mountain National Park. But Fred declined it immediately saying, "It would be too expensive". Instead, he wondered if Uncle Herman would loan us the old green International pickup from the ranch. The wish was granted and soon we found ourselves in this non-heated, rattling machine with a long stick shift that supposedly had a "fine second gear". I had no idea what that meant. He told me that whenever the pickup would go backwards by itself to, "get out, find a rock and quickly, put it behind the nearest tire." Much later on the honeymoon, when we were leaving Golden, an old gold mining town high in the mountains, the truck stalled on top of the steepest hill and began rolling backwards, just as anticipated. Remembering my instructions, I jumped out, grabbed a rock and prevented the truck, with my new husband inside, from careening off the narrow, gravel road and into the valley below.

We travelled to Estes Park and planned to go later to Grand Lake but a snowstorm had closed the pass. Two days later, the road was cleared and the indescribable beauty of the Rocky Mountains was revealed to me. I could not get enough of my new state and tears of pure joy welled in my eyes.

After the honeymoon, we spent a few days at Uncle Herman's ranch near Castle Rock, and my brother, Max, and sister, Anne, came for a visit. Fred impressed us with his riding skill, but it was nothing compared to when he bravely killed a rattlesnake with a lariat.

Soon, we were on our way to Fort Collins in the, once again, loaned International green pickup with its "fine second gear," along with our few pieces of luggage. We were happy newlyweds embarking on our first adventure together.

Fred's senior year went by fast. My job at the hospital was good. Sometimes I would get a ride with the head nurse who lived close by. Other times I'd walk about a mile because there was no money for a car. The snowstorms would not let up that winter so Fred shovelled for hours every morning before going to classes while I dressed in front of the 'Electric Sun' turning my body every minute to defrost the other side. It stayed terribly cold in that miserable, dark basement, even after it warmed up outdoors in the spring.

Fred graduated with all A's and I contributed. Not only did he have a 'perfect' wife, but I helped him when he studied 'Poisonous Plants' and other tough courses. Before long, I realized that I probably was pregnant because I had morning sickness—until late afternoon. Morning—ha!

We were excited that we were going to be a family and we began making plans for the future. When Uncle Herman offered Fred a job on his ranch, we accepted. We bought an Admiral refrigerator I had seen advertised and a square tub automatic Maytag washing machine both which we shipped to Herman and Blanche's ranch.

When I moved to Colorado in 1946 a whole new experience began for me. People rode horseback. People owned ranches. Now, I knew what I wanted from life! No more pavement, no more sirens or noises from everyday city life. I fell in love not only with Fred, but also with the wide open spaces. 🐎

Castle Rock

Uncle Herman's ranch was near Castle Rock. The foreman's son, Ben, had quit and they needed an extra hand. We could live in the back part of the house rent free and during Fred's free time he could sell and buy cattle from the neighboring ranches and give a third of the net earnings to Uncle Herman. We thought it was a fair arrangement.

Moving day arrived. Our washer and refrigerator were already at the ranch so we only had to worry about our personal items. Once again, Fred borrowed the old green 'International' pickup and loaded the stuff we had accumulated. We left Fort Collins early

Uncle Herman and Aunt Blanche's Castle Rock Ranch.

for the 100 mile trip south. It was uneventful except for my morning sickness and all the dry crackers I had to eat to keep from vomiting. Once at our destination, we were greeted by the foreman, Miguel, his wife, the dog Butch, and both of our appliances which were sitting outdoors in front of our part of the house—the back entrance.

The pretty, white, two-story home with its green shutters was surrounded by huge cottonwood trees. The main part of the ranch house was permanently occupied by Miguel Esquibel and his wife. Our two rooms were at the back of the house, at the base of the stairs, so whenever any of the Esquibels wanted to go to their upstairs rooms, they had to go through our bedroom! It led to a staircase so narrow and steep that you had to turn your feet sideways and to make it even more dangerous, there was no railing!

Just for me, Aunt Blanche (Bless her heart!) installed a bathroom in the Esquibel part— off their living room. Though they kept the outhouse for us to use when the Esquibels had company, I tried hard to avoid it. I never got over the fear of some wild animal biting me on my behind!

Soon after we got settled I helped Mrs. Esquibel make a garden. The soil in that part of Colorado is full of rocks and gravel and I had my doubts whether anything would grow.

To my surprise, we ended up with cucumbers and melons so big you could barely carry them, dark green spinach, and rows of beautiful sweet corn.

The choke cherry bushes along the gravel roads were loaded with small black fruit and I spent days picking them. Mrs. Esquibel showed me how to make them into jelly using paraffin to seal the jars. I had never tasted anything so delicious. Now, years later I long for just one jar—which I probably would not share with anyone!

At Herman and Blanche's ranch I learned the basics of becoming a country woman. First of all, you had to get up long before the animals woke up because the man of the house does. While he was busy doing chores, the country woman had to make a huge breakfast. All the meals had the appearance of a Thanksgiving dinner, lots of good, rich food and so plentiful we always had enough to feed unexpected guests who seemed to realize the abundance at our table. Some, whom we called 'regulars', would say after we invited them, "Oh, I didn't realize it was dinnertime." But we knew better!

Yep, that's Me! Milking 'Ole Bessy.

Secondly, as a country woman I needed to learn how to milk a cow. I was so proud after I had milked about a cupful and I declared, "That's all there is."

Afterwards, Fred checked things out and to my surprise, he got an additional gallon out of the patient Jersey cow, saying, "It's okay, sometimes they will hold the milk when an inexperienced person 'works' on them." I decided then and there to become an expert at milking cows!

My third job as a country woman was to drive to the nearest town, about 12 miles away, and buy parts for broken down machinery. I had to answer all the questions the implement salesmen would ask so I could bring home the right item. I had to learn whether sizes were metric or not, how old the machinery was, what type, what make, and many other previously unimportant details. Even after all of that, sometimes my purchase was still wrong and had to be returned.

That year, we bought our first car and paid $500 for it. It was a little black coupe, a 1938 Chevrolet which we named 'the Jalopy.' Years later, we wondered why we bought such a lemon because it was always in the shop for repairs and certainly had little room inside. We sold it in 1955 for $100.

Nineteen hundred forty-nine was a busy year. We retained an obstetrician in Denver which made it necessary to go there for my monthly check-ups. Sometimes there was so much snow on the ground that no car was able to move. Miguel had made a huge 'V' out of wood, using 2X4's. He would attach two draft horses to the tip of the reversed 'V' and they would pull it, thus opening part of the road. Other times, the International with the 'fine second gear' would not start so we put the same two draft horses in front of the pickup and had them pull until the engine finally started.

After my appointment in Denver, we would stop for a meal at Uncle Herman and Aunt Blanche's apartment and soon rush back to the ranch, hoping that it hadn't snowed any more. Luck was always with us and we made it back safe and sound every time.

Me with our horse, Tom.

Nineteen hundred forty-nine was also a very cold and snowy winter and the baby was due in January, so Dr. Lewis suggested I should stay in Denver, at least a week before my due date. We all agreed with his advice and Fred took me to Aunt Blanche and Uncle Herman's apartment. It was a boring time with little to do. The folks were very nice but I longed for the ranch and for Fred. Eventually, two weeks late, our first born arrived. He weighed 7 pounds, 7 ounces, was slightly jaundiced but otherwise healthy. We named him Thomas Joseph. Tommy, because I liked the name and Joseph after my father.

My sister, Anne, was working as an R.N. at Chicago's Michael Reese Hospital. We called each other frequently and she offered to come and help after the baby was born. As soon as I knew the date of my dismissal, I asked her to arrive in Denver early that day, so we could pick her up at the airport. Uncle Herman loaned us his Hudson, the car of which he was so proud, and Fred drove the baby and me to the airport. Anne's plane was on time and it was good to have her with us. We drove directly to the ranch with Uncle Herman not far behind us in the pickup. Once at the ranch he got back into his car and returned to Denver.

Anne was wonderful help. She washed and boiled the diapers and hung them outdoors. They immediately froze and before long we gave up and draped them on chairs in front of the coal stove. Anne stayed with us for a week. We all enjoyed her visit and appreciated all the work she did. Uncle Herman came to the ranch to pick her up and drove her to the airport in Denver.

I nursed Tommy but the kid was always hungry so we had to buy evaporated Pet Milk and made a formula which seemed to satisfy him. My so-called 'best friend' said one time, "If you were a cow in a milk herd, you'd be the first one to be culled!"

Suddenly, I had became a homebody. I had hardly anything to do outdoors, so I baked pies and knitted soakers for Tommy to wear over his diapers because they said it was bad for babies to wear rubber pants. Naturally, the sheets of his tiny crib were always wet and the laundry grew bigger and bigger.

Meanwhile, Fred kept going to neighbors trying to buy cattle from them but it was getting tougher all the time. It seemed all the ranchers wanted to take their own cattle to the livestock barns sale in Colorado Springs and Denver. In addition, big trucking companies were becoming popular and were as close as a telephone call, so ranchers took advantage of them instead of using Fred's service.

Our income was getting less and less and we started to think about securing a job. Fred and Aunt Blanche had a serious talk about the situation and she ended by saying, "Uncle Herman and I have to make a living, Uncle Sam, (Uncle Herman's brother who was living in Wagon Mound, New Mexico) has to make a living, and Miguel and his wife have to make a living. I don't know where you come in."

That was it! Fred was deeply hurt. Hearing that from one person he truly loved was painful. It was true, however. We weren't making any money. But why couldn't Aunt Blanche have been more sympathetic?

The next Saturday, Fred drove to the Denver office of the Department of Veterans Affairs and was offered a position doing 'On the Farm Training' in the Simla area. It sounded like a good job with regular income. The pay was $270 per month plus mileage of seven cents per mile to visit the students' farms, a radius of roughly 30 miles. We were excited and looked forward to a new adventure. We were happy, had a wonderful baby, a dog named Leo, and a car.

At once, Fred drove east to Simla to find a house to either buy or rent but couldn't find one so the real estate people told him to try in Ramah, five miles west of Simla. He took their advice and located a nice, 4-bedroom house which he bought for $3,500.

In a matter of days, our future had changed drastically. Aunt Blanche's remark stayed in our minds, forewarning us to be wary of going into business with close relatives, especially if you were a newcomer, young and fresh out of college. Uncle Herman and Uncle Sam also had their rifts but they stuck it out. Once it was certain we were moving, our relationship with the folks was as good as ever. They seemed relieved and even promised to visit us as soon as we were settled in our own home.

While our immediate future looked bright, we hated to leave the ranch and its beautiful surroundings of pine trees and gurgling creeks. We knew we would miss the Esquibels and especially the two horses we rode so often, Tom and Cheyenne. 🐴

Miguel, the always successful deer hunter.

Ramah

Our House in Ramah.

It was fall of 1949. We woke up early, ready to leave Uncle Herman and Aunt Blanche's ranch. A bitter sweet feeling came over us, happy for the past times, but anticipating our new future. We were going to be on our own. The roosters began to crow and promises of sunshine appeared on the eastern horizon. The two trucks we ordered came around 6:30 A.M. One of them loaded our ten cattle, while the other one picked up some furniture we had bought from an old rancher in the neighborhood. We paid the good man his asking price of $28. For that we became the proud owners of a beautiful, yet slightly scratched and sturdy antique oak dining table with two leaves and claw feet, five chairs, a rocker, a china cabinet with a mirror and shelves on top, and a large partner desk with leather inlays. What a bargain!

We were almost ready to leave when Miguel offered us his ugly couch that he was going to throw away and since Fred never refused a gift, it also went onto the truck. The seat of the couch was higher in the back than in the front, sloping forward considerably. The once-blue velvet material was worn thin. It was the most uncomfortable, unsightly piece of furniture I had ever sat on or seen—and now it was ours! Hurrah!

The '38 coupe was loaded to the brim. We put household items and clothes into the back along with our ever-loving dog, Leo, who sat next to the rear window. Then I got in holding Tommy on my lap and finally, Fred crawled into our very crowded vehicle. We were finally on our way travelling for some 70 miles until we reached Calhan where we stopped at Farmers State Bank to sign the papers for our new house in Ramah.

It was nine more miles to Ramah, our new home which I had not yet seen. As we turned off Highway 24, and almost hidden by an ocean of huge cottonwoods, a village appeared. There were wide streets, neat houses, trees, and flower gardens everywhere! A couple of people turned their heads as the two trucks and our car passed them. I imagined that they were thinking or saying, "Who in the world are they? Where are they going to live?" In reality, the whole town probably knew all about us before we even reached our house thanks to the telephone and its party lines!

While we were driving towards our house we passed two grocery stores, a lumber yard, the post office, a grain elevator, and a dance hall. In the distance we could see a couple of churches and a tiny schoolhouse which stood by itself on a small rise. Ramah had 200 inhabitants, and now with us, it was up to 203.

After crossing the railroad tracks we soon arrived at the house. It was a tidy, two-story building, deep brown with white trim and had an enclosed back porch. There were a couple of sheds, a chicken house, a 4-wire clothes line and an outhouse. In front of the house was a smaller porch, a big lawn, and more of those gorgeous cottonwood trees.

Full of enthusiasm, Fred, Tommy and I entered our new home. We discovered two bedrooms downstairs, a dining room, a living room and a peach colored bathroom. Some steep stairs led to two more bedrooms upstairs. The kitchen was small and it had a coal stove with an attachment, supposedly to heat water.

The cattle truck unloaded the Herefords in a rented pasture which only cost us $5 per cow and $3 per yearling each month. The truck with the furniture was soon emptied and it didn't take long before everything was in place. The ugly couch was indeed an eye sore, so I quickly found an old blanket to cover it. It was only a slight improvement!

The next day, Fred drove to Simla to his new job, teaching agriculture to veterans of World War II and the Korean Conflict. Eighteen novice farmers met for his classes two times a week in the Simla Town Hall. On other days, the group visited the students' farms or they would work together building barns, cattle chutes, fences, repairing broken windmills and machinery. Fred used some class time to teach his students bookkeeping and how to complete their Income Tax records. In others, he taught basic veterinary procedures. Not only did the government pay the students to take part, ($65 if single; $90 if married) but they learned a great deal about operating their business. The students often expressed how indebted they were to Fred for all the knowledge he passed on to them.

It was May when we decided to order baby chicks. Luckily, there were still some available because most people started raising theirs months earlier. Soon our 50 adorable, yellow powder puffs came by mail in a special carton. I couldn't keep my hands off them. They were running around as if they knew where they were going while peeping constantly.

We had no experience raising baby chicks so we got some literature from the County Agent. It said, "First count them to make sure you got what you ordered. Next, give them some clean, warm drinking water. Pick up a chick and dip its beak in it so it knows where to get more. Finally, sprinkle cracked corn or chicken feed onto the floor of the container or into feeders." The booklet continued, "It is most important that the chicks be kept quite warm and it is best to have lights so they don't pile up in a corner to go to sleep."

"We can do all that," we thought. Though it was still cold in May, especially at nights, we figured our coal stove in the dining room would be fine for a couple of weeks. Next, we put the three boxes of chicks around the stove, strung some electric wires and a light bulb over each box and watched the chicks scurry about, chirping loudly all the while. What a beautiful sight it was—I just couldn't get enough. Leo, our precocious mutt, was fascinated by these busy babies and he would lie next to the boxes as if to protect them from harm.

Sometimes he would give one chick a lick and the poor thing would topple over, peeping even louder to protest the harsh treatment.

It was hard to keep the coal fire going all night so Fred got up from the warm bed a couple of times and added more coal. By morning, though the room seemed comfortable to us, the chicks were all huddled together in one corner trying to keep each other warm. We heated up the house as quickly as we could, but it already was too late for some of those 'peepers'. We could see several chicks staying by themselves, their tiny wings drooping as they uttered a single, occasional peep. Next, we noticed two chicks lying on their sides. When I tried to help them up, they seemed paralyzed. I was told much later that they had Newcastle Disease.

We had followed the instructions in the booklet, so the situation puzzled me. I rushed over to our good neighbor, Mrs. Lasky and asked her to come and see. The chubby, little, 65 year-old lady with a strong Slovak accent, came over quickly and gave a sigh, not one of relief, but one of pity. I didn't know whether this was meant for me and my total ignorance, or for the obvious ill health of so many of my charges. "Please tell me what to do," I begged.

But before she said another word Mrs. Lasky grabbed the two paralyzed babies and twisted their necks until they were dead. Then she said sternly, "The temperature changes too much; one minute it's too hot, the next it's too cold. You've got to get a brooder with a thermometer. Also, you got to get them pills to put into the drinking water. They are yellow pills made of sulfa and you can get them at Julian's Drugstore. You are goin' to lose all them chicks if you keep doin' this kind of stuff." Talk about feeling guilt and shame—I felt like a small child who had been bawled out by her mother for stealing a piece of candy.

Mrs. Lasky then turned, "I got to get back to check on my roast." I handed her a cup of butter I had churned in my Mixmaster earlier and thanked her for being such a good advisor. She mumbled a barely audible "Thank you" and was almost out of the house when she yelled one more piece of advice, "Remember, you keep them birds real warm, day and night, you hear?"

Mrs. Lasky was a really good woman. She worked hard, cooked and baked constantly even though she and her husband lived alone. Their many children were grown and had moved away but often returned to visit. She would always bake a Sunshine Cake for them. I once asked her, "Why not make a different kind of cake for a change?"

Her answer was as predictable as her baking, "Them hens of mine are laying so many eggs and it takes 6-8 eggs for a Sunshine Cake. I don't know what else to do with them. I even throw in a couple extra just for good measure." We became good friends with the Lasky family for they were down to earth and forever helpful. We developed a mutual feeling of closeness.

After Fred returned from his job that day, I told him what Mrs. Lasky had recommended so he went right out to find a brooder and before long he returned with something that looked more like a dismembered automobile. There were piles of odd shaped pieces of tin, screws, tiny chains like one used to turn lights on and off in the olden days, but no thermometer. The new one cost 75 cents at the drug store. Eventually, through some miracle, the stuff was assembled, and suddenly it looked like a brooder.

We lost many more chicks and Mrs. Lasky had to wring quite a few more necks which is something I would not, nor could not, do. The trouble with this enterprise was that we were not properly prepared, but we learned from the experience.

We put the sulfa pills into the chicks' water for several weeks and the ones who survived grew wing and tail feathers and they soon found out that they could fly or at least, get airborne. It wasn't long before they flew out of their boxes and were inspecting all the rooms in the house. One even flew and landed in the toilet. After rescuing it, we decided it was time to move my yellow powder puffs to the chicken house and its fenced yard. Leo would spend hours there while the birds would snuggle up to his warm body and roost on top of his back.

Meanwhile, Judy, our Jersey cow, was going to have a calf so we didn't have any milk for Tommy. Since we didn't want to buy another cow Fred suggested that we, "Buy a fresh nanny," a goat who was producing milk. We knew a man who raised goats north of Ramah. He would come often to our little town and without seeing the good man, people said you could smell him coming. The aroma, which comes from two glands located next to the billy goats' horns, smelled worse than a skunk and was so strong it made your eyes water.

Soon, one beautiful sunshiny morning Fred got into 'the jalopy' and headed for the goat farm. It was going to be another exciting, new experience for this city person and I was eager to learn about a different kind of animal. Fred finally returned with two Toggenberg goats. One of the nannies was bred just before Fred had put her into the car. She wanted to let the world know that she and her boyfriend had spent time together so she carried the obnoxious odor, full strength, into the car and onto Fred. Both smelled so bad that I wanted to send both of them on a rocket ship to the moon—anywhere, just so it was away from me!

The goats were wonderful mowing machines. In no time at all, they had eaten all the weeds and, if we were not careful, the flowers too. Often, they jumped onto the top of the jalopy to eat their most prized gourmet food, the lower leaves of the cottonwood trees.

Fred milked one of the nannies regularly and soon we realized that her milk was homogenized. The cream did not separate from the milk and though it was impossible to make butter, I pasteurized it and Tommy grew into a picture of health.

After a five-month gestation period the other nanny, Sylvia, presented us with two beautiful kids which we named Bobby and Susie. About a week later we staked all three in a patch behind our fenced yard. There was someone's ladder leaning against an adjoining building and lots of grass for the goats to eat. When I returned a few hours later, to my horror I found poor Bobby hanging between the spokes of that ladder. He was dead. "Another lesson learned," I uttered, wiping away my tears. We tried very hard not to make a pet out of Susie but she was so sweet that she won our hearts! Our plan had been to butcher her, but when the time came, we sold her to a neighbor. We couldn't eat our friend!

A couple of weeks later, Fred went to the weekly livestock sale in Colorado Springs to buy a goat to butcher. They sold cattle, sheep, and goats along with chickens and rabbits, all to the highest bidder. A young goat was led into the ring. She was brown and white with floppy ears, very alert but controlled and she seemed to look at every face that was staring at her. Just then, the auctioneer started his 'cry', the term for the auctioneer's song.

My 'One and Only' with our Goats.

The loudspeaker was turned up so high that the poor animal got scared and leaped up into the air, jumping out of the sales ring and right into the first row of prospective buyers. Suddenly the whole crowd came alive. This time the bidding was very active and fast and before long, Fred owned the ambitious animal.

Fred spent the entire afternoon just watching what was being sold. Then he saw three "day-old" baby Holstein calves which were being driven into the ring. Their large black eyes were shiny next to their pure white and black coat. They looked as if someone had polished and buffed their baby pink noses, in preparation for the sale. All three stood there while the loudspeaker was screaming comments about them and you could see the frightened expression on their young faces. Fred bought them for $18 each.

The goat and three calves were brought to our house by a neighbor because we only had the jalopy. In addition to not having a truck to transport livestock, we also didn't have any corrals. Luckily, the Smith's who lived across from our front yard, had an extra small pen next to their dairy, not far from our house which they let us use. It was ideal for the calves. After Fred made them comfortable by putting down straw on the ground, they laid down and contemplated their frightful day.

Meanwhile the goat was still up to her antics. She had gotten loose in the backyard and was trying to jump the fence. She just made it half way and ended up briefly dangling with her chest draped over the wooden divider. She must have known what was coming.

By now, it was beginning to get dark and anybody in their right mind would think, "Goodie, all the left over work can be done tomorrow. We are through for today." But this was not how it went at our house! Fred's theory always was, "You never know what tomorrow will bring—we'd better finish this tonight. Besides, that wild goat is unpredictable." With that in mind, we decided to butcher her that very evening. We sharpened the big cutting and skinning knives and pulled out the .22 gun and bullets. We always kept the gun in one place of the house and the bullets in another. Having a weapon around scared me, but Fred convinced me that it was a necessity.

The flood light on the house was turned on and with the whole backyard illuminated, Fred shot the goat in the forehead. To our amazement, she just stood there and laughed at us, probably thinking, "Try again, dummy, this is not the right way to kill a goat." Fred tried a second time and again, nothing happened. He then realized that he needed to choose a spot of soft tissue rather than aiming at the bony part. That time it worked. It was almost 9 PM before we had a tidy carcass hanging in our enclosed back porch. The next day, we cut the meat into portions and stored it in the freezer above the refrigerator leaving only a few chops for dinner. It was so tender that we didn't need teeth to chew it and eaten with the mint jelly I had made a few weeks earlier, it was an absolute taste delight and a gourmet addition to our diet.

The three calves were less than a week old and they constantly bawled for their mothers.They longed for the closeness when she licked them making soothing, hardly audible noises, almost like humming. We could not replace this, but as the new caretakers we could give each of them a bottle of warm milk three times a day, a poor substitute for their mom's ever-ready, warm, rich milk.

Fred bought a 20-pound sack of dried milk which had to be dissolved in warm water. The 2-quart plastic bottles had rubber nipples, and once the calves got used to them, they went after them with gusto. As the calves grew stronger, occasionally they would pull on the nipples so hard that they would come off the bottles, spilling most of the remaining milk on the ground, while the calves continued sucking in air. It was a struggle to get the nipple out of their mouths—they were enjoying their pacifier and didn't want to give it up!

When the calves were a month old, we taught them how to eat finely ground grain. We used a mixture of oats, wheat, corn, and cottonseed meal. By putting a small amount in our hands and encouraging them to eat, they caught on soon and cleaned up the trough in no time.

News travelled fast through our animal neighborhood and somehow the Smiths' chickens got the word that grain was close by. The minute Mr. Smith opened his chicken house door those birds ran down the road as fast as they could, directly to our grain troughs. They fluttered about and scared the timid baby calves until they had their fill and were happily ready to return to their home turf. The routine became a daily occurrence. Fred asked Pat Smith to keep his chickens in until our calves had finished their grain and though he said he would, he never did. So, now my newest chore was to stand by the troughs and chase away the intruders.

Another duty confronted me, now. We didn't have mail delivered to our home in Ramah so we had to pick it up at the post office every day. The large office had pigeon holes along one wall for each family, a cart for packages, and a long desk where the friendly Postmistress did the transactions. One day, when I asked for our mail, she said, "You got a letter from the U.S. Government, I hope it's not bad news." With that she handed me a bunch of letters and the usual bills, plus the letter from Washington. D.C. Since Fred was a Second Lieutenant in the Army Reserve, we received all sorts of mail from Washington, but this time it was different. They wanted to know if he would go to Camp McCoy in Wisconsin for a couple of weeks, for pay. This sounded too good to be refused. He could take time off from his job and also visit his cousins, Max and Fred, in Chicago on the way.

One month later, we drove to Limon so Fred could catch the train to his military duty. He was so excited that he couldn't stop talking all the 60 miles while driving east of Ramah. It was around 6 AM when we arrived in Limon and Tommy and I headed back home before the train pulled into the station. After all, we had all sorts of chores to do.

I finished feeding the goats and the baby chicks and milked the cow. Next, I filled a gallon can of grain for the baby calves plus bottles of warm milk. Tommy and I walked to the calves' pen and found two of the calves lying down, which was very unusual. I noticed right away that they had a severe case of scours, the term for diarrhea in cattle and horses. The third calf seemed all right. "Wouldn't you know this would happen while I am alone!" Diarrhea can be life threatening to infants and young children, and likewise to baby calves. Dehydration was the biggest threat. I had to act fast if I was going to save them.

But I didn't know what to do! I hurried back to the house and immediately crossed the street to confer with my advisor, Mrs. Lasky. She told me to cook oatmeal in water and give the sick calves nothing else but this gruel every few hours. As an afterthought, she mentioned that Julian's Drugstore was selling sulfa pills which ranchers used for their calves with scours. "Don't know if they really help, but it is worth trying." I thought I needed all the help I could get, so I put Tommy in his 'Taylor Tot', the most popular baby carriage at the time, and walked to Julian's where I bought a bag of sulfa boluses, large, oblong pills for cattle. "Give them one in the morning, and one at night. I hope they won't die on you!" the lady advised almost cheerfully. I rushed back to the calves, stuck a bolus into the back of the mouth of the two sick ones and headed for home. Next, I cooked oatmeal and poured it into two empty Coke bottles, which used to come in light green glass containers. I then rushed back to the calves and slowly poured their new kind of breakfast into their mouths. They seemed to like it. Next, I separated the healthy calf and fed it the usual milk and grain. I made several trips, carrying bottles of oatmeal to pour down throats, but the scours continued. The following day the third calf became sick.

Before long, I ran out of oatmeal and had to buy the largest box Mrs. Lasky's grocery store carried, plus I also needed more sulfa boluses. After four days of constant attention, the three calves did not die, but instead they started to improve. They continued swallowing the pills and the oatmeal for a whole week before I slowly re-introduced small amounts of watered-down milk. It was such a relief when all three appeared in good health and were back to their usual calf routine! I was proud of my efforts.

Before long, it was time to pick up Fred in Limon. He told me everything about Camp McCoy and how he had visited several huge dairy farms in Wisconsin. I secretly crossed my fingers and hoped he would never think of having one himself. It was too late...the thought had crossed his mind and soon we were making plans to begin milking cows!

Eventually, I told Fred about my experience with the calves and their scours and he was both pleased and surprised. In fact, he was downright proud of me. I needed praise more than anything because I desperately wanted to become a real ranch wife. If I could heal sick calves, I'd be a step closer to my dream!

Plummeting Temperatures

The seasons progressed and now it was winter. Actually, the calendar still said that it was fall, but Colorado weather pays no attention to that. When it feels like snowing, that's what you get! In fact, they predicted that we would have a worse winter than usual. Here it was early in the season and already the north wind was very cold and strong and blowing all night long. We could hear tiny pebbles from the gravel road hit the windowpane of our bedroom. I crawled out of the cozy, warm bed to check on Tommy and found him completely uncovered. Quickly, I went to his chest of drawers and pulled out a blue knit baby blanket a friend of mine had sent when he was born. It was perfect. I wrapped up our 'pride and joy' snugly, turned him onto his side, said a few cute words to him and left. That kid never woke up! Now shivering from the cold, I returned to the bed to find a contented, snoring husband to whom I snuggled up closely, warming my icy limbs. He too, never woke up and before long I also went back to sleep.

It was a Saturday and this meant that Fred would be home all day and could help me with my chores. However, he had a different plan. "We need to rent a better pasture for our cows and I'm going to look at one this morning. Do you want to come along?" he asked at breakfast.

"You bet I do," was my immediate answer. It was at that moment that the telephone rang, two long rings and one short—a signal that the call was for us. We had to be very careful because our phone was a party line for five neighbors and you never knew who might be listening. We tried to share the phone politely so if we heard a click it meant someone else wanted to use the phone and we ended our conversation as soon as possible.

On the phone was Fred Goldsmith, a friend from Denver whom I had dated before meeting my husband-to-be. "I'd like to come and visit you today, if you are not busy," he asked.

"Of course we're not busy," he lied. "Come on out and have dinner with us at noon," was the answer from the man of the house. I guess the plan for the day had changed!

We decided that Fred would go alone to inspect the pasture while I stayed home to clean the house and prepare dinner. I began to cook an average dinner, which at our house meant that the Queen of England would feel satisfied should she happen to come to Ramah! Next, I got my bucket and mop, filled the bucket with luke warm water, which is all we had since the attachment to the stove never heated the water very well. I added enough ammonia to sting your nostrils and quickly cleaned the linoleum floors in the living room and bedroom. A fast job of dusting and I was ready to devote my remaining time to getting myself ready.

The weather was frightfully cold and a few snowflakes started to fall. The stove in the dining room did its best and I knew that, with the oven going strong in the kitchen, it would be comfortable for our guest.

The morning was progressing well—the roast was in the oven making delicious noises and emitting an aroma so delicate it would make anyone's mouth water. "I had better change my clothes and then set the table," I told myself. With that in mind I went into the bedroom. "Went" is the wrong word, because no sooner did I step onto the bedroom floor when I realized I was on my butt, travelling this way for 15 feet until I slid into the opposite wall. I tried to get up but couldn't because my feet kept slipping out from under me as I laughed and laughed. It was so cold in the bedroom that my good mopping job had actually formed a thin coat of ice.

When Fred returned from the pasture, I told him about my escapades in the bedroom and told him that if he wanted to go in there he would need to use ice skates. He just shook his head saying, "I don't ice skate," in his bland sense of humor!

Before long, Fred, our visitor from Denver, arrived holding a bottle of Rhine wine in one hand and a most-welcome box of candy in the other. After thanking him profusely I begged him to come more often, hoping secretly that he would shower us again with more goodies. He stayed until dark when he headed back to his home in Denver. In the evening we listened to the radio show, 'One Man's Family', before we filled our hot water bottle and went to bed. I was almost asleep when Fred told me that he had rented the pasture and we would move the cattle there in a couple of days. "Okay, good night," was all I could say while I snuggled closer to his warm body which quickly carried me into a deep sleep.

The exceptionally cold winter grew worse. The ice on the bare limbs of the trees never seemed to leave and even though the sun tried to warm everything, it really never succeeded. We quickly ran out of propane gas. Fortunately, the man who delivered more bottles came early the next day. His breath seemed to freeze in midair hovering like a cloud above him. He spoke only a few words, "I just hate to work on a bloomin', bloomin' cold day like this." I agreed with him. Though I asked if he wanted to come in and warm up, he quickly declined saying how he wanted nothing more than to go home and sit by his kitchen stove.

The cold continued to plague us that winter. Several days later, the temperatures dipped to 10 degrees and now the kitchen sink would not drain. "What's next," I thought, "after all this cold weather, now we have to deal with this!" Ever helpful, Fred got the plunger and pushed down over the drain. He did this several times and the water did not budge. We thought maybe the pipes leading to the greasetrap might be frozen.

A grease trap is a system which is often used in rural areas for collecting waste water from the kitchen. A 50-gallon barrel is placed below the ground with about a foot of soil covering the top. The grease which floats to the top needs to be collected and removed from time to time so the waste water from the house could run out smoothly. It was a smelly, disgusting job—but one of those which had to be done—and now during the worst weather!

"All we need to do is locate the darn buried thing and defrost it, perhaps with a blowtorch," Fred suggested. The theory was great but how do you find the hidden treasure and dig or chop through the hard, frozen soil while keeping your fingers and feet from freezing. After all, it was "bloomin', bloomin' cold!"

Fred quickly left the house, venturing out into the cold. He visited several neighbors to see if they knew where the grease trap was located. Nobody knew. Just then Eugene, an old man who lived in a shack behind our house, appeared at our door as he did every day to refill his gallon bottle with water. He was a man of few words and when Fred told him about our problem, the old man told us exactly where we should dig, remembering how he had helped the former owner put in the grease trap many years before.

Thanks to Eugene, who stayed several hours helping Fred, they soon had the lid off, all the grease scooped away, the pipes cleaned and the system closed, while hoping for the best. We ran into the house, turned on the water in the kitchen sink and, lo and behold, the standing water was no more! This wonderful angel, in the form of an old man, came to the rescue on that miserable cold day.

We often spoke of Eugene after that. He was a man who neither asked for, nor expected, praise or presents. He was old and poor but he had compassion and empathy for other people. The world would be a better place if there were more Eugenes!

Searching For Our Ranch

'm going to take off from teaching the Veterans today and start looking at some ranches for sale."

"Are you sure we can afford one?" was my immediate concern.

"You are so pessimistic! Of course, we can, with the help of the Calhan banker."

"Good luck, and find one with a nice house, a picket fence around the yard and with lots of trees." I didn't think Fred heard my request. He took off like a barracuda in a wading pool and I wondered about his excited attitude. Well, I decided, we'll find out when he returns.

It was a lovely morning, warm and sunshiny with not a cloud in the dark blue sky over Ramah in the Fall of 1950. The leaves of the cottonwood trees in front of the house had begun to turn their lovely light yellow color and some of them were dancing about as they approached the ground. Everything seemed right with the world. I wished that I could spend some time outdoors but decided to finish sewing the pajamas I had started a couple of days earlier. I had some pretty material which used to be a sack for chicken feed and thought it would make some handsome pj's. After all, Fred surprised me with an old treadle sewing machine which he recently bought at a farm sale and even though I was not a good seamstress, I felt I better try and put some effort into using it.

My eyes wandered towards little Tommy, not yet two years old, who was playing with his colored blocks while Leo, our small yellow mutt, was beside him. Both were constant companions and they showed mutual respect and love towards each other. Tommy never handled him roughly so Leo was always unruffled and unperturbed. "What a neat pair," I thought, "I am raising a real dog lover!"

Again, my thoughts turned to the beautiful day outside my window and suggested to Tommy, "How about you two going outside for a while and playing in your new sandbox?"

100 COW RANCH

1440 Acres East. 4 miles from In-
land town. 10 miles from railroad.
300 Acres farm land. 200 acres of
fine sub-irrigated meadow with excellent hay. Good 7 room home,
electricity, hot water, 2 barns, underneath stock sheds, grainery, garage, 3 wells, reservoirs, grade A
Milk barn & cooling room, corrals
and loading chutes. Possession at
once. Price $27.90 per acre. $12,000
will handle, balance to suit buyer.

This is the ad the Real Estate man found in the Gazette, the Colorado Springs newspaper.

In a split second, as if I had counted "1-2-3-GO!" they were both by the kitchen door, eager to be let out. Fred had nailed some 4 X 4's together and had hauled a 55-gallon drum full of fine sand from the riverbed near our house. It was just enough to fill the sandbox.

Tommy was a content and quiet child and I could hear him making happy sounds outside while I continued sewing. It wasn't long before I heard someone knocking on the kitchen door and I recognized Eugene's two knocks. He was the old man who had helped us with the grease trap last winter. I recognized his distinctive sound and even looked forward to seeing him every morning when he came by to fill his gallon bottle with water. Eugene never uttered an unnecessary word. His clothes were always dark brown and much too large for his scrawny body. Summer and winter he would wear the same things.

"Come in, Eugene," I called cheerily to him from my perch at the sewing machine. He would then rush over to the kitchen sink and fill his bottle. Almost as soon as he had entered, his next word was a polite, "Bye," and he was out the door.

My pajama top only needed to be hemmed and it would be finished soon, so I decided to take a break and check on Tommy. He loved Kool-Aid. I poured a small glassful and went outside, breathing in the delicious fall air. I did not see him in the sandbox and I was puzzled why he and Leo were not in their favorite play area. I thought maybe they were in the chicken house or perhaps in the garden. But there was no sign of them either place.

I became concerned. I looked all around the house and outside a second time before I noticed the gate to the front yard being slightly ajar. Tommy was not able to open it and the only person who had been around was Eugene. My worries grew by the minute as I kept calling for Tommy and Leo. Still, no response! I set down the drink and raced down the gravel road to the small pen where we kept the three baby calves. I headed for the shallow well where Tommy and I had looked at bugs just the day before, hoping NOT to find him there. Next, I ran to our neighbor Pat's house and asked them to watch for Tommy.

> Mr. and Mrs. Herman Vorenberg went to Ramah, Colo., last Thursday to visit the Fred Vorenbergs. Little Tommy is now walking and to show his complete independence, the very first day he walked alone, he went across the street to a nighbor's with out leave or license.

Out of breath, I went back to the house hoping that the 'wayward couple' might have returned. No luck.

I made a hurried trip to the Lasky's and found no one at home. Not discouraged, I thought, "The telephone, of course." If that doesn't work, I'll try Main Street. I called Mrs. Kloster who was the manager of the tiny Post Office and she promised to get a few people together to help me search.

Next, I headed toward Main Street, passing Mr. Lasky's grocery store. By now, I was really frightened. How could a little boy and his dog disappear so quickly, leaving no signs or clues behind. My thoughts rushed to kidnapping and I fought the tears in my eyes while I tried to be strong.

Continuing with my desperate search, half running, half walking I ran towards the Rock Island train tracks and Main Street. I looked right, then left and still nothing. And all of a sudden around the bend of the gravel road I noticed a stranger coming toward me holding onto my baby with Leo prancing by his side. What joy! What a relief!

I ran towards Tommy, picked him up and hugged him tightly. "I found him and the dog sitting on the railroad tracks. I didn't know what to do, so I went to the Post Office to find out who he was and where he lived. You know, this little guy is lucky because the noon train from Denver went through here just minutes after I found him." A wave of dizziness spread over my entire body as he continued, "By the way, my name is George Olefsky. I have a small farm south of Ramah and I just came to town to buy some supplies when I saw this little kid and his dog sitting there on the tracks just as happy as can be." I thanked George profusely and turned, holding Tommy tightly against my chest as if I would never let him go. We walked home slowly.

Once inside the house, my nerves which had been in such an uproar, suddenly gave way to a complete release. I cried until I felt totally spent and exhausted. Next, I prepared lunch, fed Tommy, and put him down for his daily nap. I was in no mood to continue sewing. Fred returned from his search for a ranch—with negative results. It had been a bad day.

The next day I finished the hem on the pajamas. Though it turned out to be a handsome outfit, every time I looked at it I was reminded of that terrible day. I just couldn't forget the fright and terror. Going through such an ordeal, I continued to feel the devastating guilt, "What did I do wrong? How could this have happened?" Though it took me a while to get over the incident, I continued to blame myself for a long time until I realized that Eugene must have left the gate open. After that, we always made sure to follow him out of the yard. From then on, I must have double-checked that gate five times a day!

Another surprise was in store for us when years later, two policemen and a detective arrived in Ramah asking lots of questions about an escaped convict from a Nebraska prison. But, nobody had heard of him. It turned out that George was their man! He had changed his name, gotten married, and had become a model citizen. The news spread like butter on hot toast and almost everybody in our little town turned out to convince the authorities to pardon him. After all, over the many years George truly had proven to be a valuable asset to our community. The lives of my first son and my dog were saved by this escaped convict and I was not about to forget his kindness. We were successful and George was rewarded for his many good deeds. He was pardoned and remained in our community, working on his small farm.

Life returned to normal and our hopes for owning a cattle ranch never subsided. Fred and I were constantly on the lookout for one at a reasonable price. Real estate people showed us a few places but always the location, the condition of the pastures, the availability of water for livestock, the house, or the price was just not right. We also needed a bank which would help us with a good sized loan. Our finances were poor but we had big dreams. Living on a ranch had become an important goal for us and we wanted to raise livestock on a relatively large spread.

Meanwhile, I had almost wrecked 'the jalopy' when I drove into some deep sand. Mistakenly, I hit the brakes really hard and the car careened over the road and into the ditch. I decided it was time for me to read the driver's manual and actually learn how to drive properly! I hurried to earn my driver's license at the Simla office.

The same day a shepherd-like mutt adopted us and presented us with a set of new puppies which she had delivered under a nearby shed. She eventually brought each pup, one by one, to our front step. They had so much personality that we quickly adopted the whole family and named the mother, Ginger.

...And, we were going to have another baby!

One day the telephone rang and an excited real estate man yelled with excitement,"We found another ranch for sale!" It was located south of Calhan, had pastures which had not been grazed the previous year, a lot of water, good bottom land, and outbuildings, etc. The price was within reason so we decided to check it out.

Early the next morning Fred and I drove to a location ten miles south of Calhan and two miles east until we saw in the distance a two-story house, two red barns, a garage and some other structures. Like Ramah, it was in El Paso County and we had been told that the schools in the Miami School District were quite good. We continued down Jones Road. As we arrived at the ranch, we quickly got out of the car and began to tour the homestead. We hoped this was it!

As I stepped out of the car, my feet sank into piles of sand which lay all around. The wind had blown it there from a field, which was directly north of the house. Everything had been transformed into a bare expanse of sand. Around the ranch house, there was one lone tree and a few bushes. The whole area sported a dull shade of tan.

We now turned our attention to the house. At first look, it appeared to be a desperate case of neglect and dilapidation. It was a compliment to call it 'run down'. Ever hopeful, I thought maybe the inside was in better condition and that at least it would be pleasant and comfortable. "Let's go inside," Fred said enthusiastically. He opened the unlocked kitchen door and we stepped inside.

I found myself staring at what looked like a very primitive, enclosed porch that had over two inches of topsoil on the floor. There were six small windows facing Jones Road. The window panes rattled even though I hadn't noticed any wind! Several of the floorboards were missing and many others were broken. We walked past the porch and into the living room. It was a very dark, tiny room with ugly green flowery wallpaper— my least favorite color! The ceiling was blackened from an old coal stove in one corner of the room. There was one small window through which you could look into an added-on porch. From there you could also see some steps leading to a cellar. We cautiously walked down. "What a fine place to grow mushrooms," I joked.

Going back upstairs, silently, we entered two bedrooms on the main floor. One had a built-in closet, the other had none. Between the two bedrooms was a set of rather steep stairs leading up to two more rooms. "Where's the kitchen?" I asked innocently. Almost sheepishly, and halfway embarrassed, I was told that the former occupants had used a small area, no larger than 6 x 8 feet, a small alcove directly off the living room. It had neither sink nor stove, only a loose piece of metal tubing which hung limply from the south wall. We guessed that it probably had been hooked up to a bottle of propane gas at one time. All the floors were covered with the same fine sand that was outdoors. We kicked it away to inspect the flooring and, to our surprise, there was a fairly decent linoleum.

I had walked though the whole house, grinding the sand with each step before I suddenly realized that not only was there no kitchen, there was no bathroom! Fred, realizing my sinking mood, tried to be funny. He giggled, "It has a 'pathroom'...south of the house. A real nice one, honest. The real estate man told me so!" He led me, holding my elbow, to the outhouse which I must admit was rather decent, for a privy! It was a one-holer, with a wooden lid, situated diagonally on a cement floor which was, of course, also covered with sand. I was told that it had been constructed during President Roosevelt's WPA Project in the 1930's when he put people back to work by sending them into the countryside to build privies. I gasped, chuckled, and was amazed to the point of being speechless that President Roosevelt had made it possible for us to have a john!

There was more of the property yet to be discovered. About twelve feet farther south stood a couple of sheds in disrepair. The ground was covered with feathers so we knew that chickens had been raised there in the past.

We then ventured to the two red barns which appeared to be in fairly good shape. One had a hayloft upstairs and a milk barn below. There were six stanchions (a wooden device which could be closed around the neck of milk cows, confining them but letting them eat while they were being milked) and a cement floor which would meet the Health Department standards. The other barn was very large with 10 stanchions. It only had a dirt floor and obviously had not been used in years. Outside the barns were three small corrals and a large one, all surrounded by four strands of barbed wire. There was no watering tank and the corrals were filled with piles and piles of old manure which had not been cleaned in years.

We walked toward the next building: the milk house. It was made of cinder blocks and contained a big vat, about 8' x 8', which had been used to cool several ten gallon cans of milk.

The final building was the garage, a red wooden structure, divided by a 4 ft. partition. On one side was room for an average size car, the other was littered with old corncobs. As we opened the door wide, several mice scattered, racing for cover. The tour of the outbuildings was disheartening—each structure needing more work than the previous one.

"Do you want to see the pastures next?" Fred asked. My reply was a very quiet, "No thank you." My thoughts were running wild and I felt disappointed. We wanted a ranch so badly, but how could I ever live in a miserable place like this? After all, I was raised in a house with running water, a bathroom (not a 'pathroom'), carpeting on the floors, a telephone, and even a kitchen! This was really going back to the bottom, a terrific come down. It wasn't hard for Fred to see my deep discouragement. "After all," he said, "sweetheart, you don't make money with a fancy house. The grass is the important thing and the cattle should do well here. The pastures are full of blue grama, the best prairie grass there is. The cattle will get nice and fat on that!" How could I argue? After all, we had dreamed of owning our own ranch and Fred's enthusiasm and energy was contagious. Maybe we could meet the challenge.

We had a quiet trip back to Ramah, both of us absorbed in our own thoughts. Finally, I became silly and suggested, "You know we really could make money by raising those mushrooms in the cellar and marigolds on one of the many porches and some poppies in the bedrooms. The soil is already on the floors! All we need is an interior irrigation system and we'd be in the money!" There was only silence from my lover!

After supper that night, we talked about my feelings and the reality of our possible purchase. I was raised to believe that wives backed up their husbands and stood by them. So, when Fred said he thought it would be a wonderful place for our own first ranch, I halfheartedly agreed. Even without the nice house, picket fence or lots of trees, we were on our way to becoming real ranchers! 🐴

Chapter 2

STARTING AT THE BOTTOM

The Old Place

For days after seeing the deplorable ranch house on the 'Old Place,' I found myself struggling with thoughts of how in the world I could possibly improve it? It seemed to be beyond help!

Meanwhile, Fred made an appointment with Mr. Griffin, the President of the Calhan Bank. Though he liked Fred and felt confident in his ability, it was our close friend and neighbor, Mr. Lasky, who made a difference.

Mr. Lasky was originally from Slovakia and after moving to the area, he made himself into an American-style "self-made man." To look at him you might think he was a pauper, but the opposite was true. He had started a typical country grocery store in Ramah. Its potbelly stove drew all the farmers and ranchers from the area who came to sit and gossip and perhaps, even buy something.

The 'Old Place'.

Mr. Griffin respected and appreciated the accomplishments of Mr. Lasky so when the latter recommended us so highly, the banker was convinced and willing to give us the loan. Fred and I signed a couple of documents and in a short 1-1/2 hours, we owned a 1440 acre ranch. It was that fast, that simple.

The cost was $28,000 with $5,000 down. For collateral, we offered our 50 head of cattle. As Mr. Griffin escorted us towards the door of the Bank, he shook Fred's hand, saying that he was not worried about us, largely because Mr. Lasky believed in us. It made us feel good, of course, but at the same time we felt an urgent sense of responsibility to meet our new commitment.

I had never before felt the burden of credit. I'm sure I looked worried. Fred saw my concern and said, "Don't worry about the payments, I know we'll do all right. You and I are good workers, so cheer up, kid!" With the words of encouragement, we headed to Ramah and our neat house with a bathroom and floors without sand. Suddenly, the house had become a cozy and comfortable place and even though it was very plain, now it looked like a mansion!

The mind is a great vehicle, it enables you to not only think and rationalize but, depending upon your mood and circumstance, it can raise your spirits and block out your problems. Fred's optimism spread over me like syrup over pancakes.

Later that week, a carpenter was hired to work on the ranch house and Fred was there everyday shoveling sand. They decided to make a kitchen out of the enclosed porch on the north side of the house...the one with the six leaky windows and the slanting floor! To reinforce the roof they used a special material that came in large rolls and was glued together with black, sticky tar between the seams. We hoped the hard downpours during the summer months would respect their efforts. As it turned out, only a few weeks later, while Fred's dear Aunt Blanche was visiting us, the snow on the roof melted and trickled down the ceiling making a large puddle on the floor in the kitchen. "You can't live in a place like this!" she cried while wiping her tears.

Fred was ready with his answer, one of which he has been reminded many times, "Aunt Blanche, you got to have faith!" The next day, Fred put up more of the roofing material and it never leaked again.

Another home improvement job was to caulk all the windows, put linoleum on the repaired and uneven floor in the kitchen. A cooking stove which was made for both coal and propane gas was bought from a neighbor and placed in the kitchen. Even though there was no water in the house, we installed a used sink to gobble up the waste water which drained through a single pipe and into a bucket that sat waiting below. I was now eight months pregnant and Fred promised me, "We'll have water in the house before the baby comes." Even though we made a lot of progress and would be able to move from Ramah in a matter of days, I didn't believe his promise about the water!

When a local man, Mr. Walmsley, heard that we had purchased a ranch, he told us that he was interested in buying our Ramah house. We had bought it two years earlier for $3,500 but still owed $2,500 on it. We asked $4,000 with $500 down. He agreed and we were all pleased.

We moved to the new ranch in early March, 1951. Ten of Fred's students from the 'On The Farm Training Program' were more than willing to give us a hand. I made a dozen and a half sandwiches and Fred bought some apples, and, of course, a case of Coors Beer. Everything and everybody was ready very early on moving day. It must have been before 6 AM when the guys began to appear. By then, it was beginning to get light. The sun on the cold morning had not yet emerged, but a bright yellow hue was appearing over the plains to the east. It promised to be a clear and sunny winter day. In an almost festive mood, our helpers began to load pickups and trailers with tables, couches, and beds until all of our possessions were removed from the house, tightly squeezed and strapped onto an assortment of cars and trucks. It was not long before the caravan left Ramah, headed towards our next, new experience.

No sooner had all the vehicles stopped in front of the ranch house when Cliff, one of the young students, came up to Fred and asked, "Got beer?"

Silly, of course we "got beer." Fred dug down behind the seat of the jalopy and pulled up what seemed like tons of coats and other clothing. Naturally, the beer was buried beneath it all. It took a while before it was retrieved. Then, of course, all the guys wanted

Mr. and Mrs. Manfred Vorenberg, Tommy and little Miss Bonnie Louise, were pleasant visitors at our house last Thursday. The Vorenberg family are new ranchers south of Calhan, in the Yoder vicinity, where they purchased a many-acre ranch a year ago to operate and continue his cattle business, along with being a G. I. instructor for veteran boys in the community. Fred and Elizabeth are natives of Germany, having come to our America in 1936 and 1940 respectively with their parents. Over here they met and were united in marriage after he served in the U.S. Army. So they never waste ny time in inquiring how my ꞁier brother is, who is sta-ꞁed in Germany, since the ꞁt of this year.

their beverage and to Fred's chagrin they took their time drinking it. There was a lot of joking and laughter while the ice cold beer transformed the young men into giddy boys. Imagine my embarrassment when later a couple of fellows, who were carrying the mattress to our bed, announced with big grins on their faces, "Here comes the workbench!" Embarrassed, I pretended not to have understood as I quickly disappeared into the house. Here I was, a married woman, already owning her first ranch and I immediately transformed back into the painfully shy little girl I used be.

Before long, the furniture was in its proper place, the sandwiches, apples and beer were gone and so were our 10 helpers. Fred and I looked at each other, spoke nothing, looked at our surroundings, quietly watched a plane high in the sky and then noticed that there was a complete absence of audible sound—total silence. A strange feeling overcame us. We felt alone, abandoned. Suddenly the world seemed austere.

But we also knew it was time for us to change those lonely sensations and become positive and assertive in our new situation. In no time at all, Fred was doing household chores! He went to the roughly dug well which had an electric pump and pulled up two full milk buckets of water. He filled them so full that they splashed some of the precious fluid onto his shoes. He was too excited to notice. Proudly, he placed the half empty buckets just inside the kitchen door with words which would soon become all too familiar, "Now you've got plenty of water!" Quietly, and before even looking at the buckets, I questioned, "I'll have to cook, clean the stove, the sink, the table, and take care of a 2-year old toddler with just this...plenty?" And as I was saying this I turned and saw something which made me gasp in disbelief. In the two buckets was a yellowish brown liquid, the color not unlike a cup of tea in which the tea bag had been left too long. "What in the world is this?" I shouted to the man who had promised to love and adore me for the rest of my life. "Oh, that's just rust from the pipes. It'll clear up in no time." Gullible as I was, I believed him. That was the first day on our first ranch, 'The Old Place' and we hoped our enthusiasm and skill would grow so Mr. Greenwood and Mr. Kline, the prior owners, would get their money!

The next day we took a sample of the water from the well and had it checked by the Health Department in Colorado Springs. A couple of days afterward they told us it was safe to drink. They explained that the dark yellow color was caused by an iron bacteria and that it was always going to be in the water. This was not what we hoped to hear.

I boiled the water in an experiment to try and make the water clearer. Imagine my surprise when in front of my eyes, a chemical change occurred and the whole thing separated. The water actually became almost clear but there was a slimy green material, not unlike algae, swimming daintily on the surface! What next? I got a strainer and poured the concoction through it. The result: almost clear water. So much for my science project!

Needless to say, we never put the refreshing, yet unsightly liquid, into clear glasses. In fact, that summer and all the ones to follow, I brewed mostly iced tea. I had to make certain that I used enough tea leaves since you could not go by appearance because the water always looked the color of dark tea!

One time during a hot summer day the County road crew, who was grading the Jones Road, came to the house asking for some glasses of water. All they wanted was a cool drink of plain, ordinary water but I was too embarrassed to offer them our yellow water. "Wouldn't you rather have some iced tea? I just made a pitcherful," I urged.

"No thanks, just water," was their immediate reply. It took another attempt to convince the guys that iced tea was a much better choice! They accepted and I was relieved.

In those days, every housewife was proud to show off her lilly white sheets on the line on washdays. We were the first people to show off our yellow ones! The china dishes took on the same yellow tint and it took cleanser and a firm brush to restore the original color. The kitchen sink proudly displayed its colorful interior because I never could completely eradicate the stain which had penetrated deep into its bowels.

For all the eight years we lived there, none of us ever got to wear white blouses, white shirts, white underwear, nor white socks. I made sure I would buy them in pink or yellow and I soon learned to play around with colors like an artist. If I bought something in blue and washed it in our yellow water—bingo: green!

> .n u.   ap-
> have bee nin u   ht along and   ap-
> parently all right.   *1949*
>   Fred Vorenberg, who has been liv-
> ing at Ramah, Colo., bought a 1500-
> acre cattle ranch, south of Calhan and
> moved there last week. He will con-
> tinue in the agriculture teaching of
> farm youth.
>   Mr. and Mrs. Floyd Turner were
> Sunday dinner geusts of the P   Mc-
> Clures at Palmer Lake, an'

I am proud to say that we adjusted to the 'Old Place' in record time. Fred's love of ranching grew and his enthusiasm and joy bubbled over almost every day. It wasn't as easy for me. Had it not been for the awful looking water, my adjustment would have been easier and faster. Silently, I tried to convince myself that there were worse things in life. After all, we were a healthy and happy family. So, I told myself to 'grin and bear it'—and that's what I did. Our dream of someday owning a ranch had finally materialized. 🐂

A Nursery In The Oven

W e settled down for our first night in the 'Old Place.' All day we had noticed, by their droppings, that mice had been around. I busied myself sweeping up the messes. "We'll just buy a mousetrap today when we go to Calhan," was my mature way of thinking. Surely, one would suffice. It seemed as though several families had made their home in our home and I was sure that they didn't appreciate us moving into what they considered was their territory. On the other hand perhaps they were pleased, for now, food would be more available and they could spend the rest of the winter living in a warm house! I was certain that animals think and I imagined them getting together that first night, having a big party to welcome us.

Mice, I used to believe, were kind of cute. Their beautiful soft fur, their short legs that moved so quickly when they ran, their inquisitive eyes and, what I liked best of all, their whiskers which trembled continually while they looked at me. I had no fear, no disgust, nor revulsion as some people have. But, when I saw the mess they left for me to clean up, I began to reconsider my love for these darling animals.

"Let's buy six traps tomorrow, I think we might catch one or perhaps two, if we are lucky," was my plea. And so the good husband made the purchase, and that night I set all six traps in strategic places where I could trick the furry critters into eating a chunk of Swiss cheese. Nothing but the finest, I thought, and hoped they'd enjoy their 'Last Supper'.

Off to bed, a kiss or two and then it happened. Loud and clear. SNAP. "Got one," Fred cheered joyously. One trap went off and then another until we counted all six snaps. "Well, now we can go to sleep."

Morning came and Fred soon left the house to do chores. I dragged myself out of bed to get dressed and start breakfast, the first in our new house. I was horrified when I realized that Fred had not touched the traps. There I was staring at an array of grey bodies, with eyes bulging caused by the piece of metal that pressed on their necks. They all were stretched out in grotesque positions. The cheese was not completely gone in some traps. Others looked as if the meal had been tasty. Perhaps some of the relatives had consumed it, saying, "Too bad he or she died, but one must not waste good food."

Now, what can the city girl do with this? Fred came in for breakfast and I asked him why he didn't empty the traps the first thing this morning. His answer was immediate and assertive, "Oh, I don't touch stuff like that, it makes me sick." From that moment on, I knew I had a new job. Squeamishly, I emptied all six traps onto a piece of paper, put on my coat and carried the bodies to the milk barn where the wild cats were already waiting for Fred to milk the cows. He poured some milk into a large metal pan the previous owner had probably used for the same purpose. The cats saw me. They timidly retreated towards the barn door in case I should do them harm. But when I emptied my six bodies into the pan they lost all fear and were soon munching on the delicious gourmet treat. They selected their tasty morsels and quickly ran them out of the barn to finish eating in privacy, never to return to the milk until much later in the day. It turned out that the trapping and counting became a nightly job, followed by the harvesting the next morning. Fred never touched any mouse traps except when he knew they were new, clean, and sterile.

Each day the wild cats from the barn welcomed me warmly, me, the pregnant mouse lady. All I had to do was call them from the house and they would come running for the 'catch of the night'.

As long as we lived on the Old Place, the morning routine was just another daily job. Sometimes, I even felt like I was winning the war! I was eventually proven wrong when years later, as I approached the stove to start breakfast, all of a sudden one mouse ran out of the top part where the gas burners are. I thought, "I better clean that stove today, some crumbs must have fallen down there." I opened the oven door to cook the morning's bacon and reached for the frying pan, which was stored there due to lack of cupboard space. I let out a scream of utter surprise and disbelief. There, in the skillet, was a warm, cozy, infant nursery with four blind, pink-skinned, wiggly baby mice. The mother had all kinds of stuff around and under them, things like pieces of newspaper, hay, straw and a piece of cloth. Actually this was all kind of cute—but what to do next!

The children, Tommy & Bonnie, stared at me with disgust when I suggested they had to be killed. "No, no," was 2-year old Bonnie's reaction, "I can raise them and feed them milk from a doll bottle. Please, Mommy, let me!" I knew I had to turn down her generous offer. I carefully lifted the skillet, carried it outside by the barn and found a large puddle of rainwater that had fallen during the night. Feeling guilty, I let the babies slip into the water, nest and all and quickly turned away. I hoped the mother mouse would forgive me for the dreadful deed I had done to her new family.

On the Old Place, mice weren't the only animals freeloading on us. One very cold winter morning, I looked out of the living room window into the added-on, enclosed porch that had stairs leading down to a root cellar. The dark and cold basement had a dirt floor and was perfect for my proudly stored home-canned fruits, vegetables, jams, and jellies. Suddenly, I noticed sitting there on the top step was some kind of animal that looked like a huge mouse. He was lying, relaxed, with his belly exposed, legs stretched out to the full length of his large body, trying to catch every ray of sunshine. Though I had never seen one in real life, I figured out that the long tail meant that this was a rat and I guessed that he lived in the cellar. He stayed a long time in the toasty sun and though I never saw him again, I was sure he was down there! After this incident, I never went into the cellar without a flashlight. Fred's only comment to this short episode was, "Forget about him." But I never did.

Several years later on yet another cold day, the sun was out doing her best to warm people—and rats. I was sitting comfortably in the one-hole outhouse which had a door that opened to the south, facing away from the road, for privacy! My 'job' was done but I refused to get up and pull up my jeans. The sun felt so good on my thighs that I simply just sat there. Suddenly there was a rushing sound that came from behind the privy. It came closer and closer. From out of my relaxed state, the largest rat I ever saw surprised me. He was heading right through the open door, trying to join me in my own private outhouse. He was more surprised to find me there than I was surprised to see him. He stared at me with utter disgust. And in rat language, cussed me out!

Not a moment to spare, he resumed his trip south, towards an old building several yards away with one of our barn cats in hot pursuit. Now, I felt moved to get up and see what had happened. The cat raced at top speed until she cornered the grey thing, killed it and then simply walked away. Later, I learned that rats are poisonous, especially the tail, and that most animals do not eat them.

I decided that rats and mice thought that "people all look alike and they're all our enemies." For me, I could put up with the mice and although the rats never did any harm to us, I always felt that we both needed our own space! 🐎

Cartoon drawn by my Brother, Martin Gumbel.

My Sister, Anne

My sister, Anne, was a registered nurse who graduated from a New Jersey School of Nursing. For a while she worked at Michael Reese Hospital in Chicago and later she moved to San Francisco where she found a part-time job in a local medical center. While at work, a visiting doctor told her of a job opening in an orphanage and gave her the address. That same day she found herself being interviewed by the director, Mrs. Freed. She was young, short in stature, perhaps 5'2" with lovely features, long blond hair and a personality that would put anybody at ease. Anne was informed that Freed was looking for an R.N. to live-in. While the salary was not great, Anne did accept the position with the stipulation that she must give notice at her present position which would take, at least, two weeks. On her way home, she kept wondering, "Did I do the right thing?" She realized how much she loved children and it would mean caring for their health on a daily basis, besides she would have a place to stay and no need to spend her salary on an apartment.

The day came when she was supposed to start working and her excitement grew to such a degree that she forgot to eat breakfast! The bus took her to the orphanage and only then did she look around thoroughly. The morning fog had already lifted and a bright sun shone onto a lovely two story building which was situated in a beautifully manicured lawn. There were roses in full bloom in red and pink, and on each side of the structure were oleanders, at least fifteen feet tall, also in full radiance. Near the entrance were a couple of lilac bushes. The lovely garden and the warm California sunshine added to Anne's enthusiasm as she entered the building. Her only thought was, "Will the kids like me?"

As Anne headed towards Mrs. Freed's office, a cute little boy who seemed to be about 8 years old appeared from nowhere, asking her, "Are you the new nurse?"

"I sure am. What's your name?"

"I'm Roy, and I have asthma sometimes, but today I have a sore throat. They told us kids that a new nurse would be coming this morning."

"Okay Roy, you just wait here and we'll go to the infirmary after I see Mrs. Freed. All right?"

"All right, Ma'am," was his very polite response.

Anne was impressed and thought, "I wonder if all the children are as well mannered and polite as Roy." Mrs. Freed greeted her and both left to show Anne where her living quarters were. It was a medium sized room which held a bed, dresser, good-sized table, and a couple of chairs. In the corner was a brown leather rocker almost like the one she so enjoyed in her own apartment. Mrs. Freed showed her the walk-in closet which prompted Anne to joke, "I think I better buy some new clothes, just to fill it!" The bathroom was tiny but had all the necessary conveniences. Next, Mrs. Freed showed Anne the infirmary which was adjacent to her living quarters. There was a long wooden bench outside in the hallway just in front of a door and guess who was sitting there. It was the cute boy, Roy, who had greeted her. There he sat, grinning from ear to ear, "Remember me? I beat you to it. I mean, I got here before you did!" Anne realized then that she had a precocious child on her hands!

The infirmary was bright and cheerful with lots of pictures of animals on off-white walls to contrast the white furniture. All were highlighted with splashes of red, blue, and yellow. There was an examining table in the center of the room and a half open file cabinet against the wall. The nearby desk was a mess with lots of forms lying around in disarray, a couple of pencils and even un-opened letters. The typewriter was off to the side of the desk. Next to it was a closed door which Mrs. Freed opened, taking Anne into another room which contained four beds, one in each corner. All were neatly made up, showing off baby blue colored blankets and crisp white sheets.

The place 'screamed' for attention and Anne, a neat and orderly person, silently vowed, "Don't worry, we'll have this place in apple pie order before you know it!" Mrs. Freed returned to her immaculate office and Anne began to explore her new space. She looked around, gave a quick smile to Roy, and began to feel both comfortable and excited about her new endeavor.

During the next few months, Anne developed a wonderful rapport with the children. She got to know not only the youngsters, but also their families, if they had any. Roy was a frequent patient because he was suffering from all sorts of allergies, mainly asthma, and Anne treated him whenever he had any complaints. Roy's father was Eric Cross who came often, but alone, to visit his son because his wife was in a mental institution. They were legally separated. It took no time at all for Roy to make sure his Dad became acquainted with Anne. And it became obvious that Eric was coming to the orphanage more often than normal. Soon people figured out that it was more than a father coming to see his son, it was a man showing interest in an attractive woman...my sister.

After a few months, when his divorce became final, Eric and Anne were married. They rented an apartment and brought Roy to his new home. Everybody was happy to be a family again and Anne set about doing things for her "boys".

My sister Anne, with Roy and Bonnie during a visit to our ranch.

One day, a letter arrived at our ranch from Anne saying that the 'new' family planned to visit us while they travelled around Colorado. We were excited and I quickly wrote back extending them a hearty invitation. Our children were slightly younger than Roy, so it would be nice for them to meet their new older cousin.

Coincidentally, the next day we received another letter, this one from my mother. She wrote us about our new brother-in-law. Already, she was not fond of him. "He's not good enough for Anne, and besides, he is ugly," she wrote. We laughed at the comment, thinking how Eric already was having mother-in-law problems! Mother's letter continued. She told how she was taking a walk in Golden Gate Park with Max, Martin and the 'new family' when she whispered to her sons that she thought Eric was "hässlich", the German word for "homely."

Anne heard her remark and spoke out loud, "Thank you very much!"

Quickly, my mother then made a weak attempt to cover up her faux-pas by uttering clumsily, "I meant the goats over there." The comment was an indication of what my mother's relationship with Eric would be like. They never did make a connection, and for years they would do almost anything to avoid being together. But with Roy it was different. They were able to build a wonderful relationship with deep affection for each other that lasted for years.

Two weeks later, we prepared for the 'new family' to visit the ranch. They were going to arrive that afternoon and the house was already spic and span, the beds for the guests were made and there was lots of food in the refrigerator. Around 9 AM, I remembered how much Anne loved coffee ice cream. I decided to make a batch so it would be ready when they arrived. I quickly opened the package of Junket ice cream mix, scooped off the top and thickest part of the cream from yesterday's milk, measured the amount needed and added it to the mix along with enough coffee to make it tasty. I placed the ice cream attachment onto the Mixmaster and turned it on. Then I heard a noise outside and looked up to see the mailman leaving the mail in the box. When I turned my attention back to the mixer I realized that the sweet, thick cream had turned into butter! There I was making coffee butter!! At least, this was original!

In my shocked state, I began to remove the butter from the paddles using my finger to remove some which had stuck on the beaters. Suddenly, I must have hit the 'on' switch and those beaters went crazy. They caught my finger, squeezing it as if they planned to devour it. I let out a loud, panicked "Ouch!" and only then did I think to turn off that woman-eating monster. The Mixmaster was turned off, but I was standing there in excruciating pain with a beater on my hand. I had two choices. One, stay in the kitchen with the steel utensil dangling from my hand or, two, wait for Fred to come home and have him free me with the help of the acetylene welder. I decided to apply some grease to my now very red finger in an attempt to extract it myself. Luckily the latter worked. But it was a painful reminder for days to keep an eye on these new fangeled inventions.

A couple of nights later I had a nightmare: I had walked all the way to the Emergency room of St. Francis Hospital in Colorado Springs, some 35 miles away, adorned with that beater which by now had became part of my anatomy. As I arrived at the hospital about 50 nurses surrounded me. They were standing around, pointing fingers at me, and laughing so hard that it interrupted my dream. I awoke, drenched with perspiration and relieved that I didn't have beaters for hands! It was a week before the swelling decreased and I could bend the finger again. Fred's only comment was, "You got to be more careful." This powerful expression of sympathy did very little for my wounded psyche but this was my 'better half,' the tough guy, the man I had promised to adore!

The anticipated afternoon was here and Anne and her newly acquired family arrived. It was a pleasure to see her again and we sisters excitedly hugged each other before she introduced Roy and her new husband. Eric stood about 5'10", had thinning black hair, tired blue eyes, and a very pleasant smile. But it was his nose that was an inch too long for his narrow face that made him look less than a beauty. Indeed, I was pleasantly surprised that he was not as homely as my mother had warned. With Roy it was a different situation. The 9-year old was tall for his age with black hair that showed signs of being recently trimmed, and he was quite handsome. When he gave me a polite hug and said, "Hello, Aunt Schlitza," my love for him was complete!

At the first pause in the conversation, Eric spoke with his thick Austrian accent that cut through the air, almost interrupting our relaxed attitudes, "Let's get going and unpack. I am dead tired." With that, Anne sprang to action and started to pick up one of the suitcases. It indicated to me how their relationship would be.

While Anne and Eric got settled, I began preparing the meat loaf dinner and the kids got acquainted. Tommy went to begin the nightly chores of riding Topsey to bring home the milk cows which had spent the day grazing in the pasture. Soon he returned with eight cows in front of him. Our urban relatives rushed out to watch the 'show'.

"Look at the pretty cows and the pretty horsy," called Anne to Roy, embarrassing us with the childish way of referring to our animals.

Not listening, Tommy announced in a clear and matter of fact voice, "Daddy, you better get the bull. Bessy (every dairy has at least one Bessy!) is in heat." Before Fred could even react, Anne grabbed Roy by the hand and literally pulled him towards the house. I was dumbfounded and had no idea what the commotion was about. We calmly finished the chores and returned to the house to check on dinner.

I was met by my sister who declared, "How could you do this? You put Tommy up to this only to embarrass us, but mainly to frighten Roy. If there is any sex education to be done, it'll come from us, not you!" I was more surprised at this outburst than if I had just won the lottery. I tried in vain to assure her that there was no conspiracy. I explained how breeding cattle at the right time was of utmost importance to us and that the ranching and dairy business depended upon such valuable information. She didn't buy it, and continued to think that it was a conspiracy! Later that night, it was the coffee butter that truly broke the ice. I had decided to get up the courage and serve the unique spread to our guests. To my amazement, they loved it and we laughed about my strange concoction.

The next day began with a typical ranch breakfast before piling into Eric's car for a drive to the Garden of the Gods by Colorado Springs where beautiful sandstone formations in striking red colored rocks had become a popular attraction. For the tourists, the park scheduled Indian dancers to perform. They had bright feathers on their heads and their ankles and wrists were wrapped with bells which jingled as they danced to the rhythmic sound of their tom-toms. It was a superb adventure for all of us.

Next, our visitors wanted to see the Cave of the Winds, another popular attraction. We had never been there before which was so typical for many of the ranchers in the area. It took company for us to get out and see places of interest in our own backyard as it were.

We were travelling downhill on a rather steep and winding gravel road which had signs of 5 miles per hour on every turn. Eric was not heeding the warnings, driving much too fast and braking continually as we went along. Both Fred and I were getting scared. Half heartedly and barely audibly, I said, "There's a five mile speed limit."

Immediately, Anne turned towards me in the backseat, "Those signs are not for Eric. He's a good driver."

I turned to Fred and whispered, "Is your will up to date?" In spite of the 'good' driver's erratic maneuvering, we arrived safely at the Cave.

Though my sister and I always got along well, it irked me to see her protecting her husband whatever he did or did not do, even if it didn't make any sense. When, for example, she and I would be alone at mealtime we would sit and talk long after we had finished our food. But when Eric was present, Anne would jump up after the last bite was in her mouth and announce, "let's go." Obediently, all of us would stand up and clear the table. Later she explained how Eric didn't like to sit after he had eaten. I hoped that her husband appreciated her to the fullest during their married life. She was too good a person, too good to a fault.

The Cross' left several days later and we were so happy when they said they had a good time. We did, too, and thanks to them we were able to be tourists as well. We promised one another to get together more often, now that our families got acquainted. In the meantime, we vowed to write regularly and to keep each other informed of things, important or unimportant. My sister, Anne, and I always got along well as we were growing up and we continued to do so in our adult years.

It's A Girl

"Only one more week and we'll have another baby," I announced that Sunday morning. Everything was ready, the suitcase was filled with a normal sized nightgown, slippers, a robe, and toilet articles plus a few baby clothes and a couple of newly-washed Curity cloth diapers. The '38 Chevrolet Coupe, which Tommy awkwardly had named the 'jalopy'—(not too politically correct for after WW2!!) was ready and full of gas, just in case we needed it in a hurry.

Uncle Herman and Aunt Blanche had planned to visit that day so that she, who was willing to stay with Tommy while I was in the hospital, could learn the routine in the house and be more helpful.

> Mr. and Mrs. Fred Vorenberg
> and family are sporting a new
> auto these days.

It was a beautiful day, sunshiny and a sky so dark blue it almost looked artificial. This was mid-April 1951 and it was cold. Fred returned to the house after doing chores, with red cheeks and a big smile on his face. "Our first calf was born during the night and it's a heifer. One of the new Holsteins had it. You think of a good name." Having a newly born heifer calf is good luck. In addition, she'll help build our own dairy herd within two short years. So, I needed to think of a special name since she was the very first animal born on our ranch.

My hair was still in curlers when the folks from Denver arrived. I should have known better because they had a habit of coming earlier than expected—always. After the usual hugging and kissing, Uncle Herman brought in a basket full of goodies. We visited while I hurriedly removed my curlers and tried to look presentable. Next, we put on our jackets and walked to the barn to inspect the new calf. There she was, standing awkwardly next to her mother, our beautiful black and white spotted cow. The mother would occasionally lick her and make low cooing sounds. The name came to me in an instant, 'Prima donna'. The calf was as beautiful as her mother.

Uncle Herman was usually pleased with the meals I made, but not on that day. A typical German, he simply had to have meat and potatoes at every meal, especially potatoes. Well, this time my meal consisted of what I used to choose for my Birthday dinner when I was a child, macaroni and cheese, a ring bologna and, lastly, ice cold applesauce—an essential ingredient. This menu remained one of my favorites. Still, Uncle Herman let me know more than once that day, saying in a pouty voice, that he "didn't like" macaroni. From then on, I always had potatoes when he came to dinner...I refused to give him an opportunity to complain! And after that, he always raved about my meals!

Uncle Herman returned to Denver the same day and Aunt Blanche made herself at home in our spare room. Hours later we settled down for bed.

"Ouch, ouch!" that's all I would utter, then another "Ouch!" and Fred woke up. It was

1 AM and I knew it was time to go to the hospital. A week early. I got dressed, grabbed the waiting suitcase, and stood ready for Fred to drive the car up to the front door. It seemed to take him forever and I secretly started to make plans to deliver the baby by myself. Finally he showed up, apologizing, "We have no lights, don't know what's wrong. We can stop at the Ellicott Gas Station. The moon is out and that should help. Come on, get in."

Fred drove slowly and we felt so lucky that there was indeed a bright moon that night. When we arrived at the gas station it was 2:30 AM and, of course, no one was there. At once, Fred began honking the horn. He got out of the car and shouted toward the living quarters which were above the station, "SCOTT, Scott, wake up. My wife is having a baby and we have no lights on the car." We waited, then Fred tried again.

We saw the curtains part and there was good old Scott with his head peering though the window. "You'll probably need a fuse. I'll be right down." The next thing I knew, Scott appeared at the car door. He opened it and scooted inside, almost having to crawl under me to reach the spot where the fuse went. Embarrassed, I moved as far away as I could. Happily for all of us, it worked! The lights came on and we were on our way.

Thirty or so more miles and we arrived at Glockner-Penrose Hospital in Colorado Springs. Fred stayed with me all night, sleeping soundly. By morning he awoke and told me he needed to, "go home and milk the cows."

Hours later, a beautiful baby girl, whom we named Bonnie Louise, was born. Dr. Carpenter, who was my OB doctor, burst out laughing after he asked me where Fred was and I matter of factly answered that he "had to go home to milk the cows!"

Being at the hospital was delightful. I had no chores to do, no 'pathroom', clear, white, running water, and delicious food. I decided, then and there, to have more babies! This was a real vacation!

Poor Aunt Blanche had to pick up the routine at home with no help from me. In fact, the minute the baby and I returned from the hospital, she quickly made us go to the neighbor's phone to call Uncle Herman to pick her up! She explained to me, "Uncle Herman needs me, too, you know." We all hated to see her leave the next day. She did a fine job and all of us loved her. 🐎

To the most Beloved Wife and Mommy in the World; Thank you for presenting us with a little sister.

All our love,
Tommy and Dadda

The Cottrells

Our other close neighbors, Mr. and Mrs. Cottrell, lived a mile west of us. Their farm consisted of a small white house, badly in need of a new coat of paint, a large garage with lots of storage space, a big chicken house, and a barn built out of cinder blocks. There was a windmill and next to it a fenced-in garden and, of course, an outhouse. The Cottrells were in their 60's and out of respect and ingrained German training, we always addressed them as "Mr. and Mrs.", never by their first names. We became good friends even though they were our neighbors for only two years.

It was soon after we moved to the 'Old Place' when the Cottrells came to our ranch to introduce themselves. When we showed them our new baby, Bonnie, Mr. Cottrell said, "Wow, she almost looks human!" We laughed and immediately there was a spark of affection between us. We never let him forget his words, especially months later when she developed into a beautiful child with blond curls and blue eyes.

Our daughter, Bonnie Louise.

We helped each other a lot. The Cottrells had one milk cow and about 20 cattle, mostly Herefords and Black Angus. Since they didn't have a chute, a device to control an animal so you could treat it safely, the Cottrells would drive their cattle down the road to vaccinate, dehorn, and brand them at our place. In return he would help us with numerous jobs and was especially skilled with any task that required a tractor.

One Sunday morning, not long after we had met, Mrs. Cottrell drove up in her car. She was all dressed up, her hair was in a neat bun, and she was wearing shiny, black shoes which had never stepped on manure...a rarity on a ranch! She wore a pink necklace and a silver brooch close to her neck, and a touch of lipstick. Her blue dress, she proudly explained, was home sewn and the material was originally a sack filled with chicken feed. She proudly continued, "My daughter sewed it for me and it only took four sacks!" She was on her way to church and wondered if I would like to come along. I told her that we were Jewish and that I was not interested in going, but thanked her anyway.

"You must think of me as a terrible person because I don't go to services much," I answered.

"Oh, no, you are a "Martha" who stays home and works and I am a "Mary" who attends church." She later explained that "Mary" and "Martha" both are good people.

Several months later, Frank Herz, for whom I had cared in Germany when he was a baby, came to visit from New York City and Mrs. Cottrell asked him to go to church. He accepted. When he returned from the Pentecostal Church, we asked him how it was. He told us that, "People were crying, talking in tongue, and some, including Mrs. Cottrell, were falling to the ground and rolling on the floor." We were amazed at the stories he told. She never again asked either Frank or me to join her in church and I appreciated it, knowing now what went on!

Since neither the Cottrells nor we had a telephone, they suggested that if either of us ever needed help after dark we could flash the yard light off and on. As we were just about to finish the milking one night, we noticed that their light was blinking. Fred got excited and told me to finish washing the milk utensils so he could see what was wrong. Mr. Cottrell had problems with a stomach ulcer and maybe he needed to go to the hospital again. When Fred got to their house, Mrs. Cottrell came to the door in her pink flannel nightie and told him how she had been sick all day with the flu and that her husband had gone to Calhan for medicine several hours ago and·wasn't back yet. She was worried about him because he always tried to save gasoline by coasting down the hill into Calhan. She thought he might have lost control of the car, maybe he careened over the side and was in a terrible accident. Would Fred, "Please, check on him," she begged.

"Of course, I'll be glad to." Fred said, comforting her. He drove over to the Farrell's and asked Bill to help because his car had a search light. They left at once and when they got to the hill they slowed down directing the light all over the steep ditches alongside the road. They saw nothing. It must have been close to 9 PM when they arrived in Calhan. All the stores were closed except for the beer hall. "Let's go in and see if somebody knows the whereabouts of Mr. Cottrell, perhaps somebody saw him earlier."

As they entered the establishment, they saw only two customers in the usually-filled parlor, and one was our missing and feared-dead neighbor "Oh Mr. Cottrell, your wife is worried sick about you. You better get home."

Mr. Cottrell roared, "A man can't even have a glass of beer without that religious woman bitching at me." With that, he paid the bill and stomped out of the beer hall as Fred and Bill chuckled. Later, the episode provided many laughs...even Mr. Cottrell thought it was funny!

Now that we were living on a ranch, my frugal husband decided that I should learn how to cut his hair. "After all," he said, "even if you mess up, the cows won't mind." As luck would have it, one afternoon the Cottrells came for a visit bringing their nephew and his wife. Believe it or not, the nephew was a barber! I wondered whether Fred had secretly arranged this because the guy even had his professional tools in his car! Before I knew it, the young man pulled out his clippers and showed me how to use them, teaching me how to correct the many mistakes I would make. For years I used the techniques he taught me and after a while I came to consider myself an accomplished 'Tonsorial Artist'!

As far as the Toni Home Permanents were concerned, Fred made good on his promise and produced many a kinky curl of which he was so proud. Years later and after several hours of 'beauty parlor work,' Bonnie, then around four years old, told her dad, "You're great, Daddy, you made Mommy look like Queen Elizabeth!"

Almost every rancher in our area had a pig or two on their place and so did we. Both our porkers were getting fatter by the day and Mr. Cottrell, "Bless his Heart," offered to help butcher them.

When Fred decided to do a certain thing on a certain day, he would not let anything interfere with his plans. On the day he had planned to butcher our two hogs, a nasty and powerful north wind suddenly blew in, surprising everybody. Now, 'normal' people would cancel the task until the weather was more pleasant, but not my husband. No way! Instead, he said, "Let's hurry and get this job done! You never know what tomorrow will bring." The boss had spoken. Within minutes we were heating gallons of water. The two hogs were killed and the men fixed a contraption called a 'block and tackle' from where the carcasses, one at a time, would be attached. After the water came to a boil, the animal would then be lowered and submerged into it. After a short while, it would be pulled up and the hair scraped off. The job proved to be more difficult than usual because the cold wind would set the bristles firmer and deeper into the skin. They struggled for hours before finishing the job. The men then halved the carcasses, wrapped them into bed sheets and took them to the Cold Storage and Freezer Locker in Calhan where they would hang for seven days after which the owner of the locker would cut up the meat to our specifications.

The following day, Fred started coughing and had a low grade fever. By late afternoon his temperature had climbed to 103 degrees. Inhaling the steam from the boiling water along with the icy north wind—together—brought about either a bad case of bronchitis or even pneumonia. I rushed for the car keys and drove to our neighbors, the Farrell's, to use their telephone so I could call the Calhan druggist, Hal Thomason, hoping he was still in the store. "Can I give Fred a shot of the Penicillin from the vial I bought the other day...the one I got for the sick cow? Is it pure enough for humans?" The words just rolled out of my mouth nervously.

"Sure," was his answer as he continued, "and if he's not better in 48 hours, take him to the doctor." That's all I needed to know. It took only a couple of shots in his "you know where" plus several days of bed rest before the resilient patient was on the way to recovery. Meanwhile, I had done the chores for both of us and was longing for a well-deserved

> Friends are indeed sorry Fred Vorenberg has been confined to his home because of illness. Kind neighbors assisted Mrs. Vorenberg with chores and ranch work.

vacation in Hawaii since Fred's illness could have been avoided if he had been a little more flexible with his precious schedule.

A few weeks after butchering the hogs, Mr. Cottrell asked Fred to help him butcher his steer. "And bring your .22 rifle!" This time, the weather was perfect, warm with no wind. Fred shot the Holstein steer in the forehead and he dropped at once. The men hoisted the 800 pound animal, skinned him, sawed through the chest bones and opened the abdominal cavity. Out poured the entrails which they caught in a bucket. Next, they removed the liver, heart and stomach. "Do you ever eat tripe?" Fred asked Mr. Cottrell.

"Hell no, you can have it," he answered. Suddenly, it was time for me to learn all about tripe!

When Fred handed me the weird looking stuff, he explained that it came from the cow's rumen, the largest of four stomachs. It looked like a honeycomb and it was green in color. He told me to wash it well and then "cook the daylights out of it" because it is tough meat. I began by washing it for 10 minutes but the green color wouldn't leave. I thought I might use bleach but decided instead to boil it and dump out the green water, add more fresh water and boil it again. I did it three more times and the meat began to look less green. After that, I put the whole thing in the Mirro-Matic pressure cooker and, as I was told, continued to "cook the daylights out of it!" Later on, I made a white sauce, added some parsley flakes, lemon juice, salt, and pepper plus a small piece of mozzarella cheese. To this, I added the tripe which I had cut into 1-1/2" pieces. The meat dish turned out to be a true delicacy; one we would enjoy many more times.

Learning new things was a daily occurrence and, now it included cooking. When Fred complimented me saying, "I was getting to be a great ranch wife", I felt like I was in 7th heaven!

Later that year, we stopped by the Cottrells just to say "Hi!" and were ushered into the kitchen and there was Mrs. Cottrell, all upset, "Come in if you can find room to walk." We looked around and were shocked at what we saw. Mr. Cottrell explained how his beloved Buick had engine trouble. He had taken the whole thing apart and the strange pieces were lying all over the kitchen floor, sink, and indeed the whole house. He was sure he could fix the ailing car.

We didn't stay long, there was too much tension between the couple. But before we left, I said jokingly, "Make sure you don't leave a sponge or two in the belly of the patient!" (When I worked in the Operating Room this was a continual concern and it was the duty of the nurses to count every sponge we used.) It took a whole week before the car was completely re-assembled and, according to the Cottrells, it purred like a kitten when it drove. The operation was a success and the patient lived!

Religion caused a great deal of conflict between the couple. Mr. Cottrell loved going to movies even though Mrs. C. tried to forbid him to attend them. It was strictly against her religion. "It's bad influence and it will get you into trouble for sure," was how she always warned him, but he continued to go anyway. After they would return from church meetings Mr. Cottrell would confide in us telling how the "Jezebels" sat around acting so "hoity-toity" and how Mrs. Cottrell loved every minute of it!

Our good neighbors sold their ranch on December 31, 1952 for $20 an acre and moved to Colorado Springs. They bought a large apartment house and were happy that they didn't have to work so hard anymore. Their ranch was bought by an elderly gentleman who turned out to be another colorful human being—maybe it was the water in that house!!

When we went to Colorado Springs, we regularly stopped by the Cottrells'. One time, we knocked on their kitchen door and nobody answered. We knocked again, thinking they might be in the back of the house. We were returning to our car after a third knock when suddenly the kitchen door was flung open and a loud voice told us to come in. We stopped, turned around, and noticed that Mrs. Cottrell had been crying. Concerned and thinking someone had died, we rushed into the kitchen and asked what was wrong. I looked around. There were three women, all crying but trying to control their apparent agony. Finally, one of the ladies spoke quietly, "We was havin' a prayer meetin'!"

I apologized for our interruption but asked innocently, "Then why are you so upset?"

Nobody answered me because this apparently was customary in their religion. "You learn something new every day," I thought as we left rather quickly, feeling somewhat embarrassed.

During the next few years, Mr. Cottrell would come to our place and do most of the summertime farming. He refused to sleep on the living room couch, so we put a bed in the basement, just as he wanted. "I haven't slept with the 'ole lady' for years and she makes me sleep in the basement in Colorado Springs, so I feel comfortable there," he exclaimed.

Much too soon, we went to their funerals, one year apart. We would miss the Cottrells terribly. Not only were they good neighbors, but they were fun to be with. Both had hearts as big as Texas, with room to spare. Never did they visit us without bringing something. It might have been food, flowers, or something for the children. We were always thrilled when we would see the old Buick drive up for that meant good times and warm companionship. Though Mrs. Cottrell told me more than once that she loved me like a daughter, all of us liked, and probably loved, the Cottrells—who provided us with so many wonderful and pleasant moments which we continue to recall even to this day. 🐎

The Farrells

The Farrell family one mile east were actually the first neighbors we met, even before we moved onto the Old Place of our ranch. We only met Carol Farrell and her beautiful teen age daughters, Kay and Karin and their son, Karl. Mr. Farrell, for some reason, was never around. It was much later that we found out he was incarcerated in the State Penitentiary in Canon City. The family had a small Grade A dairy farm and Carol and Karin did all the milking while Kay did the cooking. They lived in an old school house and to our surprise, it was so modern it even had a bathroom and a telephone!! Such luxury! This soon became our vital link to the outside world.

The family made frequent trips to visit the husband and father and also to see relatives who had a cherry orchard in Canon City. The summer of 1951, the first one we spent on our ranch, Carol asked us to come along with them to pick some cherries. After a two hour trip, we arrived at the orchard. The trees were loaded, the branches bending under the weight of the fruit. We picked two buckets full of bright red sour pie cherries which we de-stoned with a gadget Carol loaned us the following day. I made a couple of pies and canned the rest.

Whenever the Farrells needed help they would drive up in their rattly old green Ford pickup and Fred was only too glad to give them a hand. Often their cattle were sick and needed a Penicillin shot or a cow could not have her calf which needed to be pulled.

Their dairy herd was made up of Brown Swiss cows and the boss of the herd was a mean bull which hated everything and everybody except his harem. He was huge and he snorted when he saw people or horses. There was no fence that could contain him and he could frequently be found grazing on the lush grass that grew in the ditches alongside the road. Only folks in trucks could convince this beast to return to his home. Cattlemen have come to understand that dairy bulls, in general, have bad dispositions, but this one was exceptionally mean. The Farrells sold him before the year was up and bought another one who was no better!

About a year after meeting Carol, Bill was released from prison and we finally met him. He was a pleasant man with an easy smile who loved to talk, but he loved his beer even more. Many times we heard Carol complain how he was a "no good bum who was so drunk last night that he couldn't milk them cows and me and Karin had to do it." She would also tell us how Albert, her husband's drinking buddy, would also get drunk but still managed to milk his only cow! Trouble was, he never could get off his low milking stool unless he pulled himself up by the cow's tail. The story went that when the animal realized he was through milking, she would turn her behind towards him and start switching that tail so he could grab it and get up. Smart cow, indeed!

There was a lot of good grass in the bottom land northeast of our ranch and it would make a good amount of hay. So, we thought of the Farrells and their old tractor which they were happy to loan us, considering how much help we had given them with their livestock. "But," they warned, "if something breaks, you'll have to fix it." We agreed.

Fred drove the tractor home and hooked the mowing machine behind it. It was not long before he was cutting the grass and having a wonderful time. This was a new experience for him. On Uncle Herman's ranch, there was no tractor so all the heavy work had to be done with horses. Now, this was progress indeed.

Fred was happily rolling along trying to figure out how soon he could buy a used tractor when...Bang! "What in the world was that?" He jumped off the machine and looked at the huge rear wheel. It was here from where the sound came...the tire was flat. This was a major problem.

Fred walked home and drove the 'Jalopy' to the Farrell's where he used their telephone. He called the John Deere store in Calhan and spoke to Bert Skaggs who promised to come and fix the tire. "A back tire," he explained, "not only needs to be repaired but also has to have a chloride solution added so that it is heavy enough to get traction in loose soil. It'll cost you $30." With a sick feeling, Fred remembered the promise he made to Bill to fix anything that broke. After a few days, the repaired tire was back on the tractor and Fred was again mowing the grass. His enthusiasm about the task was less than it had been earlier and he secretly wished for a reliable team of horses.

Actually, his wish came true a few weeks later when he told one of his students, Bill Sater, that our corrals needed to be cleaned of manure. The man offered the use of his team of Clydesdale horses and a scraper made especially for this purpose. "I'll bring 'em out tomorrow if you need 'em and you can keep 'em as long as you want."

The next afternoon a two ton truck drove up to our house with two huge heads looking over the solid sides. I never saw or was so close to such big horses. It made me feel quite insignificant. They looked at me; I looked at them. Both animals seemed identical. They were a soft brown color with one white spot between gorgeous, big eyes. Completely at ease and relaxed, they waited to be unloaded. Bob lowered the back end of the truck which made into ramp, backed out the horses and led them into the barn. What a well behaved team and so beautiful, I mused. I fell in love with them.

After Bob unloaded the scraper and the harnesses, he showed us how to hook them up. We hoped we would remember all the details. He refused to stay for supper and left. Much later that evening, after the chores were done, we checked on the horses and found them munching on mounds of hay, barely giving us a second look. "I never thought that huge horses like these could be so calm," I said to Fred.

Enthusiastically, he encouraged me, "Let's see how well they work in the morning!"

The next day was quite chilly for summer and the wind, which had started during the evening, seemed to get stronger by the hour. The routine morning chores were done and Fred was getting ready to clean the corrals. A few minutes later, I saw him pulling the two feisty horses behind him. Next, he tried to hook up the harnesses but had trouble because the horses wouldn't stand still. Both of them were dancing around, becoming more restless as the wind, blowing from the north, hit them squarely into their faces.

I was watching from the kitchen window and wondered if Fred shouldn't wait for a calmer day. The horses obviously did not like the weather. But 'friend-husband' did not give up his plan for the day and he decided that 'wify' might be of assistance. He yelled for me— I guess he did—all I could see were his lips moving as he looked towards the house with a desperate expression on his face. I wondered what in the world I could do to help him.

I quickly put on my jean jacket and went outside. Imagine my horror when I was told to, "Get in front of the horses and hold them by the bridle to keep them still."

"Who, me?" I screamed, "Stand in front of these wild beasts?"

"You'll be all right," he yelled back, "just hold them still long enough so I can hook up the harnesses and the scraper."

I shouted back at him, raising my voice above the summer wind gusts, "Will you have time to come to my funeral?"

I don't even know whether he heard me above the wind. Regardless, I was prepared to go to my grave, brave to the outside world, but scared to death wondering how it would feel being trampled to death by 4,000 pounds of horseflesh. The horses continued to prance nervously while Fred tried to control them by the reins. I got in front of them and tried to reach for the bridles but the horses' heads moved up and down and from side to side. Besides, I was much too short. I felt like I needed a ladder.

"Have you got them?" I faintly heard.

I yelled back, "No, I can't reach them." He apparently heard me and somehow managed to come where I was standing while still keeping control of the horses. One of them lowered his head for only a second and Fred quickly grabbed the bridle and pulled his head down. A minute later the other horse, obligingly, also lowered his head, only for a split second but long enough for me to grab his bridle.

"Now, hold them." I was told while the Boss ran back and attached the harnesses to the scraper. It seemed to take forever before I was assured, "Now, get out of the way." Those were the sweetest words I had heard in a long time!

As I ran for safety, the horses took off as if they were in a chariot race in ancient Rome. Naturally, they went in the opposite direction from where Fred wanted them to go. Poor Fred was half running, half being dragged behind them until those frenzied animals were finally stopped by a tall wire fence. Eventually, they calmed down and behaved like a decent team. Perhaps it was because the wind was subsiding, but more likely, they had enjoyed their fun with us, the unskilled strangers.

Regardless, Fred got the corrals cleaned before the afternoon was over and he was proud of the huge manure pile that would be so useful as fertilizer on our wheat fields. As far as I was concerned, after this horrid experience earlier I was glad to be alive. Once inside the house I had suddenly realized the need to change my underwear. After so many years, I had actually encountered a task that could cause me to wet my pants!

We called Bob to pick up the horses right after Fred finished using them. Their appetite for hay, the size of Pikes Peak, was something we could not afford. The next day the beautiful, challenging animals were back with Bob! We decided from then on to borrow

Bill's tractor until we could get one of our own. The horse episode was just too much for us.

Here comes my question: horses versus tractors. The horse is reliable, ready to go and usually cooperative but they need to be fed whether they work or not. The tractor is faster, has more horsepower and can be used constantly but it breaks down and parts need to be replaced. As it turns out, the tractor has won the march of progress and draft horses have almost disappeared everywhere.

The Farrells quit milking and sold their dairy herd because they could not make enough money, the same sad song as so many other small dairymen who confessed that they also were in financial trouble. Bill and Carol decided to move to Colorado Springs. They bought a comfortable house and he secured a job while Carol, missing her country life, slowly eased into being a city woman. They rented their farmhouse to a family from Yoder and leased us the pastures for $1.25 per acre per year. A year later, they raised it to $2. It was on Labor Day that their then-empty house burned to the ground. The cause of the incident was never discovered.

We saw the Farrell's frequently and were pleased that they adjusted well to their new environment. It seemed as if all our neighbors were leaving the country. Such a pity. They had worked so hard and managed with so little, and yet it was not enough.

When will our time come? 🐴

Not A Dairy, Too!

Though the 'Old Place' was primitive, getting used to it was not too hard, except for two things.

One was the constantly frozen pipe that led from the kitchen sink through the east wall to the outside of the house. From there, Fred had added on a 1-1/4" pipe which he laid downhill so it could drain an additional 50 feet. Sometimes this narrow pipe would stop up and no waste water could flow from the sink in the house. The culprit was the build up of frost or snow. When this happened we had to dig out the pipe close to the house, defrost it and hope the water would drain.

The second continual problem was the outhouse. Using it in the winter months meant having to thoroughly bundle up and by the time you would be ready to close the kitchen door behind you, a gust of icy wind would hit your face and the urge "to go" would leave at once! "I can wait another hour," was my decision quite often.

Fred Wagoner was our new mailman. He was tall and thin, very friendly, and handsome. We looked forward to seeing him wave to us while he deposited our mail in the aluminum mailbox on the Jones Road at 9:15 AM sharp. He was hardly ever late. I often wondered how he always managed to be on time, considering he had to make over a 50-mile round trip every day.

Mail was very important to us, especially now that we were so isolated. I always loved writing letters whenever there was time and I naturally hoped for a letter in return. Whenever we happened to be out of stamps, we simply put the change in the mailbox and our dear friend, Fred, would do the rest.

> Friday, Fred Vorenberg, who is a second Lieutenant in the reserves, left for Camp McCoy, Wis., for two weeks training in the Artillery. *1950*

One day, we received a letter from the War Department informing Fred that he needed to get a physical exam in preparation for being shipped out to Korea. We immediately answered this order by explaining that we just had bought a cattle ranch and that we had two young children. There was no answer so Fred had to go to Fort Carson, south of Colorado Springs to get the physical. During the next several weeks, we anxiously waited for news from day to day. Here we were with a ranch, what would happen if Fred had to leave, could I do it alone? It took more than a month before we heard from the War Department, telling us how Fred had earned a deferment from the service. What a relief! Instead, they would keep him in the Reserves, which was fine with us. Though Fred had spent two enjoyable weeks at Camp McCoy, Wisconsin the previous year, our future had taken a different turn and, needless to say, we were overjoyed by the Army's decision. "I'll bake a cake and we'll celebrate. What kind do you want?" I asked.

"Chocolate, of course." was Fred's immediate answer.

Soon after we had moved to the ranch Fred bought four more milk cows, making five cows that needed to be milked twice a day. We sold the cream in Calhan and gave the skim milk to our three hogs. Our chickens got a bucket full of bran daily and we poured some of the skim milk over it to make a mush. They loved it and thrived on it. Before long we were able to sell a boxfull of eggs to the Safeway store on Tejon Street in Colorado Springs, receiving 35 cents per dozen.

Then Fred came up with another idea, "How about selling Grade A milk. There's money in that." he said, remembering all the successful dairies he had seen in Wisconsin last year.

"Oh goodie, I thought!" I had heard dairy people talk about getting up at 4 AM to milk their critters, only to have to do it over again at 4 in the afternoon. I had also heard how tough the Dairy Board is on farmers and how particular they are about the equipment. I never shied away from work but I hated to get up that early. "Are you going to get a hired man to help with the milking?" I asked stupidly.

I could have easily predicted his answer, "Yes, you!"

In order to sell Grade A milk, we had to improve the milk barn by painting the walls and installing a $420 milk cooler which could hold four 10-gallon cans. The big milk trucks would come daily to pick up the filled cans and leave empties. This all seemed like a big order. We decided however to go ahead and improve the milk parlor so it could accommodate four cows. Eventually, the Dairy Board approved our operation and we ordered ten young Holstein cows from Wisconsin.

Fred Vorenberk was a successful hunter, bagging a nice fat doe on his first day out.

Before a cow gives milk she has to have a calf first. So, after receiving our dairy herd we anxiously watched for the signs of pregnancy. Meanwhile we milked the cows we already had on hand until, after several months, nine of the ten cows had their calves. One of these was born sick and died after a few minutes. The mother, we found out later, had Brucellosis or Bang's Disease so we called the Vet who branded a "B" on the cow's face before she was culled. The tenth cow never did have a calf.

That fall, my 'one and only' told me how he would like to go to Uncle Herman's ranch to go deer hunting. "I'll ask someone to help you with the milking." The hunting season opened the next day and Fred was on his way. Mr. Cottrell came quite late the next morning, but I didn't care, as long the cows didn't tell Fred! We moved the cows into the holding pen in front of the milk parlor and one of them jumped over the four strands of barbed wire fence, clearing it like a ballerina. As we brought her back into the pen she immediately repeated the same stunt, earning the name of "antelope." From then on we made sure that she was the first one into the parlor to be milked. Afterwards, every day, she would do her high jump act and wait for us on the other side. It was a game she loved and I swear I could hear her chuckle every time!

Since Mr. Cottrell was late that first day, Tommy had already fed the chickens and had let them out of their coop. Soon, they realized that the cows were eating grain while they were being milked. The chickens pranced into the milk parlor hoping to steal some spare kernels. They startled the contented bovines who were used to eating in peace. One of them suddenly moved back a few inches, stepping onto one of the hens. She squealed and

> Mrs. Herman Vorenberg returned to the ranch from her visit with Mrs. Fred Vorenberg and little Tommy. Lt. Vorenberg has finished the training at Camp McCoy in Wisconsin and returned to his home to await orders. During his absence his wife did a fine job of carrying on his work at home of which he said she had the 'spirit and courage of a sodier.'

bingo—there was a beautiful white egg rolling towards me...but the hen was dead! "Enjoy a chicken dinner, on us." I told Mr. Cottrell as I handed it to him.

Mr. Cottrell helped me two more days until Fred showed up with a deer. We had liver and onions that day and the next few days we enjoyed the fresh meat. We hung the rest of the carcass in our enclosed porch for a week to age the meat, and thus make it more tender.

Afterwards, it was cut into the desired portions and taken to a freezer locker in Calhan.

We milked our nine-member Wisconsin herd for a year but it was very difficult to make enough money with such a small dairy. We thought perhaps we could do better by raising beef cattle. So, we found someone who was interested in buying them. The day we sold the cows was a happy day—and I baked another chocolate cake!

Fred continued with his 'On the Farm Teaching' job and every time one of the guys had something new to sell or to give us, Fred would bring it home.

> On Monday Fred Vorenberg of near Yoder was a pleasant visitor in our neighborhood. He tells us that his wife and children, Tommy and Bonnie, will be leaving soon by plane to visit Mrs. Vorenberg's mother and other relatives in San Francisco. 1953

Soon our ranch had three very old ducks, a couple of grey geese who were quite antisocial, and Lucy, an adorable guinea hen which became a real friend of mine. In the evening, she would hop onto my lap and stay an hour at a time, making all sorts of contented music. She would follow me everywhere. One day she wandered onto the road when a pickup, that was driving by accidentally ran over her. My special Lucy was gone.

> Mrs. Fred Vorenberg, Tommy and Bonnie returned recently from San Francisco, where they visited relatives for the past several weeks. The trip was made by airplane and was a very thrilling one.

On a ranch it seemed like you have to deal daily with life and death and it affected us all. But for me, my love and respect for animals and birds was so sincere I didn't mind being totally surrounded by them 24 hours a day.

Ranch life was certainly agreeing with me. It was an answer to my prayer and I loved every phase of it. Fred and I agreed that ranching provided contentment and happiness and if you try hard enough, success. Not necessarily wealth. Challenges appeared often and we learned fast to tackle them. This was our dream, our niche! 🐂

Snake In The Garden

Wherever I lived I have felt the urge to grow a garden. Being outdoors, working the soil, and planting things has always given me inner peace. It's a special place to think and let my mind wonder without interruptions. There are no demands from the outside. It is just you, an insignificant, yet important, person.

In Colorado, no one does, or should, start a garden before the middle of May. In fact, June l is even better. The weather often plays tricks on you and snowstorms can come as late as June 1st. Cold weather slows down germination of the seeds, so if you can hang on and wait until the nights are warmer, the young plants will grow more evenly and speedily.

On the Old Place, there was not enough water by the house to supply all that is needed for a garden so we decided to use a windmill which was a quarter of a mile away in the southwest pasture, on Jones Road. The garden was to be my project and I looked forward to all the joy I would get out of it. As a child, my father had shown me how to divide each patch, where to stamp out paths between the beds and where to snip off suckers on tomato plants, among other things. Even my Dad would have been stumped here in the country. Deciding where to place the plot was very difficult, for though it was near the water tank the cattle had trampled the short, dry grass, made bare spots, and there were puddles of water standing close to the tank. The ground was crusty, hard, and very dry and I wondered if it would even grow anything at all. Because it had never been cultivated I borrowed a handplow from a neighbor. In those days everyone borrowed things from each other.

Fred volunteered to do the plowing and this was the only help for which I asked. After he announced, "Honey, the job is finished. It's ready for you," I cheerfully gave him a thank you kiss, loaded up the old red Ford pickup with a rake, a shovel, a hoe, a hose for watering and last, but not least, packets of seeds and boxes of bedding plants. It was late afternoon by then, the sun was close to setting, it was warm and pleasant and the most important thing was that all the chores for the day had been finished! The rest of the family stayed at home while I excitedly drove off to my new endeavor.

Once at the garden, I opened the wire gate to the pasture, drove through and made sure to close it securely behind me, for we learned never to leave gates open! Cows must be able to smell a place through which they can escape and walk for miles, all to the chagrin of the boss, the kids, or the hired man who then have to spend valuable time rounding up the wanderers. I parked the truck and what I saw next made my enthusiasm sink below sea level. There were huge clods of soil every which way, all in disarray and so big—they must have been 2 foot square lumps. I didn't know how to attack this job that was supposedly "finished." Everything looked so depressing! I remembered my father's advice, "Never give up just because things look tough," so I gathered my courage, picked up the hoe, and began the impossible job of trying to chop up the clods at least into smaller ones. I thought my poor tool would give out before I did. Perhaps, watering would help. I slung the hose into the tank, lifted one end out and directed the stream onto some of the clods of dirt. All of this frustration made me quit rather soon and I headed for home.

"Well, did you get it all done?" asked my dear husband who cheerfully greeted me in the driveway.

All I could manage to say was, "No!" He noticed that I was not too happy.

Later, he uttered one of his favorite expressions, "It's the best I could do."

I was too exhausted to say any more, so I unloaded my truckful of tools, bedding plants, and seeds, stormed into the house and sulked.

Preparing the soil took me several long, hot, and sweaty days and eventually the clods became fine and soft dirt that felt smooth as it flowed through my fingers. I added old manure from the corrals and built a new wire fence to protect the future plants from the cows. The plot was finally ready for planting. I was proud of my accomplishment and soon Fred and I were overjoyed when the tender seedlings appeared.

Work in a garden never quits, so I watered daily and pulled weeds. Later, I made trenches around the plants so more water could be channeled to them. And how they grew! They bloomed and made a great harvest. There was an abundance of green beans, carrots, leaf lettuce, cauliflower, cabbage, parsley and tomatoes all exploding from a corner of the dusty prairie. Everyone was proud of me. Fred would tell all the neighbors about me and how much money we were going to save just on food alone. And I swore then, that I would grow a garden every year. I felt glorious and warm.

It was late one day and sunset was approaching when I was there again working in my garden. While kneeling on the ground weeding I suddenly heard a noise and realized quickly that this was something ominous, something to be feared. In a flash I became petrified. The sound came intermittently and it reminded me of a baby's rattle. Perspiring profusely, I quit weeding and froze, unable to think of what to do next. Instinctively, I knew it was a rattlesnake. I had been told many times that they were seen frequently in these parts of East Central Colorado and that one should remain perfectly still when confronted by them as they might just slither away.

I slowly got up, grabbed the hoe next to me and started chopping furiously in the area where I suspected the snake might be, for it was now well past sundown and getting dark. After a lot of hits and misses I finally saw the now-wounded reptile. My heart was pounding. My blood pressure was sky high and I was so full of energy that I could not stop the chopping. Finally the battle was over and the city girl had killed her first rattlesnake.

As I calmed down, I remembered how I had seen dead snakes hanging over pasture fences. I had never understood what it meant before. But, now I knew it was a trophy, a conquest over danger. I proudly carried my dead reptile to the Jones Road fence and draped the carcass over the top wire. The only missing parts were the lower third of the snake and its most sought after part, its rattle, which were scattered amongst the vegetables in my garden.

The next morning was 'Show and Tell' and the whole family arrived at the spot only to find that the darned two-thirds of the snake had disappeared! It was nowhere to be found.

Fred's explanation was that "the peristalsis had moved it off the wire and some wild animal had eaten it." That made sense. To this day I get goose bumps just thinking about the encounter with my first snake, which fortunately did not destroy my love for gardening. 🐎

ISOLATION

Two Unforgettable People

A bright moment occasionally interrupted my daily routine while reminiscing of the two people whom I left behind in Germany. One was my friend, Hedy Cleer and the other was my teacher, Fraulein Kate Seiler. It was like a holiday when Fred Wagoner would pull up and deliver a letter from either one. I would stop all the ranch work, the housework—everything, just to sit on the nearest spot to read and reread their messages.

Hedy Cleer was my best friend. She was tiny, slender, and the shortest girl in our class. Her hair was blond, combed back and held in place with a ribbon that matched her plain cotton dresses embellished with pictures of flowers. She was very bright. She could solve any math problem in record time while I sat wondering how to do the first step. I knew I wasn't, and never would be, a math scholar. In those early days I hoped that someday I would marry a man who was clever in that area so I wouldn't have to worry about it. Luckily, that is exactly what happened!

Hedy and I spent a lot of time together while we were attending the Lyceum in Bad Homburg from age ten to fifteen. It was an all-girl school with twenty-five in our class. She

My best friend, Hedy Cleer.

was an only child and naturally adored by her parents. They lived in a tiny town north of Bad Homburg, called Dornholzhausen. I spent many days with her and became fond of her parents as well as the dogs, a schnauzer and a clever dachshund. The latter used to climb into the oven, which Frau Cleer heated for him because he was always cold. The first time I saw the dog in there I laughed out loud and said in German, "Anybody wants a hotdog?" It was then that Frau Cleer warned me to never touch the oven door because he would bite my hand off! I didn't try it.

After we had moved to Frankfurt in 1935, the Cleer family visited us only once. The conversation was very subdued. The strain of the political situation made it impossible for a Christian and a Jew to be seen together. It was too risky for all of us, so we decided to stay in touch by correspondence. Such a pity, such a disappointment!

Hedy and I wrote to each other for a while until Hitler and his henchmen decided to start intercepting the mail. A new law was in effect that no Aryan could contact non-Aryans by written correspondence or otherwise. The concentration camps would welcome the offenders. After hearing this, I wrote Hedy a letter and I remember tears falling onto the white paper as I asked her not to answer the note. I wished her well in her future, hoped for a possible reunion some day, and told her how I would never forget her. Secretly, I had hoped for an answer but it never came.

During the war my brother, Max, was stationed in Frankfurt and he stopped at the Cleers in Dornholshauzen to give them my address. It was years before I got the first letter from Hedy's mother. Hedy had been sick with an extended illness and had died. I was devastated. She was such a sweet person and was dealt such a blow. Frau Cleer continued corresponding with me every few months for several years until this, too, stopped. In spite of all the hatred of the Nazi regime, they could never pull apart the friendship between Hedy, her family, and me.

My English Teacher, Kathe Seiler.

Kathe Seiler's letters stopped me in my tracks as well. She had been my English teacher and I was one of many students who adored her. Her short, dark hair was combed back and she dressed simply, but classy. I'll never forget the day she entered the classroom wearing a bright pink angora sweater. Our "uh's" and "ah's" gave her a reason to wear the beautiful garment often. She was tall and had extremely heavy legs which she tried to cover up by wearing long skirts, even though they were not in style at the time. She always wore a man's watch with a wide, brown leather strap. Fraulein Seiler was very strict but had a heart of gold. Besides teaching English, she made geography come alive. She was such a joy that we all tried to make good grades in her classes.

She made no bones about disliking Nazis. In fact, it got her into trouble. All the teachers were supposed to give the Hitler salute with an extended right arm and the loud pronouncement "Heil Hitler" immediately after entering the classroom. She, however, would come in and sloppily throw her hand in the air and mumble something. Someone must have reported her because one day her salute abruptly changed, suddenly taking on the "ordered attitude".

Another time Dr. Sandman, the school principal, and Kathe Seiler entered the classroom and asked me to wait so they could talk to me. They told me how all the Jewish-owned stores in town had been closed and were being guarded by the Gestapo. "Don't walk home on the business street but take the long way to your house," they warned. After that, Fraulein Seiler regularly gave me advice how to deal with the hostile environment and I felt safe in her presence. Her constant concern strengthened my resolve and gave me self-confidence.

After the war, I wrote to Dr. Sandman and asked for my teacher's address. I'll never forget the first letter that arrived from her. It was exciting and I was thrilled to hear of her activities and her health. We developed a lively correspondence and I received many letters for years. She was always interested in my life, always cheering me on. Then one day, I received a note from her niece who had found my address among her belongings. Fraulein Seiler had died from cancer. It was one of my saddest days.

A teacher can "make" a person and influence his or her life to the fullest. Fraulein Seiler was that kind of an individual. How fortunate for me! I still have all her letters and have read them over and over again. Tears well up in my eyes every time I think about this marvelous person who gave me more than she ever knew. 🐎

Ranching Is Never Boring

After another snowy winter, it finally warmed up enough to think about planting trees around a couple of dams. There wasn't a single one in the entire pasture and we always felt sorry that the animals were exposed to the merciless summer sun all day long and they didn't have any shade after their thirst was quenched. We ordered and received 50 willow and 30 buffalo berry saplings and with great enthusiasm we set out one morning to make our wish of growing a lush green grove come true. Fred dug the holes and I planted the trees. Both of us watered them well. It was a big job and it took many hours. We knew we would have to water them often so Fred offered to do it every time he checked the cattle.

But things did not go well. The dams were over 1/4 mile from the house, and we often missed going to them every day. Between a lack of water and hungry rabbits it soon became obvious that the elements were winning while we were failing miserably. We never tried to repeat the effort of making a more pleasant resting area for the cows, but we hoped they'd forgive us.

Not long thereafter, our west well quit pumping the ever-important water. In order to rectify the problem, the pipes leading down deep into the well needed to be pulled up. On the bottom of them is a cylinder whose 'leathers' need replacing every so often. Though, I never learned what they are and what purpose they serve, they are important! There are professionals who do this work regularly with good equipment so they get the job done fast and well. But, my friend with whom I share the marital bed wanted to save money and said, "We can do it just as well, it will just take us a bit longer!" So, Fred hired the 12-year old, somewhat-unwilling, neighbor boy to help. Of course, Fred needed me too, even though I didn't have any idea of how to fix a well. Every so often, a voice barked at me, "Hold this. Pull on that. Let it go now." I did what I was told. Then suddenly the rod which is inside the pipe slipped and in a moment, it zoomed towards my right foot. The thing burst through my leather shoe and slipped between my 2nd and 3rd toes and, but luckily, not on my foot proper. The pain shot towards my head and I crumbled down to the ground grabbing my toes. It bled for the longest time. Fred knew I wouldn't be able to help any longer and he had the hired kid drive me home to suffer by myself. I swore that I would never work on wells again!

While the guys worked over two more hours on the project, I managed to make supper. I couldn't put any weight on the injured foot so I used a chair, kneeling on it with my right leg and maneuvering around, slowly but surely. After a couple of days my entire leg swelled up. Fred took me to our doctor who merely gave me a Penicillin shot and told me to stay off my feet for a few days. Fat chance! Physically, I survived, but the mental scars remained.

We didn't have much money and we tried to save wherever we could. This led to many dangerous situations which could have been avoided if we had spent money for the proper equipment. Similar accidents on wells never happened again because the next day Fred bought a vice grip and a pipe vice. He felt bad about the whole episode for years but it was all in the learning of how to run a ranch properly.

Fred's idea of ultimate enjoyment was having me cook new foods. We had always loved eating pickled herring so one day Fred surprised me with a wooden container full of 9 pounds of fresh herring. I had never pickled anything before. Now I needed to learn in a hurry because it was summertime and the fish wouldn't stay fresh long. I found a recipe in The Settlement Cook Book by Mrs. Kander, whose motto was, "The way to a man's heart is through his stomach." Well, as a good wife, I read the directions carefully and proudly produced 6 jars of the most delicious pickled herring. I was quite pleased with my accomplishment and wanted to show it off to our friend, Mrs. Cottrell. I gave her one of the jars and a few days later asked her how she liked it. "Well, I guess it was all right. Do you want the jar back?"

"You mean," I questioned her, "you ate the whole thing already?"

"Sure, I fried it the day you gave it to me." Well, I could tell—anybody could—that she didn't think much of my achievement and I lamely explained that pickled herring is supposed to be eaten as is, and never fried. I don't think I ever convinced her. There is a German saying, "Was der Bauer nicht kennt, frisst er nicht," which translated means, "What the country folks don't know, they won't eat!"

One time, Mr. Cottrell asked Fred to help him butcher another steer. Usually, as neighbors help each other, they would be given a good-sized piece of the liver, a delicacy in our household especially fried with lots of onions. On this particular butchering day Fred returned, with the liver plus an unbelievable sight: Four feet, the hooves! I felt a wave of nausea arising from my stomach to my throat and if we had had indoor plumbing, I would have rushed towards the bathroom! Since this was not the case, I turned away from that dreadful sight and swallowed the saliva which had arisen in my mouth. "These make the best soup. My mother always cooked the feet!"

"Well," I thought, "must I compete with my mother-in-law?" Because the situation was so repulsive to me, good 'ole Fred decided to do the cooking himself. First, he scalded the feet in order to peel off the horny part and then put two of those "things" in the largest kettle we had. It bubbled for hours and the next day, after it had cooled all night in the fridge, we tried the dish of jellied broth. I must admit, it was really quite good. We froze the rest and I, courageously, cooked the remaining two feet the following day.

When Bonnie was close to three years old, she could out-talk anybody. In fact, we called her "Walkie Talkie". She bossed her brother who was two years older and often tried to do the same with us which didn't go over very well. Both Fred and I were fairly strict parents and even though I didn't always agree with Fred's opinion, I always backed him up. I have since doubted whether that was a good idea, but we used to listen to trusted theories from childhood pedagogues and educators.

Mrs. Farrell watched "Walkie Talkie" at her house all afternoon one day. A big job was awaiting them, namely that of weeding out her children's old and outgrown playthings.

Minimum Requirements For "Ranching"

1. A wide-brimmed hat, one pair of tight pants and $20 boots from a discount house.
2. At least two head of livestock, preferably cattle—one male, one female.
3. A new air-conditioned pickup with automatic transmission, power steering and trailer hitch.
4. A gun rack for the rear window of the pickup, big enough to hold a walking stick and rope.
5. Two dogs to ride in the bed of the pickup truck.
6. a $40 horse and $300 saddle.
7. A gooseneck trailer, small enough to park in front of a cafe.
8. A little place to keep the cows, on land too poor to grow crops.
9. A spool of barbed wire, three cedar posts and a bale of prairie hay to haul around in the truck all day.
10. Credit at the bank.
11. Credit at the feed store.
12. Credit from your father-in-law.
13. A good neighbor to feed the dogs and cattle whenever the owner is out in Colorado fishing or hunting.
14. A pair of silver spurs to wear to barbecues.
15. A rubber cushion to sit on for four hours at the auction ring every Thursday.
16. A second-hand car for going out to feed the cows when your son-in-law borrows the pickup.
17. A good pocket knife, suitable for whittling to pass away the time at the auction ring.
18. A good wife who won't get upset when you walk across the living room carpet with manure on your boots.
19. A good wife who will believe you when you come in at 11 p.m. saying, "I've been fixing the fence."
20. A good wife with a good full-time job at the courthouse.

She offered all sorts of toys and books to Bonnie who eagerly accepted everything. Upon her return home Fred asked her why she brought all that junk home. Her answer was firm and direct, "Kids are kids, they like toys... and they are not junk!" That was Bonnie all right, she never lacked for words, even at a young age.

One evening, while I was bathing Bonnie I noticed a lump in her groin, the size of a nickel. It felt hard to the touch, but it didn't produce pain. At once, I remembered my classes of 'Medical Diseases' and how one of leukemia's early warning signs is a lump in the lymphatic system. This scared me to death and both Fred and I worried that a dread prognosis might be in our future. I couldn't sleep that night and the next morning I got up early to take Bonnie to the pediatrician. He examined her while I told him about my fears and my half-hearted diagnosis. He tried to calm me, saying that it could be leukemia but probably was not. He told me to take her to Glockner-Penrose Hospital for a blood test. After a short drive, we entered the huge doors and were greeted by a nun who met us like we were longtime friends. She took us to the lab which is a mysterious and confusing place for any child, but not for mine. Bonnie's eyes were riveted on the nuns in their flowing black habits; their huge white coronets and chains about their waists as the amazed child whispered to me, "Look at those Santa Clauses!" Later, back at the doctor's office to get the results of the blood test, I was overjoyed to hear that the lump was caused by a lymphatic infection and Bonnie only needed a penicillin shot.

Before we left the doctor's office I told him how Fred had remarked, "You worry too much about the kids' health."

The good doctor replied, "You tell him, as a nurse, you are trained to observe every sign and symptom and report them." His words made me feel much better. The day turned out to be one of relief and gratitude. After a swift 35-mile trip home I informed Fred of the good news and also told him what the doctor had said about me and nurses in general.

His answer was to the point, "I told you, you worry too much," and as an afterthought which came loud and clear, "The next time I marry it won't be to a nurse!" I felt like answering, "Thank you very much!" but I didn't say a thing and hoped that 'Good 'OLE Fred' meant to be funny.

Life on a ranch could be mysterious. Strange things sometimes happen. We noticed that every morning for about a week, the door of our feed room was open about 12 inches or so. We stored sacks of different kinds of grain and several uncovered barrels of cattle feed there, so we were careful to close the sliding doors every evening after the chores. Obviously, while we were sleeping something was going on. One morning when I was up earlier than usual, I happened to glance out of the kitchen window to see a medium-sized dog slipping out of the feed room door. It was our neighbor, Lew Eis' dog who apparently had learned how to open the doors. He must have been quite hungry and quite athletic to accomplish the feat so often. The mystery solved, we secured the door with a device even the smartest of dogs would be unable to defeat—baling wire!

Sometimes I wondered, what's next? I was getting an education on these 1,440 acres of drought-hardened soil with cacti showing off their beautiful soft yellow and purple blossoms. With neighbors far away enough not to hear the children's yelling, my singing, nor the dog's barking, we would watch sunrises and sunsets that produced colors any artist would appreciate. This is freedom; glorious freedom and we drank it in, day after day, never tiring of the sights and sounds.

Jim Gochnauer

An interesting couple in our neighborhood was the Gochnauers who lived four miles from our ranch. The first time we met them was at a farm sale when Jim was buying a calf for one of his boys' 4-H projects.

The sale had a party-like atmosphere because everybody had dropped whatever was scheduled for the day to attend what actually was a social gathering. Men crowded around, laughing and spitting, and occasionally bidding on items the auctioneer's helper held up. There were tools, sacks of feed, rolls of wire, and even household goods for sale. Everything seemed to find a new home. The women stood in their own circle visiting with one another, talking mainly about their children, exchanging recipes and the latest gossip about the Rawleigh man. Everybody was laughing; everybody was happy.

Soon afterward, we visited the Gochnauers in their neat, white house that was overshadowed by an abundance of greenery: bushes, flowers, and trees of all sizes. It seemed as if someone had taken several handfuls of seeds and let the wind scatter them, and they now were growing into lush exhibits of color. It was a delight to one's soul, an oasis, especially in this very dry area.

Jim, a tall and very friendly man, had a healthy and slightly sunburned complexion from all the time he spent outdoors. His wife, Fern, was equally friendly and asked us to have a seat on their soft couch. There were a lot of crocheted doilies protecting the arm rests of easy chairs and one large doily rested in the center of the dining table. On top of it was a massive, empty crystal fruit bowl. The whole house was in "apple pie" order. We enjoyed our visit and we quickly learned a lot about gardening in Colorado, especially when and where to plant vegetables. "You got to get them green beans in early, right after the last frost," Jim would say and I innocently would question him, "How do you know when that is?"

His answer was short and to the point, "Just take a chance and hope for the best."

The next day Mrs. Farrell came to borrow a few bales of hay. I told her about our visit with the Gochnauers and she immediately told me the rumor that was circulating through the neighborhood. Apparently Jim's dad did not trust banks, so he put all his savings into an empty coffee can and buried it somewhere on the Gochnauer's homestead. She told me how poor Jim had spent years searching for the can and had finally given up when someone suggested that he get a metal detector. Well, he got one the very next day. He tried his luck but still didn't find the spot. Perhaps the whole thing was a hoax. Regardless, if he was to find the container there couldn't be a substantial sum of money in it because whatever the amount, it certainly would not buy much these days.

When Fred found out that Jim owned a metal detector, he borrowed it to find a pocketknife he had dropped somewhere in our corral. He had searched high and low, but it was nowhere to be found. In only a few short minutes, Jim's handy tool pointed it out, buried deep under sand that cattle had trampled. After all, the metal detector came in handy, at least for us!

The Gochnauers sold their place on the north side of the Big Springs Road and built a new house on property south of the road. We were anxious to see the new addition to the neighborhood. It turned out to be a lovely place filled with all the modern conveniences—a dishwasher, washer, dryer and Mixmaster. On the far side of the living room was an organ on which Fern rehearsed the many hymns she performed each Sunday in church. She showed us through the entire house, opening all the built-in closets, her special workroom where she kept the supplies for her 'fancy work', and Jim's own room. Here he had a huge desk with a comfortable leather chair, lots of books on tree planting, literature on windbreaks, and a whole shelf of brochures from Colorado State University in Fort Collins which was always sending him information.

Next, Jim took us outside and showed us all the new, young pine and spruce trees he had planted. He told us how his dad taught him all he knew and he hoped to make a business out of his budding tree farm. Years later, he succeeded and was supplying trees all over the state. He became an authority on the topic, was interviewed and photographed and even had written many publications.

We became close friends and one day, during a visit to our place, Fern told us about the tragedy that had hit the family years ago. It happened one summer evening when their first son, a toddler, wandered off into the pasture behind the house. After searching and calling for him, the frantic parents discovered their lifeless son's body in one of the ponds. The whole community had gathered around the grief stricken family and it was said to have been the most sorrowful funeral ever in these parts. Although they wouldn't talk much about the incident, you could tell they'd never quite gotten over it.

Later, there were four more children, all college educated and with good jobs who eventually married and had families of their own. In their later years, the Gochnauers made good use of their travel trailer by visiting the kids yearly, taking dozens of pictures and showing them to interested neighbors, and perhaps, to not so interested ones. We always considered the Gochnauers not just neighbors, but friends.

You can see their groves of trees which stretch out for miles around from every direction. Jim made the bland valley take on a look of lushness and vitality. His efforts are being enjoyed by many and his father would be so proud. Jim did it all, even without the now-famous coffee can!

Milton Kipples

About eight miles from us lived the Kipples, a middle aged couple. We met Milton when he came to our ranch to welcome us to the neighborhood. He was a pleasant person, not very big, perhaps 5'6", thinning black hair and dark piercing eyes which seemed to penetrate your very soul. When he talked he always smiled and exhibited the most beautiful set of white teeth which he proudly announced were "store boughten."

Milton was unforgettable. He had a high pitched, twangy voice caused by enlarged adenoids in the back of his throat and sinus trouble making him reach frequently for the red and white handkerchief that always dangled from the pocket of his well-worn bib overalls. His one pair of brown cowboy boots had remnants of hay and manure and were in need of several layers of boot polish. His gait was unsteady and I constantly feared he would step on his own toes and fall to the floor.

But the most fascinating part of Milton's physique was his nose. Actually, it wasn't his nose proper that got my attention, but instead it was a small pea-sized wart under his right nostril. Every time he smiled, the sprouting piece of flesh would move up and down, blowing in the wind. From the side, it looked like a big drop about to be pulled by gravity to the floor. I wanted to offer him a hankie, quickly, before it fell. And then I realized the darned thing, indeed, was attached. Often I found myself staring at his nonessential appendage and wondered if it ever needed grooming!

After the original visit he came by often, coincidentally, at dinnertime. He never refused an invitation which made me wonder if his wife either was a bad cook or didn't cook at all. We never did meet the 'the wife' (it never was MY wife). According to him, she was a "stay-at-home wife" who always worked around the house and garden. She also did all the milking and took care of forty chickens and five ducks. She had to, for good old Milton was never at home. He went to every cattle sale, farm auction, and community event possible and spent the remainder of his time visiting neighbors. All in all, he was a good guy who wouldn't hurt a flea but I did feel sorry for Mrs. Kipples who fell in love with someone who certainly was not much of a catch, to say the least.

Milton owned a two-ton truck which usually ran well, except for sometimes in cold weather when it wouldn't start. Then Fred would run down to his place and pull it with our pickup until the engine would turn over. Several times during fall and winter Fred hired Milton to haul feed from either a field or from the Co-op feed store and unload it by our corrals. He was usually reliable. His happy mood was contagious and it was easy being with this good-hearted person.

One evening he stopped by our place. He talked and smiled up a storm as that little wart under his nose happily danced about. But things were different. He told us how 'the wife' had thrown him out of the house. "What happened?" both Fred and I simultaneously asked, anxious to hear all the gory details. It seemed 'the wife' had invited a friend of hers from Denver to stay at their house for a week. Before she arrived, the extra bedroom was fixed up beautifully with a bouquet of daisies from the front yard and brand new sheets on the bed.

"You would have thought with all the fuss that the Queen of England was coming!" Milton explained.

"So, tell us more, what happened?" We said, encouraging him to get to the point.

"Well," he grinned, "The friend arrived a couple of days ago and last night 'the wife' and I did 'you know what.'" He stopped, apparently embarrassed to mention the word "sex", but recovered quickly thanks to the high level of toxicity in his body. "Later in the night, when I was sure 'the wife' was asleep, I sneaked into 'the Queen's' room and did the same thing to her!"

Both Fred and I burst out laughing, relieved that the children were in the living room. "Then what happened?"

"Well this morning when 'the Queen' came downstairs, first thing, she told 'the wife' what I had done—over breakfast. Can you believe it?

'The wife' got the broom and chased me out of the house yelling, "Don't you never come back again, you bastard."

"She threw the pickup key at me and I drove off, wandering around the countryside until I finally ended up in Calhan. I couldn't eat anything, but I drank one drink after another at the beer joint and I think I'm a little drunk now." 'Little' was a major understatement!

Fred encouraged him, "Go home and try to make up with 'the wife' and if it doesn't work you can come back here and sleep on the couch." He left.

As each hour passed, I became more hopeful Milton would not show up. I was relieved since I didn't want to interfere in a marital situation. Later in the week, Milton told us 'the queen' left long before she had planned. And, everything returned to normal between Milton and 'the wife.' 🐴

The Marshall Ranch

It had been at least a year since we had moved onto the Old Place when we decided to make an effort to meet the last of our close neighbors. Their house was close by the road, down a short driveway, a one-story brown frame building with white trim. It had a well cared-for look with bushes and a few medium-sized trees that surrounded the entire house. There were a couple of large red barns and a chicken house with a garden on one side, but no outhouse—quite unusual in these parts!

The minute Fred stopped the pickup, a tall, 80'ish very thin person wearing bib overalls approached us from the corral. He introduced himself as "Mr. Marshall" and told us that his wife was in the house but that she wasn't feeling well. We could barely hear him over the sound of bawling cattle. "I'm weaning calves off their mothers today," he said, explaining the reason for all the noise. The calves were hungry and the cows' udders hurt because they were so full of milk. This painful process required separation for several days of the babies from their mothers. Both suffered. We spoke with Mr. M. a few minutes longer and then went our way. We hoped to meet his wife on a later visit.

After several weeks we stopped to see the Marshalls again. This time it was quieter, no bawling cattle. A bunch of cats were sitting around the front door meowing in a steady chorus. There must have been at least six, all different ages, colors, and temperaments. As we approached some of them ran off while the others came towards Fred trying to rub against his legs. He did not appreciate this. Fred actually hated cats and rabbits and wasn't even comfortable around dogs. With ours, he merely 'put up' with them. Mrs. M. opened the door and asked us into the kitchen. She was a neatly dressed lady but looked frail, thin, and pale. Walking seemed to be an effort for her and she sighed quietly as she sat down. The kitchen was clean with no dishes standing around. Everything was white—walls, cupboards, appliances, and even the curtains. Only the tablecloth had color in light embroidery around the edges, of course against a white background. She offered us a cup of coffee but we declined explaining that we were on our way to feed cottonseed cake to the cattle and had one more bunch to feed. Mr. Marshall suddenly appeared from a back room carrying a leather belt in his hand but was not joining us in the conversation. He barely said "hello" to us. In fact, he was quite absorbed in what he was doing and while he was punching holes in the belt, he let out a few choice words under his breath. We were surprised—but never since then did he ever use profanity in our presence.

We soon got up and went out the front door. All the cats had disappeared. I got in the driver's seat of the pickup because Fred still had to feed the last 50-lb. sack of feed which was in the back of the truck. Five or six empty sacks were piled in a big heap on the floor of the rider's side. As Fred entered the truck, he kicked the sacks towards my feet—thank you very much!— to make room for his. We drove out of the driveway and onto the Big Springs Road, a gravel road. It was around 11 AM and I was getting hungry, having eaten breakfast before 7 AM. "Let's hurry!" I said, as I gunned the motor and was quickly going over 30 miles an hour. Suddenly there was a great flurry of activity. Dust filled the cab as a cat literally exploded from the sacks. At once, she leaped at high speed towards the open window on my side and out she flew like lightning. At the very moment the cat appeared Fred quickly yanked open his door and jumped out of the pickup. I braked hard and stopped to see what was going on. It was a challenge for me to keep a straight face. There was Fred, rolling over and over and not far from him was the cat, doing the very same thing as if it had been choreographed. I backed up to where my very 'brave' husband was now sitting on the ground, grinning, while the cat took off in a streak towards her home.

"Why in the world did you jump out?" I asked, unable to believe anyone would put his life in jeopardy like this. "You could have broken every bone in your body!" I scolded.

Almost childlike, he cracked a smile saying, "Didn't you see the cat?" I could only laugh! He got up, brushed the dust off his clothes, and climbed back into the truck. Not a broken bone, not a scratch. Unbelievable! This was a true phobia—indeed a feline phobia!

Fred later told me the story of how, as a young boy, he found the family cat sleeping in his favorite chair. Little Freddie wanted to sit there, too. He grabbed a wooden stick and hit the cat. The frightened animal leaped off the much sought-after chair and ran out of the house, never to return. His folks reprimanded him severely and blamed him for their pet's disappearance. Whether his phobia was triggered by this incident is anybody's guess but I found it hard to believe that a rancher whose entire lifestyle meant dealing with animals could display such an aversion to cats.

After that, we visited the Marshalls on a regular basis and were enthralled as he would take us from one tale of olden times to the next. He especially liked to tell stories of the cattle drives he worked on, moving thousands of longhorns all the way from his native Texas to Montana. He talked about the long wagon trips to get supplies from Calhan and described the unique characters who homesteaded our area, living only in sod houses. He pointed out where we could find the many one-room school houses which were scattered every few miles and how he always saw kids on horseback, often riding double, passing his house on their way to school. We would leave his house; our imaginations filled with images of how it used to be living in our area only a few years prior.

The Marshalls were a very close couple, but they had their unique habits. Often, when they would go to Colorado Springs for groceries, they'd leave so early in the morning that we would see them coming home just as we were going to town—and it wasn't even noon yet!

Not too long afterward, Mrs. Marshall died leaving Mr. M. a widower at loose ends. This new lifestyle was tough on him. His face took on a strained, worried look and before a year passed, he too, was in ill health. We began to shop for him whenever we went to Colorado Springs. Sometimes, it was hard for him to realize that the price of groceries had gone up but he always repaid us the amount we had spent. We began renting his pastures and always made it a point to stop at his house to check on him.

Twice I called the Calhan ambulance to take him to the hospital. One time he had fallen down hours before and hurt his back. In the second incident, he had a slight heart attack.

The ambulance was quite old and broken down but Calhan was glad to have one regardless of its condition. The man who drove it was pleasant and sympathetic, but he was in no hurry. Each time after we—slowly—loaded Mr. M. into the vehicle, the driver would complain that there was no lock to keep the stretcher in its place and he warned the patient that he might be moving around within the ambulance on the hour-long trip. The nurse in me spoke up and I volunteered to ride along with the patient to keep him company. Whenever the driver would turn a corner that darned stretcher would also turn—right into me or in some other direction. By the time we reached the hospital I was completely exhausted from all the exercise I got trying to push the stretcher and its heavy load back into position.

Occasionally Mr. M. had relatives visit from Denver and Texas. He got along well with all of them, so they visited often and we came to know and even became good friends with them. On one of her visits his niece questioned him whether he had any decent clothes other than the bib overalls he always wore. He said "No, why would I need something other than these? I have plenty of them."

She insisted, "We'd better go to town today and get you a suit so you'll have something nice to be buried in!" He finally agreed to it and they went to Springs and bought a modern looking grey outfit which he wore right away. They celebrated the 'event' by having dinner at a nice restaurant, something he very seldom did. He modeled the suit, shirt, and very colorful tie for us. I must say he looked quite dapper and was so proud of his purchase. Such a change from his usual country outfit!

Sorry to say, it was not long before Mr. M. died and was now able to use his beautiful new outfit for good. We bought 80 acres of his ranch for $13,000. The rest of his acreage and the house were sold to some people who, instead of keeping chickens in their chicken house, raised marijuana!

Help!

On the Old Place, with its lack of comfort, one winter seemed to go on relentlessly. Everything was white from frost, snow and clouds. The especially strong north wind had stirred up snow and built large drifts which were already reaching the windows of the barns. This kind of weather quickly froze any part of your skin which was exposed. Earlier in the day, Fred had returned from chores, his eyebrows and eyelashes covered with ice and the scarf around his neck was frozen stiff. All I could think (but would never dare say), What a way to make a living! This was one of those days when desperation was not far from one's mind, especially mine.

The snow kept falling harder and the wind whistled furiously around the house but Fred was still preparing to do the daily job of checking different herds of cattle on horseback. "Why don't you take the Jeep, it's so nasty today," I asked. For a city person it seemed like a logical suggestion.

"One never uses vehicles in the pastures, it destroys grass," I was told, as my determined and all-knowing, husband bundled up again. He opened the front door; breaking off icicles which had formed above it then closing it tightly behind him, making sure it stayed shut. He walked out into total whiteness, which in seconds completely engulfed him. I wondered if I would ever see him again.

A NEW MARKETING IDEA

A Colorado Farmer had been taken in so many times by the car dealer that when the dealer wanted to by a cow, the farmer priced it to him like this:

Basic Cow	$ 200.00
Two Toned Exterior	45.00
Extra Stomachs	75.00
Product Storage Compartment	60.00
Dispensing Unit, Four	40.00
Spigets $10.00 each	
Genuine Cowhide Upholstery	125.00
Dual Horns	15.00
Automatic Flyswatter	35.00
TOTAL$	595.00

In situations like these I got busy. In the matter of a short time, I had started a large pot of split pea soup with an extra large ham bone, encouraged the three oldest kids to build a fort with their Lincoln Logs and made double sure the fire in the coal stove was still going strong. I tried to turn the radio to the Denver station, KOA, which usually gave the best weather predictions for our area. All I could hear was the crackling static and an occasional voice, which would break as the electric wires touched from the strong winds. Fred was a good rider and Topsey a willing horse, but I was worried. All I could do was sit and wait.

After what seemed to be hours, Fred appeared at the door. I hardly recognized him. He was covered with snow from head to toe. I helped him take off his frozen garments while he warmed himself by the stove drinking hot cocoa, which I quickly made for him. "Did you find the cattle?" I asked.

All he could say was, "We have a problem. One of the steers was looking for water and he wandered onto the new pond, which was covered with ice. You know the place—the pond that smart ass conservationist told us to build last summer—that one!"

Water is at a premium in Colorado. You could count on roughly 12 inches of moisture a year. Summertime would be dry except for occasional severe thunderstorms followed by downpours, which usually came between 2 PM and 5 PM. These rains, which old timers called toad stranglers or gully washers, would fill what little holes they could find and then race, loaded with debris, under fences, through corrals, and to the next neighbor's place continuing on to who knows where. Last summer we took the pushy bureaucrat's advice and built a good-sized pond before the summer storms started. It was filled in no time.

On the ride, Fred noticed all the cattle standing close to the pond. After counting, he was missing one and eventually discovered a very dead steer that had fallen through the ice! The pond had been frozen solid for a while and Fred chopped the ice daily near the edge so the cattle could drink the water. Apparently the steer could not wait and had wandered to the area in the center where the ice was thin. "...And tomorrow you're going to help me get him out" he said, "or that carcass will spoil the pond water."

Yippee for me, I thought.

By the next morning, Sunday, the storm had passed. The wind had stopped and the moon was out. It was pitch dark and cold in the house and the children were still asleep while I stepped into my long handled underwear and Fred made the usual morning noises, meaning that the coal stove was being lit in the living room. We hurried outside, milked our ten Holstein cows, fed the cattle which were being kept in the barns and got the kids up for breakfast. We ate the usual—oatmeal, sausage or steak, eggs, homemade bread, homemade salt free butter, homemade jam or jelly and some kind of fruit. The Law of the Ranch says that people never eat before the animals do and we stuck to that religiously.

Now it was time to get going on the grizzly job of retrieving that blooming steer from the pond. "I'm riding down. You and the kids come in the Jeep and bring a rope," were the orders from 'Headquarters' as he left the house. The Jeep was a vehicle, I swear, that had no springs. The heater never worked and the metal construction around it rattled making an awful noise while we drove anywhere and especially over pastures. However, it was reliable and cooperative.

Unwilling to leave the children unattended in the house, I settled them into the Jeep. They were dressed as if on their way to the South Pole and excited about another new experience. About halfway to the pond I could see Fred on the ground. He had taken a bar to break the ice around the animal and was now chopping away. Suddenly I could not see him! Then he appeared again! Then he was gone again! What was going on? I stepped on the gas; the kids banged heads on the metal roof while the Jeep raced over the bumpy pasture.

Fred was in the center of the pond, his elbows supporting his upper body on the ice and the rest of him dangling in the frigid water.

"Throw me the rope," he yelled.

Good idea. I quickly ran to the pond, my heart racing madly, with rope in hand I tossed it towards him as hard as I could.

"Now pull!" he yelled again. Another good idea. I did. Nothing happened.

"Tie the rope around the saddle horn and let Topsey pull me out."

I ran to the horse, led her carefully onto the edge of the pond where she slipped on the ice and fell smashing flat on her side and refused to try it again. What next?

"Try the Jeep."

I tied one end of the rope to the hitch close to the rear bumper, got into the rattlebox and stepped on the gas with a bit too much power. Expecting to go a short way, all of a sudden I was speeding along with a cold, dripping, wet husband flopping on the ground behind me. It had worked—best idea yet.

"I'll drive home, you ride the horse" he said with his teeth chattering. Soon we were back home once again; Fred in a dry set of clothes sipped another cup of hot cocoa. We still had to get the dead steer out of the water. Fred happened to think of Ed Miller, who raised hogs. Quickly, Fred drove over to use our neighbor's phone and called Ed explaining his predicament and suggesting that perhaps the dead animal would be good hog food. All he had to do was to get it out of the pond!

Ed Miller came the following day with his tractor and Farmhand, a powerful attachment to the body of a tractor which is able to reach and lift heavy loads. It didn't take long before the job was done and Ed's hogs were feasting on frozen steer meat.

Things changed after that winter. Fred built a fence around the pond as soon as the ground thawed, he started taking the Jeep to check cattle in snowstorms, and Topsey never stepped on ice again.

But it was the smart-ass bureaucrat who suffered the entire next year because all the neighbors for 20 miles in every direction learned about Fred's close call. They told each other, "I'd never take that damn guy's advice ever again." So whatever he suggested, folks would answer back, "Now, will that work better than Fred's pond?" 🐴

NEW ENCOUNTERS

Visiting Clergy

Jehovah Witnesses

anches can be lonely places. Neighbors can be miles away and company, whoever it is, is at a premium. So, though I'm not a religious person, anyone, even a clergyman, was welcome. One Sunday morning, I was alone when a couple and a young teenager drove up. All were dressed immaculately and as they walked towards the kitchen door I had a feeling I might know who these people were. In fact, our closest neighbors had told us about some Jehovah Witnesses who had been to their place on the previous Sunday, trying to convert them. The missionaries explained their philosophy and read verses from the Bible, and gave them a publication called "The Watchtower" before trying to sell them other materials. I froze as I recalled my recent conversation. Immediately I thought, "Oh, no! These must be them!" Sure enough, I was going to meet the people of whom I had heard so much.

The three people introduced themselves by name and told me that they were Jehovah Witnesses. They were polite and well mannered as I led them towards the garage to lean against the wall. You see, I had been told to NEVER invite them into your house because they would linger for hours. That was the reason why I led them to the garage wall now— in hopes it might be so uncomfortable that it would encourage them to leave, soon. Unfortunately, they didn't seem to mind, in fact, they seemed to appreciate that I was willing to listen to them.

We started talking about the weather, schools in general, Dixie, our German Shepherd who loved people, and then it came: religion! I could hardly get a word in edgewise, but eventually I was able to utter, "We're Jewish." Well I thought and hoped that this would end the conversation, but instead, it only fed more fuel to the fire. "Oh, we love the Jews. They're such good people and we think the world of them. Did you know," the man continued, "that not only a lot of Jews were killed by Hitler but so were Jehovah Witnesses?" He was talking so fast and furiously that I didn't have a chance to answer him, even if I wanted to. His wife then turned towards the boy and said, "Here son, read the nice lady something from the Bible."

The mother handed the well-worn book to her son who knew the exact page to read. Meanwhile, the couple made themselves more comfortable by cozily sitting on some small barrels and pieces of wood that also leaned against the garage. All this scared me half to death because I realized that this was going to take a while! I did have things to do. Visiting with these people would be ok for a few minutes but I didn't appreciate Bible class and religious school being forced on me here next to my own garage! I began to struggle with myself and wondered how fast I could send them off to pounce on another 'victim' down the road.

The boy read fluently and with well-trained pronunciation. It was obvious that he'd been taught to idolize every single word. Trouble was—he went on and on and just as I was about to straighten out, thinking that this was the last line, he would continue onto the next page. My frustration increased and I tried to think of something to say or do to get out of this distasteful, annoying situation. My mind went blank; I really didn't want to be rude to these people. I felt like saying, "Leave now and don't come back. But...!" After all, they were being sent by their church to do this kind of work. I just couldn't say anything; I was a coward when it came to things like this.

I turned longingly to the kitchen door and noticed something blue floating in the air, followed by the definite odor of something burning. "My roast!" With that, I ran into the house to view the terrible damage. My beautiful dinner was black, ruined, the kitchen was full of smoke and now there was nothing for dinner. I turned towards the still-open kitchen door and noticed that my three visitors had quickly placed a "Watchtower" on the handle of the garage door and were speedily heading towards their car. They never said goodbye, just left!

That was the only time I ever burned a roast—not a bad record for over 50 years of preparing them. Now, whenever I see what looks like Jehovah's Witnesses coming down the street, I immediately get ready to thwart any and all of their pushy antics.

The Reverend John Millingham

Years later, every month like clockwork, the Reverend John Millingham from Ellicott Baptist Church on Highway 94 would come for a visit. He was always in a happy mood. He was elegant, around 6 feet tall, good looking, and charming with a thin mustache and he often dressed in a dark business suit with a colorful tie, usually red. His face had a ruddy complexion as if he had been in the sun too long.

One day during the summer, while I was doing my most disliked task, that of mending jeans, the Reverend knocked on the door. As I opened it, he immediately asked me, "Are you too busy to have company?" Though I didn't feel like being interrupted, I decided to take a break and asked him into the kitchen. We had some chocolate cake left, but I thought if I offered it, he would stay too long and I wouldn't get my work, though disgusting, done. Well, the good man was always kind and generous and I remembered the fresh fruit he had brought us the last time he visited, so I made him a cup of instant coffee and gave him a thick slice of Fred's favorite chocolate cake. He praised my baking and told what a wonderful Jew I was! (Why, because I could bake?) The conversation went on and on and eventually I remembered the sick steer which had needed medicine an hour earlier.

As a nurse I knew the importance of giving medication on time. This was my chance to free myself from this lengthy conversation. I told the Reverend, "I need to give a sick steer a shot and I'll be back as soon as I can. He's just in the corral across the driveway." The sick steer had a severe case of pneumonia. His fever was up to 104 degrees; he had trouble breathing and was losing weight. We put some molasses on his grain to encourage him to eat, but it didn't do any good.

With all the dignity a preacher could muster, he said, "It's been known that not only people, but animals also profit from prayer. Would you mind it if I prayed for his health?" I agreed, hiding a smile. We went to the steer. I gave him the shot and the Reverend prayed out loud. Would the Reverend's prayer help? Who knows the power of such fervent and intense activity, so well meant, so sincere?

To my chagrin the Reverend followed me back to the house and into his chair to finish his coffee. Thirty minutes later, during which we did not mention anything religious, he finally decided it was time to leave. I walked him to his car, thanked him for coming and wished him well. After all, he was a nice person who spared no compliments. After bidding the Reverend a fond farewell, instead of returning to the house I circled back to the corral to check on the steer. To my chagrin, there he was lying on his side—dead. So much for the power of prayer!

Rabbi Goldsmith

As I mentioned earlier, Fred came from a very religious orthodox family and he wished we could attend the weekly services in addition to the yearly High Holy Day ones, which we never missed. We had too many chores to do and the distance to the Colorado Springs Temple was just too great. However, we decided to try going once a month on Friday nights during springtime. We would change the schedule and do the evening chores earlier.

It was the first time we left the children with a sitter. We chose Susie, a 16 year-old neighbor girl who all the kids liked. We felt comfortable that things would be all right. Fred and I quickly got into the car and drove off to childless freedom for one night.

It felt unusual to be in our best clothes, for those were rare times. Usually in summer I wore jeans and a blouse and in winter my 'wardrobe' consisted of jeans, sweatshirts, and a few well-worn sweaters. We often felt uncomfortable at the Temple. Once there, many people who knew each other were in deep conversation. We spoke to some acquaintances whom we knew the best. They were pleasant but not overly friendly. They tried to make conversation but their questions like, "How are the cows?" seemed impossible to answer. Fred immediately expounded on how, "The cattle market was down again last week." Oh, to see the look on their faces as they struggled for a polite response! They had absolutely no idea what he was talking about. Finding something in common with the folks at the temple was always a challenge. It didn't bother Fred, but it did me. "You are too sensitive," he would say, trying to bolster my shyness.

Services were over by 10 PM It had been a good evening, almost inspirational. The sermon had been thought provoking so Fred told Rabbi Goldsmith how much he enjoyed it. Without asking me, he then asked him to come to the ranch for Sunday dinner. The Rabbi accepted. Fred asked him to be there by 12 Noon while I quickly sketched a map to the ranch.

We were ready for the long drive home. Some good-byes were said and we were on our way going east on Platte Ave. Suddenly, our thoughts were interrupted by a whistling sound and we found ourselves going right, then left. The car went out of control but after a short while Fred managed to stop it. There it was—another flat tire!

It seemed we were getting flats at least once a week. Somehow the tires seemed to know exactly where to pick up old nails, staples or anything else to puncture them. There was quite a bit of traffic on Platte Avenue and we needed to be careful so Fred wouldn't be hit while changing the tire. "Here is a flashlight, you direct the oncoming traffic," was my order as Fred knelt down onto the ground in his best and only suit for this, our special night out!

For a while Fred fixed the flats himself. He bought a kit with glue, colorful patches, and the necessary equipment to inflate inner tubes. But it didn't take long for us to realize that the homemade patches didn't have the strength to keep up with the pastures and gravel roads. We began taking the constant stream of damaged tires to Warren Garage in Calhan who made a lot of money fixing ours!

I worked hard getting ready for Rabbi Goldsmith's visit and prepared what could be done before he arrived. The Sunday was beautiful and sunny and I spent even more time than usual putting the finishing touches on the meal fit for a king. We never had much money but we didn't scrimp when it came to food, especially when we had guests. If a dish looked a bit pale I would simply add another egg yolk or another dollop of thick cream of which we had plenty, because our cows produced such rich milk from the lush pastures they enjoyed.

Noon arrived. Then 12:30 PM came and no rabbi. We were being patient and polite but we were beginning to wonder how long we could hold out. When you get up before 6 AM, you are hungry by noon. And for Fred, when he says to eat at 12, it didn't mean five minutes afterward! It was one o'clock, then 2 PM. Still no Rabbi. "Let"s have an apple before we all starve. He must have gotten lost." With this, I washed and cut up a few apples and divided them among us.

My beautiful meal was beginning to look as sad as we felt when at 2:30 PM up drove a fire engine red Buick, and out stepped a very chubby man, all ready for the ranch—decked out in shorts! Rabbi Goldsmith was a very pleasant man, quite corpulent, no, more than that—he was fat! Always well dressed, he loved to hug the ladies, but his most prevalent quality was his stubbornness. Nobody could change his mind in most situations and he always had an answer to everything. Now it was mid-afternoon, and here was the usually well-dressed Rabbi looking like a fat, little kid. As we struggled hard to keep a straight face, we hurried him into the house, accepted his apology for getting lost, and we all sat down to the meal from which there were no leftovers.

In between bites, the good Rabbi told how much trouble he had finding our place. He forgot to bring my map so he thought he'd ask people on the road, but he didn't see anyone. Finally, he stopped at a farmhouse. He heard a terrible noise as he brought the

Buick to a halt. He told us how three mangy dogs approached him with saliva dripping from between their yellow teeth. They barked at him furiously while he was still in his car. They so terrified him that he immediately decided to start the car and get away before those three monsters demolished his beautiful Buick with him inside. After this hair-raising experience, he decided to keep driving and promised himself never to try to get out of his car wherever there might be dogs. "Country dogs are vicious animals," he said. We all smiled, knowing that was not true.

"Finally," the Rabbi continued, "I met a cowboy on horseback who told me where you lived and here I am. I'm really sorry to be so late." After another mouthful of roast and mashed potatoes, he uttered, "This is the best piece of meat I've had in a long time!" I am a sucker for compliments, so I forgave him for fouling up my special meal.

"I want to see your place, your barns, your cows, your chickens...I want to see everything! I've never been on a ranch before and I want to find out how a rancher lives and feels!" After his enthusiastic request, we set out to show him the barns. While the rabbi stood there admiring the size of our bright, newly painted red barns, I suddenly noticed that he was standing squarely on top of an anthill.

Ants are common in Central and Eastern Colorado. Their hills are cone shaped and can be up to 1-1/2 feet tall. On this particular day, we could see ants carrying white oval shaped larvae into the sunlit area. But when the Rabbi stepped onto their home, the ants became frantic and scurried around picking up their unborn kids and moving them down inside the anthill for protection. I called to the Rabbi, alerting him that he had better move off the anthill and do it quickly. But as I mentioned before, he was a stubborn man. "Oh, they won't hurt me, besides, I am tough!" By the time we had finished the tour of the "barns, cows, and chickens" he was itching severely. His legs turned blue and then bright red. He sat in the kitchen, trying to make conversation, but he obviously was greatly distracted. I put baking powder compresses on his chubby legs. He appreciated the cool comfort to his now-burning anatomy. He was not that tough after all!

Even though we invited the good Rabbi back to the ranch on numerous occasions, he always had an excuse. We knew the real reason "...ants and mean dogs were more powerful than God!" 🐴

Soil Bank

The federal government was always cooking up new programs for the already suspicious farmers who wanted to run their farms as they saw fit, without interference from the big shot. This time, it seemed the bureaucrats in Washington D.C. decided there was a glut of grain on the U.S. market. On television, they showed mountains of feed being stored on the ground, out in the open. They aired pictures of rats and mice gorging themselves on spoiled grain alongside storage facilities that were filled to capacity. As a solution, the government wanted farmers to pull fields out of production for ten years and place them into what would be called, the 'Soil Bank', in return for yearly payments. In case of an emergency, like a severe drought, the land could be used to graze cattle. White posts in the corner of the selected fields would tell inspectors if the farmer was complying with the program. Once the farmers heard that there was a stipend, many tempered their skepticism about the Soil Bank and jumped at the opportunity. We, also, joined and placed our two fields of 50 acres each into the Soil Bank for 10 years at $1000 each year. Our 'city cousins' grumbled, "You farmers are always complaining and now you are getting paid for doing nothing." They were right, of course, but it was an enormous help in our shaky financial condition.

Our neighbors, the Farrell's did not believe in the Soil Bank as they thought more money could be made raising a crop, so during the summer months Fred helped Bill plow and plant his land. The paycheck was small because he, like everybody else, was very short on cash. To make matters worse, it looked as if it was going to be another dry year, not a good sign for dry land farming.

Meanwhile, the animal population on our ranch was exploding. Someone gave us a couple of white rabbits and in true-rabbit fashion, they produced six babies. When it came time to butcher the fast growing soft cuties, my brave husband refused to do it. He objected, "I don't touch rabbits and I don't touch cats. It nauseates me. You do it." I did it...and we all, including Fred, enjoyed the fried delicacy.

Four gray geese joined our animal kingdom—for which we paid $10. They immediately started laying huge eggs as they built a nest in the haystack. All the geese, even the 'resident gander' did duty keeping the eggs warm. We had to keep them moist, according to a pamphlet from CSU, because there was no pond where the geese could go for a quick swim. So I inherited another daily job, that of pouring water over the eggs and turning them, in case all the other 'Moms' forgot.

After a month, the first bunch of goslings began chewing their way out of the hard shells. Talk about a nervous mother goose! She ran around trumpeting her news to the animal world. All the eggs hatched, except one. I carefully picked it up, listened for a sound, and heard a weak "peep." I decided to help it out of its tight cage and broke the shell like you do when you peel a hard-boiled egg. Out popped a beautiful, yellow, fluffy gosling. Someone with 'goose experience' told us that goslings think the first animal, or person, they see is their mother. They are immediately 'imprinted' and they will follow it or her everywhere. Knowing this, I quickly disappeared and left a confused baby bird stumbling over the other siblings, peeping desperately for moral support.

The following day, the proud mom walked her six babies around the ranch, one behind the other. Before long the show was over and they returned to the nest. The goose did not mind us being close but when any of the collies came near she hissed at them so furiously that they retreated immediately, their bushy tails between their legs.

Also, included in our animal harem was a beautiful gray cat that came to our place and stayed. After a while, we noticed she was pregnant. The children were anticipating the happy event of her litter and, to them, it seemed to take an eternity. Then it happened. She came to the house for breakfast and one of the kids yelled excitedly, "Look Mom, she's empty!" And she was! We fed her lots of milk and she left, not to reappear for two days.

"Why isn't she coming back? Where do you think she is?" the children asked.

I answered that she probably was nursing her babies. "Is she a nurse now?" the kids asked. I had to explain how kittens needed milk, just like babies do. After much searching, we finally located the well-hidden nest, away from danger and warmly nestled amongst empty feed sacks in a corner of the barn. We trained all the kittens to go to the milk barn for food, and every time the cows were milked we filled a special pan just for them. They grew up fast. And they should have because they got all the milk they needed along with an unlimited supply of mice.

One morning at 9:15 AM sharp our mailman, Fred Wagoner, drove up to the house instead of the mailbox by the road. This could only mean one thing. He was delivering something too large for the mailbox. Fred and I knew what it was but the children didn't. Two weeks earlier we had ordered 50 chicks for $13.30 ($9.50 plus $3.80 for freight). We said nothing to the kids while they surrounded the mailman's car. He opened the back door, stretched far inside, gave a grunt, and finally pulled out a large box. There were small holes all over the top and you could hear a constant peeping. "I got to check how many are dead," he announced as he lifted the lid and exposed a bunch of baby chicks, scurrying around in a great big hurry. The kids asked me why Mr. Wagoner expected some dead ones and I explained that the hatchery guaranteed live chicks and would replace the dead ones. Fortunately, they were all alive and the children were so delighted they forgot all about the kittens. The chicken business was assigned to me and I quietly challenged myself, "Let's see if I can raise all of them."

Next, we took the box into the heated chicken house where the warm brooder kept the babies under a large, round, metal hood until they grew bigger. We took each chick from the box, dipped its beak into the drinking water so it would know where the water was, and filled feeders with special mash. They had not eaten for a while so the hungry chicks began to peck, eating every morsel. It was hard to get the children away from the chicks— but I had to admit, I was just as spellbound.

Tommy was now in the second grade. Both he and Bonnie were great help and could milk the cows. They seemed to enjoy ranch life. I put them in charge of watering and feeding the chicks, of course, under my supervision. They were delighted with the responsibility and I knew they would do a good job. I always felt children should be kept busy and that they should be willing and dependable when asked to do things. Mainly, I wanted them to be kind to all animals, small or large.

I had been raised in the city, surrounded by noises of cars, buses, and streetcars. The only responsibility I had when I was young was to wash dishes and in the winter I had to bring up coal from the basement. We didn't have any animals, not even a dog. At an early age I came to understand that my family didn't care for pets. I vowed to change that when I became an adult.

New Encounters

Kids Thrive On Danger

It promised to be a beautiful, bright spring day in 1955. The sun had been warming people, animals, and the rest of the world for hours. The blue sky was cloudless and winter was becoming a memory. In Colorado, this season does not necessarily mean that it will be predictably warm with the pastures greening up, followed by a pleasant summer. No siree—spring means: enjoy every day while it lasts, for very often, it can be interrupted by a sudden snowstorm, often unannounced by the ever-vigilant meteorologists from the radio station. Those spring storms would blow in with such fury and were very wet and sticky; good for the dry soil but so hazardous that it was necessary for both man and beast to seek immediate shelter.

On this particular day, however it was not the case, so I decided to get the wash on the line early in the morning. Everybody in the family was busy. Fred, when he wasn't repairing something, was checking cattle; Tommy was a first grader at Miami School, and baby Susan was doing her thing: sleeping. Bonnie, then close to four years old, was my "assistant" and she was helping me gather the soiled clothes. She was such an enthusiastic helper that I had to watch her because she 'found' all sorts of things she thought needed washing. Nothing was safe, not even a pair of kitchen curtains which she pulled off the rod.

It was time to get started before the huge pile on the floor got any larger. Actually it looked as if each article was giving birth to another one right there before my eyes—Horrors! I quickly moved my square tub Maytag towards the sink, hooked a small hose to the faucet, turned on the hot water and added soap to the first load of clothes. It churned happily for ten minutes. After the wash cycle I changed hoses to use the 'sudsaver' function, a popular feature on washing machines at the time. I then diverted the soapy water into a metal container which sat on the floor so the solution could be used again in the upcoming cycles.

I rinsed the first load and then put it, piece by piece, through a wringer to eliminate excessive water, then dropped it into a laundry basket to take to the clothesline. Before going outside, I sucked up the suds solution via the saver hose and started on the next load. With the machine busily washing, I picked up the basket and urged Bonnie to follow me outside. Somehow, I just didn't trust that inquisitive child alone in the house, call it intuition...or perhaps apprehension.

I was deep in my thoughts, enjoying the warm spring breeze when I heard a horrible scream. I dropped the shirt I was hanging on the clothesline and rushed towards the wailing sound. As I threw open the kitchen door, there stood my child with her arm caught in the wringer clear up to her armpit. In a flash, I hit the red release button that relaxed the tension between the two wringers so I could carefully back out Bonnie's arm from the wringer's grasp. On examination, it did not seem broken or even squashed so I thought I'd just watch it to make sure the circulation returned. Almost at once, Bonnie's tears were gone, her violently red face was back to normal and she produced an angelic smile while her blonde curls danced on her forehead. I felt like scolding her, remembering all the

91

warnings I had given her to never touch the wringer. Why didn't she follow me into the yard when I specifically asked her to? But, I decided she had learned her lesson and I didn't need to say anything more.

That same afternoon William House, a good friend, dropped by. Over coffee, he told us that he would like to sell Topsey, the horse he had loaned us. She was calm and all of us liked riding her, especially the children. William asked $60 for her and Fred immediately accepted. We now owned our first horse, a beautiful white Quarter Horse mare with small brown spots all over. In the past, she had led Williams' racehorses on a track, so she was comfortable around a lot of noise and crowds of people—a perfect horse for kids.

Every afternoon Tommy's chore was to bring the dairy cows in from the pasture to be milked. Fred would saddle Topsey for him and he'd be gone for at least 30 minutes gathering the bovines. Eventually the cows would appear with Tommy following behind. We'd see him and then hurry to open the corral and get things ready for the milking. One time, as Tommy was pushing the cattle across the road, one of them started running in the opposite direction. At once, our little cowboy went after her with Topsey running quickly to surround the stray, just as any good cow horse would do. She turned the wayward animal and chased her, at full speed, all the way back to the others that had already drifted into the corral. There, the heavy gate hung between two big posts and 4 feet apart was

Our horse, Topsey.

stabilized with a thick, twisted wire between them, about 6 feet off the ground. With Topsey running at a full gallop, Tommy realized he could not fit under the wire and that it was going to catch him and pull him off the horse. Quickly, he leaped off the right side of Topsey, moments before she entered the corral, then quickly crawled underneath the bottom strand of the wire corral, rolling away from Topsey's fleeting hooves. A split second later, the riderless horse tore into the corral, her sides heaving as her lungs screamed for air. She soon calmed down, stared at the still open gate behind her, and probably wondered to herself, "Where is that little boy?"

After this scary episode, Fred removed the wire from the posts and we began seriously anticipating other dangers around the place. We needed to be more diligent to prevent other near-accidents that loomed around every corner of the ranch. How lucky we were that our little ranch hand had the presence of mind to act so quickly!

Spring is probably the busiest season of the year. Recovering from a long, cold winter is almost immediate and very welcome. The world greets new life—animals and plants alike. Optimism is at its highest and it's a good season to be alive! 🐎

Gret

One afternoon as Fred was driving home on Calhan Highway, a gravel road full of holes left from a downpour a few days before, he noticed a lady with two beautiful collie dogs, walking in a driveway which lead towards a neat white house. Not having seen anybody there since the last owner left, and knowing my love for dogs, he thought he would introduce himself. After the usual greeting, he asked if he could bring his wife over sometime to meet her. With a hearty laugh, she responded, "Please do, we don't know too many folks around here, yet!"

From left to right: Merril, their daughter Annie, Husband Joe, their son George, Gret,
daughter Mary with Eddy on her lap, and Clifford.

"I met someone you GOT to visit," was Fred's greeting as he bounded into the front room that same afternoon. He told me about the new owners of the old McNeal place and how she loves dogs. That was all I needed to know.

The next Sunday afternoon we visited our newly found neighbors, roughly three miles southeast from our place. As we were driving up the long driveway towards the house, we could hear dogs barking, announcing our arrival. Soon the door opened and a man, at least six feet tall, greeted us followed by a lady almost as tall, perhaps 5' 10" or 11'. They were Sam and Gretel Stouffer who had a little girl, Annie. I knew immediately that we were destined to not only be neighbors, but also great friends. Fred and Sam talked about ranching while Gret, as she called herself, and I chatted about dogs. She was as fond of them as I was. We decided to drive to Colorado Springs to visit the collie kennel sometime soon. She knew the owners and would occasionally stop by to see their newest arrivals. Meanwhile, the children were getting to know each other and they played quietly in the corner of the living room while the four of us enjoyed a cup of coffee and a piece of chocolate cake, a surprising coincidence since this was Fred's favorite flavor. It certainly made a hit with him. Besides, Gret cut the slices so thick you would have thought all of us had been on a month's hunger strike! We didn't know whether to eat them or climb them!

Sam told us he was a Coloradoan and that Gret came from Ithaca, New York where she graduated from Cornell University in Animal Husbandry. They had met on the western slope of Colorado, fallen in love, and married. Now, at their new ranch, they owned close to seventy head of Hereford cattle and several dozen chickens. We could tell that Sam and Gret were going to be good operators and that they weren't afraid of hard work. It was getting late and we knew we had to go home to do the chores that were waiting for us, as always. We promised to visit one another again, soon.

While driving home, we talked about the comfortable house the Stouffers lived in. The kitchen was painted a lovely combination of white and yellow. On the first floor there was a tastefully furnished living room and a good-sized bedroom with a bedstead and dresser painted a delicate light gray. And there was a bathroom! There also were two more bedrooms upstairs. Everything was neat and it looked like Gret had done nothing all day but scrub and clean house. Even the dogs looked freshly brushed.

It was not long before Gret and Annie came over for a visit. I hurried and put on the coffeepot, placed a few leftover cookies on a plate, and settled down for a friendly and lengthy conversation. We made the splendid decision to go to Colorado Springs the next day, visit the collie kennel, and do our grocery shopping.

As arranged, at ten o'clock, up drove a big green Buick. There was Gret dressed in jeans and a hot pink blouse with bright red lipstick and curled hair yelling to me, "Are you ready?" Of course, I was. It was easy and relaxing to be with Gret. Her contagious laugh, her openness, and genuine wholesomeness was a welcome release from ranch work.

North of Colorado Springs, not too far from I-25, going towards Denver, was the collie kennel. A lot of muffled barking greeted us as we parked next to a long, window-less building. There were several metal enclosures and dog runs. All were empty. As we entered the front door, we were greeted by a couple, both quite short in stature, about 5'4". The man, Mr. Walker, spoke with a thick Scottish accent to which we had to listen closely to understand him. The wife said very little.

Annie and Susan.

Obviously she had less control over the business. Her duties, no doubt, consisted of doing most of the physical work. I felt sorry for her. While enjoying a cup of coffee and chatting about collies, Mr. Walker told us about one of his dogs that had recently been returned because she was unfriendly with teenagers. He now had an idea. He would give her to me, free of charge, if she was bred by one of their best dogs and he could have his pick of half the litter. He also wanted me to exhibit one of the pups at an upcoming dog show, to promote the kennel. I was being offered a registered dog, the breed I had always admired and wanted to own. How could I not agree!

The 'little woman' was sent to get the dog. "This is Lady," she said. Immediately this magnificent animal and I bonded with each other. She was tall for a female and had sable and white coloring. Two almond-shaped brown eyes accentuated with the longest eyelashes I ever saw gave character to her smooth, delicate, and long face. She stood there, waving a bushy tail. If she could have talked she would have pleaded, "Please take me!"

I bent down, stroked her forehead, and with a quiet voice I asked, "Hey Lady, how would you like to be a ranch dog?" I swear she understood that this meant she was going home with me.

Mr. Walker handed me Lady's registration papers along with her pedigree and I appreciated that he had faith and trust in me to follow through with his proposal. He then explained the dog's dislike for teenagers. It seemed when a certain group of youngsters passed her yard, they teased her by throwing sticks at her and making threatening noises. I assured the friendly Scotsman that Lady would be well cared for and loved by the whole family.

So the three of us left with Lady in the lead. She walked right up to Gret's car, waited for the car door to be opened, and with an air of aloofness, hopped into the back seat. Gret and I had a quick hamburger at a Dairy Queen, did some grocery shopping, and drove home where we enjoyed a jubilant reception from the children and a very reserved one from the husband. Lady was excited, too. She wandered all over the place, in and out of the house, and finally lay down in front of her doghouse in which I had quickly placed an old woolen rug.

Later that afternoon, I went to check on Lady and she was nowhere to be found. Frantically, I called for Fred to get the jeep and the two of us sped to the south pasture where I thought I had seen something moving. As luck would have it, we soon found her about 1/2 mile from the house. The minute she noticed the jeep she turned and ran towards us. I took this as a sign that she was glad to see us. She then leaped into the vehicle. But when we got back home, I knew I had to impress on Lady that roaming around was not allowed. I took her to the doghouse. There, I grabbed her by the loose skin of her neck, shook it, and told her to stay by the house, and that she was a "BAD DOG". In an instant, the proud collie began to look like a bloodhound, so sad she made me feel guilty. She let out a very low growl which caused me to back off. Soon it was time to reconcile and show her that everything was all right. Lady never again left the house and always stayed close by. She was a marvelous companion for the ten years of her life. Such a short ten years!

Gret used to come to our place more often than I would go to hers. She always had interesting and funny experiences to share, always punctuated by her contagious laughter.

One Monday morning she again came for a visit, having left Annie at home with Sam. "That kid is mad at me, again," she said, "so I thought I'd let Sam handle her for a while.

Then he'll find out what I'm talking about."

"I'm curious, what in the world was she up to now?" I questioned her with a grin on my face.

"Well," Gret continued, "last Friday Annie said a string of profanity, words that I'd had never heard her say before." Gret didn't know where she had heard those expressions! To impress the importance of not swearing, Gret sent Annie to her room and told her to stay there one hour. "Don't leave your room until I come for you," was the last thing Gret said before closing the door and going to the kitchen to read the latest 'Good Housekeeping' magazine.

She wondered, "Am I too harsh on my daughter?" She leafed through the magazine and came upon an article, "Are We Too Tough on Our Children?" How timely and appropriate! She started to read but didn't agree with the author's permissive attitude and decided then and there that the writer probably didn't have children. If she did, she wouldn't make such lame excuses for poor behavior. Gret continued reading her favorite magazine when she realized that the hour of Annie's detention had passed.

Gret went to Annie's room to tell her she could come out. But after opening the door and looking around, she discovered that the room was empty—no Annie! Was she hiding under the bed? In the closet? She was nowhere. She thought that maybe Annie had sneaked out quietly, not making a sound. Gret was certain she would find her outdoors playing in the sandbox. No Annie there either. She next circled around the barns and other buildings with the same result. But, what was this? Finally, she noticed a distinct mark, a groove, in the loose sand by the house. Gret followed the score for a few feet and realized it continued down the driveway. She thought she should get in the car and follow the track, just to find out where it went. Maybe Annie was hiding in the car. But she wasn't there either. Gret got in and drove down the driveway in hot pursuit of the telltale mark in the road. To her surprise, the groove turned south onto Calhan Highway. The gravel road (I once was told by a road maintenance man not to call it a "dirt" road) made it easy to see. She followed it until she was almost at Highway 94, a good mile away from her home. This busy thoroughfare started in Colorado Springs and lead through Yoder, Rush, Punkin Center and on to Kansas. Now Gret became worried. Did Annie cross the highway or was she back in the house or in a barn? Perhaps she had missed her somewhere. And where did that groove in the sand lead to? As Gret was worrying about Annie, several cars zoomed by, followed by a cattle truck and another car coming from the opposite direction. She sat in her car with the motor idling, thinking about what she could do next when suddenly her eyes focused on a small child about 1/2 mile away on the other side of the highway. It must be Annie!

Gret gunned the motor, sped across the thoroughfare and in no time was close enough to recognize Annie. When she reached her, she stopped the car and got out. There was one tired looking child riding, of all things, her favorite toy, a stick horse.

"What in the world are you doing?" Gret almost shouted with concern. She had to control herself even though she was relieved to have found the child.

"I'm running away from home. You don't want me anymore."

"Where are you going?"

"I'm going to the Higgins'. I'm going to live with them," was Annie's determined and immediate answer.

"You don't know if they want you. We got to ask them first. In the meantime you better come home with me. Hop in and bring your stick horse." Annie did. Gret turned the car towards home. She felt relieved, the terrible fear vanished and at the same time she tried to suppress a chuckle. "What is this kid going to do next?" she thought.

The Higgins lived about 1-3/4 mile from where Gret picked up Annie. Fred and I visited with the family after this event and informed them of almost becoming foster parents. They felt honored—at first—but then they decided, "We've raised one family and that is enough, besides Annie is a handful. No, thank you." Annie's stick horse escapade became a priceless story, one which prompted many laughs.

Gret and I continued our coffee klatches with news, old and new, of our families. She often spoke of her parents, especially her father who was an attorney. Every summer he and his wife would travel around New England and whenever they came upon a church which needed a coat of paint, they stopped and paid to have it done. I had heard so much about her parents that when they visited for a week, I felt like I already knew them.

One spring morning both Fred and I returned early from checking cattle at a pasture we rented for the year. We were on Calhan Highway when Fred suggested, "Let's stop at Sam and Gret's place. We haven't seen Sam in a long time." That was fine with me because I was anxious to see Gret's 50 new baby chicks she was keeping in her house.

We parked in the driveway and walked through the fenced-in yard. The collies came to greet us, barking happily. Fred, never comfortable around dogs, told me to lead the way and he would follow. "Keep the dogs with you," he pleaded. As we arrived at the back door I started to knock. No response. I knocked ever louder, still no answer. "Perhaps their radio is on and they can't hear us," was Fred's reasoning. And with that, he opened the unlocked door. Before he could call out Sam's name, a gray cat zipped past us and disappeared into the house. Horrors! Baby chicks, and now a cat on the prowl! "You got to find her and get her out of there. I don't think anybody is home," I urged him. Both of us tiptoed inside, looking for the cat in every corner and trying to locate the box with the few-days-old chicks. I soon found the yellow peepers, content and undisturbed, not realizing the danger they were in. The hunt for the cat continued while, at the same time, we hoped our friends would NOT return just then. It would look awful if they suddenly appeared while we were roaming through their house. I kept calling "Here, kitty kitty", but "kitty" had no intention of revealing her hiding place. We crawled on hands and knees, looked under cabinets in every room urgently shouting, pleading "Here, kitty kitty." I returned to the box of chicks every so often and checked on their safety. It wouldn't take long for the cat to grab one and devour it.

Finally, we checked the bedroom and as Fred bent down to look under the bed, he yelled victoriously, "She's here!" I crawled under the low bed and tried to reach her but she moved away. I think she was just as scared as we were because of all our excited shouting for the illusive "kitty".

I finally retrieved her and carried her quietly in my arms. She soon purred like a buzz saw, and now I was sure I could carry her out of the house without her trying to escape from my arms. What a relief! And we were not even caught running through all the rooms.

"Let's get out of here!" Fred announced as we hurried back to the pickup, where we started to laugh. It was funny, now.

Annie and Mary, were typical sisters. They loved each other and sometimes, they didn't. They played tricks on each other and occasionally on different people. Annie was the champion, though. She had lots of ideas and put only the most treacherous ones into practice.

One day, she wanted to show little Mary how to brand cattle. She had the willing partner lie down on the ground while the 'cowboy' made a fire and placed a one-inch thick stick into it. She took her 'branding iron' and held the hot end against Mary's upper thigh. Naturally, the pain was immediate. Mary screamed and quickly ran into the house where Gret treated the wound with bag balm ointment and covered it with a Band-Aid. Fortunately the 'brand' soon healed. Annie's punishment was strong enough so that she did not repeat the stunt and Mary learned not to be so trusting of her sister. This episode was neither forgotten nor forgiven for several years.

Another time when Annie was going to Miami School, some 25 miles southeast of Calhan, she and a bunch of boys decided to 'hang' a boy. He was the son of a rich rancher, a town bully whom nobody liked. It was during recess when most of the kids were on the swings or playing baseball. The vigilantes chose the big cottonwood tree in the school yard, thinking it would be just perfect for a 'hangin tree'—just like they saw in so many Westerns. They found a rope and made a noose. Then they borrowed a little red wagon from the school office and forced the 'prisoner' to stand in it. Annie slipped the loop over his head and they were starting to move the wagon when a girl who was watching the preparations suddenly realized what was happening, ran to the principal, who luckily stopped the 'execution' just in time. You can imagine the uproar this caused!

During the years that we were neighbors Gret and her family spent many important, and not so important, occasions together. She was an inspiration to me, a bright person, another ranch woman whose terrific sense of humor, common sense, and compassion was an asset for me, her neighbor, her friend. 🐂

New Arrivals

It was such a cold January night that it was hard to keep the living room warm for Lady, our collie, who was going to whelp at any moment. We had made an enclosure for her and covered the floor with several layers of newspapers and during the past few weeks we had encouraged her to stay inside at nights, just as the folks from the kennel advised us to do. They had given Lady to me, papers and all, and only had asked that they receive half of the litter. It was a great opportunity for us, especially since she was bred to their best sire.

"Was that a whimper?" I thought as I listened to a sound outside our closed bedroom door. "There it was again!" Both Fred and I jumped out of bed to check on our patient. She was so nervous, she ran around the living room and soon went to the area we had fixed for her. The pups arrived and I would say after each was born: "One for the kennel, one for us..." We now had five blind, sable and white little balls of fur. Lady was still busy cleaning her babies and making low grunting sounds when we decided to return to bed for what was left of a short night.

Imagine our surprise when hours later, we checked Lady and found that she had given birth to a sixth pup! Now, there were three males and three females, falling over each other like dominoes.

After six weeks, the folks from the kennel came and picked out their three pups. They were surprised how alike they all were and how much they had grown. They asked us to bring the best one to the next collie dog show to promote the kennel. We agreed. We sold one female pup in Denver and gave a male to Uncle Herman and Aunt Blanche, Boy, his name, stayed at their ranch. We kept the other male, Pete.

One bad blizzard after another hit our area that winter, each two weeks apart. We had no mail, no electricity for 34 hours, and no school for ten days. One night a fierce wind blew out the entire bedroom windowpane and the daytime temperature never rose above fifteen degrees. Between storms, Gret came for a visit and told us that 22 of their neighbor's cattle drifted to their house and some wandered onto their partially enclosed porch. Unfortunately, they all died. The storms had blown in so fast and so strong that losses were severe throughout the county.

During early spring, Mr.Watts a neighbor who raised sheep in the Arkansas Valley, south of Colorado Springs, gave us two tiny, baby lambs. We fed them milk from a baby bottle. Imagine our surprise when one day we saw one of them being nursed by Lady, our collie dog. We wondered, "Did she still have any milk? Did she miss her six pups? What made the lamb try a new source of nourishment?" And then on another chilly day, I found both lambs snuggling on Lady's warm belly encircled by her legs, surrounded by lots of warm fur. Her satisfied look was a picture of peace and love.

Every so often we were confronted by new emergencies. One day, Fred noticed a yearling calf that was not eating like the other cattle, and had an unusually large head. Upon closer inspection, he discovered that a snake had probably bitten the calf. Fred brought the already weak animal into the corral where the poor thing dropped to the ground. We asked the vet for advice and bought a small bottle of Potassium Permanganate (KMnO4). We filled a syringe with the solution, fixed a tiny needle onto the tip, and injected small amounts two inches apart into the entire head and neck where the swelling was severe. The vet had warned us that the yearling would probably die. He was right. Sometimes larger animals like mature cows or horses will survive snakebite even without the medicine, but that was not the case for yearlings. On a ranch, rattlesnakes were about as welcome as a root canal! During our 36 years we killed a goodly number of the unwelcome critters!

This was the year of more wonderful guests including the Masons from El Paso, Texas. Fred was a neighbor of Lee's when they were boys in Meimbressen, Germany. Both had immigrated to the U.S. and they were reunited in 1944 while serving in the Army during World War II. They happened to meet at Fort De Russey P.X. on Oahu Island, Hawaii where they shared many memories. We showed Lee, Hilde and their daughters, Carol and Linda, the foothills around the Broadmoor Hotel in Colorado Springs, had a picnic in North Cheyenne Canyon, and visited the Zoo. Sorry to say they did not stay longer.

My ex-roommate, Rosalind, along with her husband, Joffe, and their boys visited again for a few days. One night during a vicious thunderstorm, a flash of bright lightning hit our electric water heater in the kitchen and started a fire. While Fred and Joffe attacked the blaze, I got the kids out of bed and brought them into the living room where they huddled together, frightened. Suddenly, I realized that seven year-old Tommy was not there. I returned to his room and shouted for him to come. He was sitting on his bed, putting on his shoes. He looked up at me and quietly explained, "I was having trouble with the shoestrings." Finally he appeared, decked out in his blue pajamas, socks, and shoes, perfectly calm as if this was just a drill while the other kids stood in their pj's, barefoot and scared to death. As a youngster, Tommy never got excited. Who did he get that from? Not me and, certainly, not from Fred! The fire was soon extinguished and the thunderstorm moved on, leaving us with 1/4" of wonderful rain.

Our first snowstorm arrived in September. Though it did not cause too much trouble for us, it produced an outbreak of the Asian flu that made it necessary to close both the rural and urban schools while the hospitals tried to cope. The private rooms became doubles and the halls were lined with beds containing feverish, coughing sufferers. We hoped to stay healthy while the kids enjoyed their impromptu vacation.

Our cellar was stocked with last fall's canned pears, peaches, plums, and applesauce, as well as pickles and jams. We butchered nine turkeys and seventeen capons and put those into the freezer locker in Calhan as our big freezer was filled to the brim. We could have fed an army and still had enough to last all winter!

Improvements and repairs were always needed on the old house and now the roof was leaking! The ugly green wallpaper in the living room was peeling and so before more things went wrong we 'attacked' both at once. We hired a man to shingle the roof and another one to texture the walls in the living room.

In early December, I baked Christmas cookies and fruitcakes and sewed doll clothes while Fred bought 47 calves. The poor babies bawled incessantly for their mothers but calmed down after a few days. Now, they were on their own. When calves were being weaned, it was hard on them and you had to pamper them with warm, dry barns along with plenty of feed and water plus TLC. So ended another year. We hoped for fewer chuckholes in the road of life from now on.

I had invited friends from Colorado Springs to celebrate New Year's Day. Our conversation drifted to this fantastic new invention called Television! Just a mention of the word stopped country folk in their tracks. It was magic. Though most of us had heard or read about it, few ever had watched it. The people spoke of this marvel of a product with respect and hoped to someday be the owner of such a luxury item. Imagine my surprise when Fred announced that we ought to buy a set.

It arrived on February 8, 1955 in a huge box with "Hallicrafter" boldly printed on it. A second, smaller and longer box contained the antenna that we needed to install on the peak of the roof. Fred immediately got in touch with the Calhan electrician, George, who hooked up the system, telling us how lucky we were and how few folks in Calhan had a TV. That night we watched Groucho Marx and his antics. What a delight it was! Suddenly we had a connection with the world—we were not so all alone.

Television programming and reception were quite primitive. Only three black and white stations were on the air and very often the picture was quite fuzzy, introducing us to a new kind of 'snow'. Programming began around 9 AM and concluded around 11 PM with a special salute to the nation followed by a test pattern and a humming tone.

Television changed our lives and our routines. Fred especially enjoyed a program that I thought was extremely stupid called 'Beat the Clock.' Here contestants had to accomplish a variety of tasks before the bell rang. If they were successful they would receive generous gifts. "Be sure and call me when 'my' program comes on," he always reminded me. I assured Fred that I would, even if it meant walking through 'hill and dale', mud, and manure until I reached shouting range. Then, this guy, this ex-German who never stopped a job until it was finished, would drop everything and, as if a magnet was pulling him, would race to the house to view his foolish 30-minute show.

Our favorite programs were "I Love Lucy", "Jackie Gleason", "Gary Moore", and the "Breakfast Club," but westerns were especially appealing to us. It was like looking at our life in a previous era. One I especially liked was "The Rifleman" which left me drooling over this courageous, handsome, and tall man, wondering why there weren't more of him around! I silently suffered from one week to the next waiting impatiently before he would show up on TV again, heroically toting his rifle.

We never missed Liberace who combined excellence on the piano with showmanship into an hour-long extravaganza. And then there was Guy Lombardo and his Royal Canadians with Kenny Gardener as the main vocalist, a tenor who would smile and send shivers surging though my very soul.

Fred's favorite television shows were sporting events. When, for example, the New York Yankees won the World Series over the Milwaukie Brewers by six to two games, he was ecstatic. He watched them all—from football, basketball, to whatever else appeared on the screen called "sports". For me, I confronted yet another hurdle, that of learning the rules of all the games. I came face to face with something else new in which I was uneducated and frankly, uninterested. It took me a while but I learned and I especially came to appreciate the Denver Broncos and their quarterback, John Elway.

What TV did for me in those early days was miraculous. It seemed as if a whole New World was thrust upon me. Suddenly, I felt rich and very content. I had a good husband, healthy children and a TV! 🐴

Another Drought

955 was one of the driest years ever. The pastures in El Paso County were like straw. Even during the summer, ranchers had to buy expensive hay to feed their cattle because the grass would not grow. The cattle got thin, milk production went down and the dry land farming we did, without irrigation, was futile. On top of it all, the price of cattle dropped to an all-time low: 12 cents per pound for steers, 8 cents for heifers, almost half of what it was the year before.

The desperate ranchers and farmers kept their eyes directed to the sky, especially when a few clouds wandered across the blue firmament. Sometimes when what looked like a thunderstorm was approaching; everybody would say a silent prayer and hope for the precious rain to burst from the dark sky. Usually the thunder would rumble, lightening would flash, and a few fat drops of wetness, several inches apart, would fall. Then a strong wind would appear and blow those wonderful black clouds away. It was like a game, the world toying with our psyche and emotions.

Some folks kept their sense of humor. One day, Jim Gochnauer came by and announced that he had a 3-inch rain. Dumbfounded, we answered with a question, "Really?"

"Yep," he replied, "the drops were three inches apart!"

The drought was not only felt in El Paso County, but it was widespread. The banks that loaned the money were not cooperative. In fact, even though these were desperate times, they now decided that livestock was not good collateral. People tried to sell their places hoping to eke out what little money they could rescue. Hopes for a job in town were on folks' mind. The struggle for survival affected everyone.

Our neighbor, Bill Farrell, drove up one Wednesday morning with an important telephone message from Aunt Blanche. "Fred, you are supposed to go to Denver right away. Something's wrong with your uncles." Bill, having delivered the urgent plea, was in no hurry to leave. Instead, he got out of his pickup, closed the door and lazily leaned against it.

"Guess what I did the other day?" he finally said. Fred did not care to find out and answered him that he didn't have time to visit because he wanted to get cleaned up and dressed for his trip to Denver. He turned and started to walk towards the kitchen door when Bill called out, "I got me a job in Colorado Springs."

"A job?" Fred turned back, uttering in disbelief. Here was a man who was not too keen on working hard. "Yup, me and Sam Stouffer are going to start next Monday. You're surprised, ain't you?" He also told us that he and Sam, Gret's husband, were going to share rides to Colorado Springs and both would be working for a moving company.

"Good for you, Bill!" I shouted from the kitchen.

Fred excused himself and again approached the open kitchen door, hoping he would not be interrupted again. But before he closed the door behind him good 'ole Bill yelled, "Have a good trip!" and left.

It was no more than 30 minutes when Fred appeared in the kitchen where I was preparing lunch. A couple of salami sandwiches were ready for him to eat on the way.

Also, a thermos filled with his favorite, hot cocoa. I looked up and saw standing before me a handsome man, clean shaven, surrounded by the scent of the Skin Bracer Aunt Blanche had given him a long time ago as a birthday present. He was dressed in his one and only decent suit —the light gray one he wore at our wedding with the black shoes I helped him buy before we were married. The crisp, white, slightly starched shirt was highlighted by a blue and yellow tie, one I always liked. He carried an overnight case filled with toilet articles, underwear, a pair of jeans, a work shirt, and boots. "I better hurry, don't know how long I'll be gone. You and the kids take care of the place and if you get in trouble ask a neighbor to help out. I can't imagine what the problem is with Uncle Herman. Hope he didn't have another heart attack." He set down the case, kissed the children and told them he loved them. I accompanied him to the car where we said a swift good bye and he was off.

Now the welfare of the family and animals rested on my shoulders. I was concerned but confident, hoping for the best. My thoughts suddenly gave birth to worries. "What if——!" I had no car to go for help, no telephone to call neighbors. I tried to reason with myself. The weather was no problem, the kids were in good health and I could always ask Fred Wagoner, the mailman, for help if I needed it. I reassured myself that things would work out fine. Oh, from where did this new country woman get all her confidence?

I needn't have worried. The kids were cooperative. They helped with chores and Tommy acted like 'the man of the house'. The next morning around 10 AM, Gret drove up for our 'Kaffee Klatch' and we had a good visit as usual. She always seemed to be in a good mood and invigorated me like a breath of fresh air. Her visit lasted about an hour during which she told me about Sam's new job at the moving company and how glad they both were. When she was ready to leave, Gret promised to come over every morning to check on me until Fred returned. What a relief to have such a good friend!

Fred left on Wednesday and now it was already Friday. "Time really went by fast when you are busy," I thought. There was no news from Denver and we all began to wonder when Fred would return. All the evening chores were done by 6 PM because we decided to start them earlier than usual so we could play outdoors a while. A beautiful sunset illuminated the western part of the sky. Light fluffy clouds seemed to change into different formations powered by a soft wind. As the children and I watched the exquisite show, almost spellbound, we made a game out of 'who can identify the shape of an animal, person, or thing'. The kids all saw different things at the same time and we laughed so much our sides started to hurt.

We were having so much fun that we didn't notice Fred driving into the driveway. Once the children saw the car, they all ran to greet him. He was hailed akin to an astronaut stepping off his space shuttle. All of us were happy and relieved that we could answer that everything was fine when he asked the all-important question, "Did you have any trouble? Any problems?"

"Of course not," was my fast reply. "What's wrong with Uncle Herman?"

"I'll tell you later. Now I need to get something to eat. Got something for a worn out traveler? I'm bushed." I heated up some leftover stew, sliced half a tomato onto a bed of lettuce and poured a tall glass of milk. Halfway through the meal Fred told us about the trip. He went into detail between every third mouthful while I struggled for patience. Uncle Herman was deeply depressed about the cattle business and kept talking about losing their ranch and all his savings. The situation was so desperate that he cried. But Uncle Sam, Uncle Herman's brother who had just moved from Wagon Mound, New Mexico to Denver, was also in terrible shape. The day Aunt Blanche called, he suffered a nervous breakdown and they took him to the hospital where he was receiving electric shock treatments. Fred felt so sorry for both of them. Never had he seen them so upset, so devastated!

Fred could only talk with Uncle Herman about his problems because we couldn't help him financially. He suggested they drive out to their Castle Rock ranch in hopes a change of scenery would do him good. It was a fine idea. The trip helped Uncle Herman realize that a lot of ranchers were in the same financial bind. Aunt Blanche was especially pleased with Fred's visit since she was out of patience and didn't know how to cope with all the stress. She said she was "going crazy with their whining and crying. We really needed your help, Fred." He was glad he went.

It was beginning to get dark outside. Fred really was very tired and was in bed before the kids were. He slept until 7 AM the next morning.

A couple of weeks before Fred's trip to Denver he had heard that the McNess Company was looking for travelling salesmen to sell their products. We thought that it might be a good job, one that would help until the cattle business improved. Fred could do this in his 'free' time. So he wrote and told them he was interested in the job. We didn't think any more about it until a panel truck drove up one morning and stopped by the house. It was a green Ford with huge yellow printing on both its sides proclaiming, "Try McNess Products...They are the best!"

"It looks like you got a job, Fred." I yelled to my prospective 'travelling salesman' who was doing the accounting in the back room.

Excitedly, we rushed out to greet the driver. All of us surrounded the truck and stood in awe as the man opened the door revealing boxes and more boxes of mysterious products. The unloading began and everybody helped place the cartons in a neat pile next to the truck. The printing on each box was different: vanilla extract, pudding mixes, vitamins, soaps, animal medications, antiseptics, ground pepper, worming pills for animals and more.

Since one of our upstairs rooms was empty we decided to use it as the storage room. We carried all the 'stuff' up the stairs and put it in the room. Then the driver handed Fred the paperwork, wished him "Good luck", and told him, "I left the carrier in your kitchen. Fill it up with the products you think your customers will want." And he was off, leaving us feeling lost. It all had happened so fast.

We returned to the kitchen to look for the carrier. There it was, a heavy black wooden box 12"X 36" with a thick metal handle. The thing weighed like lead and the color looked like it had been recently painted.

The entire family climbed the stairs to get a better look at what was to be our supply room. Fred started to arrange things on the floor since we had no shelves, separating the foods from the medications, etc. A space around the four walls was now completely covered so he moved some boxes into the middle of the room.

"Give me a hand," I was told.

But I didn't. All I could say was, "Es wird mir ganz uewwel!" which is German slang for, "I'm going to be sick!" I stared at all the confusion spreading over the linoleum floor while wild thoughts tumbled through my brain, "Has he gone overboard this time?" A moment of silence and then I broke out into a nervous giggle in which Fred eventually joined me. Then we both went to work and straightened things out as best we could.

The next morning Fred, who was full of enthusiasm about his new job and with energy galore, loaded up the car with all sorts of items from the 'supply room'. The black carrier was filled with small bottles and boxes, mainly household articles. He lifted it, producing a string of cuss words, then set it down and complained about its weight. "That thing must be made of iron with a fake coat of wood!"

By the time my 'salesman' was ready to leave he was already tired but he didn't complain. I gave him sandwiches and a thermos filled with tea and off he went out to his new career.

Now, it was time for me and me alone! What a 'delicious' idea! My thoughts ran wild—what to do. "Maybe Gret and I could go somewhere" and then as quickly as the idea came, "I can't leave here, I don't have a car and it is too far to walk to her place." So, the only thing to do was to write letters which I enjoyed doing anyway.

The first one went to my mother who lived in California. She was always amused by my experiences which I described in great detail. Had I been raised in the country instead of the city, many things would not have been so fascinating to me. For example, once when Fred was hand-milking a nervous cow she suddenly jumped with both hind legs high into the air and landed with one foot in the bucket half full of milk. The funny thing was that this didn't upset him at all, he simply lifted out her foot and continued milking! Things like that seemed hilarious to me and were worth describing in detail.

I must have written four letters, long ones, before I felt like listening to some of my records. My favorite one was the "Barber of Seville" which reminded me of New Orleans. The next record I always loved was Ezio Pinza's Italian songs. I remember seeing him perform at the New Orleans Symphony accompanied on the piano by Mr. Kitzinger, a friend of my Uncle Jos', who lived in London, England. I also listened to Ezio Pinza's famous rendition of "Some Enchanted Evening." Somehow music always released me from my troubles and worries and helped me imagine being in the most wonderful places.

Late in the afternoon my 'McNess Husband' returned somewhat harried and looking tired. "I don't know about this job. I drove miles in between ranch houses, saw ten people and only sold two items. I took orders for things I didn't carry with me, and for some that the guy didn't bring out. Now, I have to order them from the main office and go back to deliver them after the outfit in Denver sends them to me." He was really depressed.

I tried to cheer him up but I didn't do a good job. "Perhaps the next time will be better. Don't give up, yet."

Fred made fifteen more trips that month with almost the same results. People didn't need travelling salesmen anymore like they did in the past when transportation was inadequate. Nowadays they could drive to the nearest town and do shopping where they would find a better selection and at cheaper prices. The faithful customers were the old-timers who looked forward to the Raleigh man, the Watkins man and last but not least, the McNess man. To those ranchers it meant more than buying supplies, it was a social event. They would visit over coffee and share the latest gossip from around the area.

After one long month of disappointments, Fred packed up part of the 'goodies' from the upstairs spare room and took them back to the main office in Denver. They, in turn, sent a man out to our place to pick up the rest.

Other travelling salesmen did stick with it. About once a year, a Raleigh man would come by our house. We bought something, occasionally a green tin of Bag Balm, which was wonderful for cuts on animals and humans, or some tins of pudding mixes which were especially good. But we always bought more than this because we felt sorry for him. We knew what he was going through!

"There ought to be another way to make money," mused Fred one morning over breakfast. Then I blurted out, not meaning a thing, "Sure there is. You can sell the ranch, maybe sell the kids, move to a dingy apartment in town and get a job selling ribbons at the May Company but I don't think you'd like that!"

That was one of Aunt Blanche's frequent remarks, "Be a ribbon salesman!"

I meant to be funny. Having been born without a sense of humor, my 'one and only' husband responded with, "I wouldn't be happy doing that!"

But selling the ranch came up often. It seemed to be the only way to settle our debts with the Calhan Bank. We considered many possibilities for improving our financial status. Perhaps we could make a dude ranch out of our place, but the area was not pretty enough. We didn't have the trees, creeks, and beauty needed for tourists. We also considered operating a nursing home, but that would have taken too much money and business know-how that we didn't have. Actually, these ideas were neither practical, nor were our hearts in them.

We finally put an ad in the paper and listed the 1,440 acres with a real estate business. There were a few 'lookers' but nothing became of it. We had paid $28,800 and Fred asked $36,000 because of all the improvements we had made. So, we kept the ranch and hoped for a better year. After all, our dream was to own and live on a ranch and we always knew that the rains would return to give us better years. 🐎

Music and Art Touched My Soul

Music played a big part in my home in Germany. A huge gramophone sat on a pedestal in the living room, never to be touched by anyone other than my parents. The monstrosity was a massive square object of beautiful, brown wood. On top was a picture of a white terrier dog, his eyes and ears focused on a funnel-shaped device which was attached to an old fashioned phonograph. Underneath was printed, "His Master's Voice."

To use the record player, we first raised the heavy hinged wooden lid exposing the very bowels of the machine. A scent of old wood and mustiness emanated from within. Next, we searched for the crank, put it into its designated slot on the outside of the machine and turned it until Mother, who was usually the one who used it, complained about her arm and shoulder getting tired! Finally, we inserted a tiny needle in its proper place. You needed a fresh one for every two records. Finally, a black disc appeared. I had no idea where the records were stored because my mother guarded them like a police dog watching an intruder!

We had a lot of records of opera, especially arias. When Mother wasn't listening to Enrico Caruso, she was playing songs sung by the famous German tenor, Richard Tauber. She played the Strauss Waltzes and Beethoven's symphonies almost every week.

Before my mother was married, she sang with a large group of semi-professionals for several years. Most of all, she loved opera. I remember hearing her singing arias while she worked in the kitchen. She sounded so great! My love for music was never as well developed as my mother's. She taught me to recognize certain composers and I can readily identify Beethoven, Mozart and many others.

While I don't care much about opera, I do love all kinds of classical and semi-classical music. In Nurses Training, half a dozen of us were given free tickets to attend the monthly concerts of the New Orleans Symphony. It was a real treat for me. Other times, I attended performances free because I collected donations for Polio research. All I had to do was pass a small basket from row to row during intermission. A small price to pay for such great rewards!

Music is important even when you are not gifted in the art of playing an instrument. It is in the appreciation of listening and the involvement in thought and spirit which can do so much to improve your feeling of well being.

I will never forget when in 1986, the 82-year old Vladimir Horowitz returned to his home country of Russia and performed in the Great Hall of the Moscow Conservatory. As he was playing the encore, "Traumerei" (meaning "Reverie") many in the audience, men and women alike, unashamedly wept as they let their emotions drift. I often hoped that Fritz Kreissler knew how many hearts he melted and how many lives he touched by his musical score.

Music does not have to be the classical type, it can be the popular kind or whatever you enjoy. Let it surround you. It gives you inner peace, comforts you when you need it, and encourages you when you are down.

Whenever times got tough on the ranch I decided to devote more time to the music I loved. I could always eak out a few minutes to listen to some of my favorites. Music touched my soul...I embraced it.

Another form of expressing my self was through an attempt of ART at which I did not become the 'Talk of the Town' as it were. I did not inherit the wonderful expression of painting from my mother as did my sister, Anne, and my brother, Martin. There is no way I could ever learn to draw a decent cat or dog—maybe a house or a tree, but that's it.

I had to wait until something simple came along. And when I attended our club meeting one afternoon, some lady showed us how to do liquid embroidery. That was fun. All you had to do was squeeze a fat tube onto some lightly blue painted design. I bought several colors needed to decorate a small tablecloth and six napkins. After I completed the job, they looked so nice that they appeared to be hand embroidered cross-stitching.

A couple of my ceramic clowns.

Knitting sweaters was actually my favorite past time. And I was good at it. Everybody in my family wore MY sweaters, caps and socks. Those items felt cozy in those icy Colorado winters.

Ceramics was another thing I learned. A retired teacher in our neighborhood volunteered to instruct us club members who were willing students. Within weeks we were producing colorful vases, figurines, etc. One of the pluses was that this lady owned a kiln and would not charge us for baking our more or less perfect creations. My personal accomplishments consisted of numerous pitchers and a few figurines of clowns and dogs, of course. But, how many of those can you give as gifts? Much too soon I gave up this delightful hobby in order to resume my knitting again.

Years later, after we moved to El Paso, Texas, I met a lady who would teach me how to applique sweatshirts, cotton bags, aprons and windbreakers. For that undertaking, you had to buy certain things, for example: the item to be painted, the fabric—usually a cotton print, sheets of bonding material and finally, different paints. There was some ironing-on to do and lastly came the painting. I sold quite a few items but mostly gave things away as gifts. My grandchildren were the most enthusiastic recipients.

And finally, having joined CLL which is short for "Center for Lifelong Learning" at the University of Texas, El Paso (UTEP), I took a course among others in calligraphy which I still enjoy doing nowadays.

These things are my artistic efforts, not too much to brag about, I guess. But I did the best I could with my meager talent. Regardless of the outcome, just trying new activities is healthy and I would encourage everyone to persevere. 🐎

Chapter 5

COPING AND GROWING

Oscar, The Inseminator

Colorado State University in Fort Collins always did a great job supplying us with the latest information, plus advice and recommendations on both old and new ranching techniques. As in other occupations, it was imperative to have an open mind, able to learn and act upon new information if it's right for you, so we were constantly experimenting. When CSU published an article on improving a dairy herd by artificial insemination, we decided to try it.

We contacted the local expert on the topic, Oscar Simmons. He said we needed to determine the cow's cycle and her optimum time. He would bring all the equipment and we could select the semen we wanted by looking at pictures of Holstein bulls. In less than a week, one of the cows started to come into heat and Fred remembered Oscar's warning, "Its got to be done early in the morning." So he drove to the Farrell's to call Oscar.

The following morning at 7 AM sharp an ugly brown pickup drove up to our house. A big, rotund man, close to 240 pounds stepped out and headed for our kitchen door. I opened it and he immediately introduced himself, "I'm your inseminator!" I was startled. I stammered trying to respond as he immediately asked if he could come in the house. "I got the book with pictures and performances of all the bulls."

"Oh goody," I thought. I offered Oscar a seat at the kitchen table while I hurried to get Fred who was feeding cattle on the south side of the big barn.

Both of us returned to the house and found Oscar arranging his books, articles and wares, as if he was going to make a big sale. He jumped off his chair, removed his heavy green parka and cowboy hat, both which had seen too many years, while briskly shaking Fred's hand saying again, "I'm your inseminator!"

All of us went through 'the book', but every bull looked the same to me. They were all Holsteins and most of them were between two and five years old. If someone had asked me to choose, I would have closed my eyes and pointed but 'friend husband' pretended that the photos varied and told the good man to use the semen of Number 875. It was decided.

In a flash, Fred and I were in the barn and the chosen cow was secured in the stanchion. Fred gave her two handfuls of grain to calm her down. "You stay with Oscar, I've got to finish feeding the cattle," Fred directed.

"Don't you want to watch this?" I asked in disbelief.

"I know how it is done," he curtly replied and was gone.

Oscar took his time getting organized so I was alone with the cow as I scratched her side, talking to her, hoping nobody would be listening, "This is progress—no more bulls for you, kid!" And wouldn't you know, here came Oscar, who had obviously overheard, because he was grinning from ear to ear.

Oscar was carrying a big tank which he set down with a grunt. He shed his parka and hat again, and started talking about everything but the work he was about to do. He donned long, plastic gloves, pulled off the top of a steel container and steam from the dry ice hissed as it escaped into the air. He next pulled out a thin glass pipe which was filled with bull # 875's contribution. It took no more than a couple of minutes and the procedure was completed.

Oscar turned to me, made an embarrassing remark and started walking towards me. "I've got to get out of here," my instinct told me, "this guy's job has gone to his head—or somewhere else." I left in a hurry without saying a word. Back safely in the house, I watched through the window as Oscar and Fred talked energetically, occasionally laughing out loud in a lewd way. Men!

Dear big, fat, crude Oscar did his job right, the cow was pregnant. Now, we hoped for a heifer calf that would be added to our dairy herd. But after nine months of waiting, she had a bull calf. The fine animal, became a big, strong and outstanding steer that was sold, along with the rest of the yearlings.

Oscar returned many times, but he always did his job in the presence of Fred, not me! The next cows he inseminated all produced fine heifer calves. Though we were satisfied with the program, Fred decided he could do the job on his own. However, before long it became too time consuming to track the cycle of every cow and heifer, so we bought an extra bull and let nature take its course. Oscar was out of a job! 🐂

Black Blizzard

"The wind velocity in Cheyenne, Wyoming is 70 miles per hour," Weatherman Bowman announced early one morning. "Big deal," I thought, "the wind always blows in Cheyenne." In fact, the motto of their community was 'The Windiest City in the West'. But as Mr. Bowman continued with his forecast for the day, it became clear that those of us in east central Colorado might be in for some foul weather. It was still dark outside, there was no wind and the temperature on the outside thermometer was normal for this time of year, a mere 28 degrees.

With morning chores and breakfast over, the sun made its appearance and a delightful glow of pink mirrored itself against Pikes Peak and the lower contiguous mountain range. The sky was a cloudless expanse of sapphire blue and all seemed right with the world. It promised to be another beautiful Colorado day, and one could only hope that the predicted storm would miss us.

Another calf rescued during blizzard in the "Bovine Motel."
Cartoon by my Brother, Martin Gumbel.

My plans for the day were to mop the linoleum floors in every room of the house, a job I intensely disliked because keeping the house clean was a constant war. So, after it was accomplished I always felt valiant, almost like a soldier returning home from a victorious battle! It seemed like every grain of sand, mud and yes, manure, adhered itself firmly onto all of our shoes until the 'goodies' were displayed in every room. I usually placed some papers on the floor next to the stove in the living room where we would shed our wet or dirty shoes and exchange them for slippers. However, the good husband, when reminded of this minor inconvenience, would answer, "I got to go outside again in a few minutes, anyway." Even though the "few minutes" often turned into over an hour, I concluded that arguing or trying to prove my point was a useless waste of time.

So, while the ammonia water stung my olfactory nerves, I kept mopping until the job was done. During all this, I had the radio on to sweeten the task and to keep my mind occupied with more pleasant things. It worked. Just as I was about to put away the mop and bucket, a sweet 2-1/2 year-old voice came from out of nowhere asking, "Why are you cleaning the house? Is somebody coming?"

Wow, a remark like that made me think, "Is that the only time I clean house?" or "Is this ridicule coming from this little tyke? Or, "Do I deserve this?" To which I answered to myself, I sure do. I should have done this days ago. But I merely said, "Nobody is coming. It was just dirty."

I must say, the more the floors sparkled, the more my attitude was refreshed and instead of being weary I found energy that had been well hidden until now. "I'm going to darn those socks in the basket, all six pairs, and afterwards I'll write some letters," I said planning the rest of my day. But first, I'll check the mailbox to see if Fred Wagoner brought some mail, hoping for more than bills.

I slipped on my fleece-lined jacket, dashed out through the kitchen door and at once was accosted by a strong wind. The lovely, clear sky had suddenly changed from blue to a light gray and the temperature had dropped considerably. "Could the weatherman be right?" I wondered. I rushed to retrieve the mail. All we had in the box were the electric bill and an advertisement for bedroom furniture. We needed both like we needed a hole in the head!

For some reason, after only darning a couple of pairs of Freds' socks, my energy level dropped to zero and my thoughts drifted aimlessly. I looked out the window which had begun to rattle. I saw that the sun, which had been so bright earlier, had vanished behind dark clouds and some cattle were drifting towards the south fence. The wind increased steadily and I noticed dead leaves and other refuse being blown from the summer wheat field, now barren with only weeds to hold down the topsoil. "Thanks a lot, Cheyenne, for sending us some of your wind." I thought out loud just as Fred entered the kitchen and asked me to help move the livestock to barns, sheds, and windbreaks for protection.

By the time I returned to the house a few snowflakes galloped horizontally mixing with blown sand from the north. Together it became sticky mud. Within less than 20 minutes every window was caked-solid with the unattractive goop and the entire house became darkened as if it were sundown. Fred finally came in from the barn and reported that the cattle's eyes were almost closed with mud. He was at a loss of what to do next. "Perhaps the wind will lessen and at least some of the topsoil will stay on the field," he hoped. He continued, showing how bad he felt for the cattle, "They are standing around like statues behind windbreaks and even in the barns but they can't see anything because of the sand in their eyes. It's terrible!"

Instead of dying down, the wind got stronger. The windows to the north, now completely caked with mud, rattled on. The house, which never 'heard of' insulation was becoming colder, the oil stove in the kitchen gave one big huff, regurgitated clouds of black soot, and died, covering everything in its path with a layer of black filth.

"At least the power is still on," we consoled each other, "and we have plenty of coal for the stove and propane gas to cook with. We better run lots of water into kettles and buckets just in case the electricity goes off. This looks like it might last a while."

I quickly put on an old warm coat, the brown, wooly one I had bought in England and ventured into the now freezing, cold kitchen. Lady, the collie, followed me and went towards the door waiting to be let out. Nature was calling! I opened the door for her and she took one disgusted look at the wild display of Mother Nature and backed up, thinking, "I can wait!"

Lentil soup with potatoes and a ring bologna was my swift choice for the next few meals. The aroma was delightful even before the soup was done. The radio crackled news about all the wind damage and that it probably would continue to cause problems for the rest of the day and into the night. Horrors!

For a while, what little snow had zipped past the house, now had quit, but the dirt, powered by the relentless wind was forming drifts all around buildings, outdoor machinery and, to our dismay, the outhouse.

Towards evening, the snow returned, just enough to make more mud which was sticking on the electric poles. The wires were dancing so hard we were afraid they would break.

There was nothing more we could do for the animals. The kids were going to use the 'kiddy potty' so Fred and I decided to make a run for the privy. A 'run' is the correct word because you couldn't just walk; the wind made you run! It pushed us so hard we almost missed the—by then—much sought after john. Fred and I held onto each other as we struggled not be blown away and to stay in one place as we tried to open the door that had been blocked by drifts of sand that were over two feet deep. We needed a shovel to get it away from the door. Fred looked around, found a 2 x 4 board and was able to move enough of the precious topsoil so he could partially open the door. It was a tight squeeze but we managed to slip inside. What a relief—in more ways than one!

Trying to get back to the house was even harder. It meant going north against the powerful force of the wind while the flying sand stung our faces like a thousand needles. We struggled, holding hands against the strength of the storm, and there, found Lady, whom we had pulled earlier out of the house against her will. We hoped she did what she was supposed to do—her only chance until the next morning. We went to bed early that night. Trying to fall asleep was difficult as the noise of the wind, the rattling of the windows, and the sand hitting the windowpanes was so loud that just as soon as you drifted off, it would wake you up again.

Morning came and the wind had died down to a soft breeze. Drifts of sand, up to four feet high, were all around us. And it was bitter cold. Luckily, the electricity remained on, which meant the water pump continued to work.

The cattle appeared tired, almost listless. The snow and sand had made a wet brown mud that ran from their eyes and down their tired faces. But, we were pleased that they all survived the storm. They slowly ate the hay Fred placed in front of them but they had to wait for fresh water because the tanks were full of sand, some of which had frozen within chunks of ice. But luck was with us and soon we were able to empty the tanks and pump in all the fresh water we needed.

This was indeed a storm to remember. Most blizzards do harm, but this one was especially vicious because it stole important topsoil from fields already hurting for nutrition. Since our windows, mainly the ones facing north, were not airtight, much had entered our entire living quarters—without an invitation— and made itself comfortable everywhere, especially onto my newly mopped floors! Hurrah for country living! 🐂

Mr. Akers

Mr. Akers was the new neighbor who bought the Cottrell place and took possession of the day Stalin died in Russia, March 1, 1953. Fred and I drove over the next day to introduce ourselves. Before we even got out of the car, an elderly man walked to us, greeted us as if he had known us for a while and invited us into his house. We told him we didn't have much time to visit but just wanted to welcome him to our neighborhood. Here was a man, 82 years old, he told us, standing at least 6 feet tall. He wore blue overalls, a wrinkled denim shirt over a red, white and black flannel jacket. His cowboy boots looked like they'd been worn for many years and used to be brown. It was hard to tell. The skin on his face showed his age, his eyelids drooping. He looked tired. A faint odor of pipe tobacco travelled towards us. He told us briefly that he lived alone and how his wife had died a few years earlier and that some of his children lived in the next county. He planned to raise chickens, sell eggs, and plant a garden. "And if you folks ever need help, I'll gladly give you a hand, just don't ask me to ride horseback." We shook hands and drove off.

Fred and I stopped by Mr. Aker's place every so often just to see how he was. We always found him outdoors doing something, often working with the crates and boxes on the shelves in the barns, ready to receive the chickens he had ordered. He owned a hand plow which he planned to use in the garden as soon as it got warm enough. The entire place looked neat and orderly. We never entered his house until much later.

Mr. Aker's place had a great well. Not only did it deliver all the water anyone could want, but also it was clear and tasted delicious. I remember Mrs. Cottrell telling me that when they bought the ranch they needed to drill a new well. They had no idea just where. Mr. Cottrell had decided on a spot close to the house but it didn't seem right with Mrs. Cottrell. She said, "We'll let the Lord tell us." Then she went outside, spoke in tongue telling the Lord how they had spent a lot of money buying the ranch and all they were asking for was the best spot to drill a good well. She then asked him to stop her while she was walking. Lo and behold, something told her to go no farther. She stopped, marked the area with a cross and ran to her husband saying that she knew exactly where to drill! Amazingly, that is the exact spot where the well drillers found the water. The well continued to produce the same generous amount of clear, tasty water, never being influenced by dry or wet years while neighbors struggled to retain even minimal supplies in the semi-arid climate. And there we were, not but a short distance away, with our skimpy and...yellow...water!

The irrigation, plus Mr. Aker's ability and love of gardening helped him yield a fantastic array of produce. I never saw cabbages so large and heavy nor so many zucchini squash on one plant. The tomatoes, he grew along the garden fence, were loaded with bright red fruit weighing down the branches. They seemed to say, "Come, pick me."

Though Mr. Akers knew a lot about gardening, he knew an equal amount about life itself. To visit with him was always fascinating because you always learned something. He told us, for example, about the Indians and how they predicted the weather according to which way the clouds rolled over Pikes Peak, the 14,000 foot mountain to the west which was so predominant in our vision. He told us how and where to plant trees which would serve as wind breaks so they could catch the snow and slow down the unrelenting winds. He knew how to build houses as well as almost every other skill needed around a ranch. He had done it all and you could sense the pride he took in having accomplished so much.

The summer of '54 was hot and very dry. The lack of rain for weeks on end had caused the grass in the pastures to turn brown. In fact, it looked dead and you could see the soil between the patches of grass. Some ranchers again had to buy expensive hay from the Western slope of Colorado to supplement the lack of decent pasture. Around our ranch the only substantial food for the animals was in the ditches on either side of Jones Road. Every morning, Fred would turn the cattle onto the road to graze. They had a tendency to drift apart, all going in different directions, so we had to have someone stay with them to keep the herd together. Usually this chore went to Tommy, or next best, to 'the wife'.

I was pregnant, once again, with #3 and ready to deliver any day. It was July 14, 1954 when a relative of Mr. Akers drove up to our house with the bad news that he was sick with chest pains and that they had taken him to Penrose Hospital the day before. "Would you be so kind to do his chores and gather eggs for the next few days?" Of course, we said yes. So, around 2 PM we gathered Tommy and Bonnie and drove over to the Aker's place. It looked neat, like usual, and many chickens were busy catching grasshoppers while the rest were sitting around the shady areas. We needed to collect eggs, clean them, and place them in special egg boxes and then had to water all the chickens. We found several buckets and all of us, even the kids, filled them with eggs from the chicken house. Next, we thought we'd check the garage and there we found eggs all over the ground. Laughingly, I suggested, "Maybe we better look in the john!" The door to the privy was open and, guess what, there behind the seat was a hen. She was annoyed with me and she clucked, spread her wings, and acted angry. I was not going to argue with her and was almost out of the door when I gave a quick look back to see if the hen was going to chase me when I noticed six tiny, yellow baby chicks. They couldn't have hatched more than a couple of days earlier because they still hadn't grown feathers. All I could think of was, when one needs privacy what better place is there than a privy, especially, now that the boss was absent! Next, both Fred and I looked for chicken feed but couldn't find any. "He must keep that in the house," Fred suggested.

While we were checking every corner for eggs—those hens didn't use the boxes they were supposed to—we suddenly heard some rumbling. It sounded like thunder. "Oh, please let it be, we need rain so badly," we all seemed to say in unison. There were some dark clouds coming from the west and you could feel a slight breeze. It smelled like bouquets of lilacs, reminding me of my years in Germany where our backyard was filled with rows of tall bushes.

Fred finally announced that we must have found all the eggs and he suggested that we, "Go to the house to wash them and hopefully find the packing boxes and the chicken feed." He carried two big buckets full of eggs and I grabbed two filthy, though happy, little hands belonging to two grimy kids and we entered the unlocked house. The sight which greeted us took our breath away. The air was filled with dust stirred up by surprised, flying chickens. Feathers were all over everything, there was chicken manure on the linoleum floor and, to my surprise, no eggs anywhere. All four of us just stood there, speechless, trying to avoid breathing the dust. It was obvious that Mr. Akers didn't have allergies! Luckily, neither did we. On closer inspection, there were empty pans and dishes on the floor which probably had been filled with drinking water. I picked them up and went into the kitchen to fill a couple of them. As I set the water containers down, more hens came flying towards me even out of the bedroom. They were terribly thirsty—poor things. We were all so amazed; it was hard to get to work. There was so much to see. I thought of how my brother, Martin, would have had fun painting this scene!

"Look, Mommy, there's Mr. Aker's bed in the corner. He mustn't sleep in the bedroom." Tommy observed. And sure enough, there in the living room was a double bed with a blue and green quilt and a filthy pillow on which a hen had made herself comfortable. Not bad living quarters for a bunch of chickens! There must have been at least 30 of them living in the house and once they quit flying around, they actually became quite friendly—or maybe they were just hungry! We found three sacks of chicken feed in the kitchen and fed the hungry birds. Both children carried full cans of feed to the outside birds, including the 'outhouse hen'. We also located rags to wash the eggs and hurrah—there were several egg boxes in another corner of the living room.

All of a sudden the kids came running into the house. "It's raining!" they shouted, knowing how much we had talked about wanting some moisture. There was another thunderclap and rain began to pour. We all ran to the window to watch it fill holes in the road and ditches. We were jubilant and Fred started dancing. He grabbed me, but my pregnant belly was in the way! Lightning seem to be directly over us but we didn't mind. Our children never feared thunderstorms as so many do. To us all, it meant green grass which we always needed in East Central Colorado. It was a time for happiness.

"We better get started washing eggs," I encouraged everyone, pulling their attention back from the rain. This was a tedious job. A lot of the eggs had yellow, sticky yolk on them. So many had broken because they had been laid in all those strange locations. Every so often, our eyes would be drawn to the window. It was still raining hard. The sky was so dark we turned the lights on in the house. Finally, we finished the job. Every single egg was packed and ready to be taken to the store. I was aching all over, especially my back. This had been a hard job and I was longing to lie down for a few minutes. Though I needed to recuperate, this luxury had to wait.

Eventually, all of Mr. Akers' chores were done and it was time for us to head home. The rain had slowed to a drizzle. The sky was a dark-gray-blue with lightning in the distance. We piled into our car after we closed the doors to the chicken houses—both of them—the chicken house and the people house with chickens, and we were on our way home. When we came to a low place in the road, we noticed water running across from the north to the south pasture. This always happened after a rainstorm, but sometimes there would be so much water that swept through with such great force that it pulled up fences and made huge holes in the gravel roadbeds. "You better not have to go to the hospital tonight, this looks like it will get worse. There's a lot of run-off coming yet," my Beloved One warned me.

"Don't worry, I feel fine," I reassured him as we drove through gullies full of mud. The rest of the afternoon and evening went as usual: chores, supper, clean kids, playtime, and off to bed.

At 1:30 AM, July 15, 1954, something woke me up and it wasn't a person telling me a new joke. No siree, those were definite labor pains. "Wake up, Fred. Guess what?" Almost immediately and without thinking, he began worrying about the roads and how damaged they were from the rain.

"I surely hope the road isn't washed out or we'll have to ride horseback to the Farrell's and borrow their car. From there on we shouldn't have any trouble to get to Colorado Springs, all good roads."

My daughter, Susan Ruth in the much-used "Taylor Tot"..

All I could answer to that was, "If Mary, in the Bible, could ride the donkey when she was 'with child', certainly I could ride a horse." Fred was dressed long before I was. He drove west to where we had seen the water rushing across the road and found that it was completely washed out. He turned around and drove to the east to check another low place. We were in luck. It would be rough but it was passable. Fred returned to the house with the good news. We picked up the suitcase and we were off.

Susan Ruth, a beautiful 7-pound girl, was born later that night. And once again, we had another ranch story for my doctor! 🐂

Lew Eis

After Mr. Akers was released from the hospital in July of '54, he sold his chickens, moved in with his daughter and put his place up for sale. Fred asked Uncle Herman to loan him the money to buy it, but he refused saying, "I wouldn't buy a ranch in that part of Colorado." Enough said!

It was soon thereafter, that a well-dressed man drove up to our place and introduced himself as Mr. Eis, the new owner of the Aker's place. He had just returned from making the deal at the bank, paying $8,000 for 640 acres. He knew we were renting the pasture and had 30 head of cattle on it. He told us to "move them at once." This attitude was something we weren't used to. Ranchers and farmers just didn't talk like that and we wondered what sort of a neighbor he would be. We moved our cattle the very next day and we weren't sure we wanted to see Mr. Eis again.

About a month later he reappeared and asked us whether we were interested in renting his pasture. Fred agreed to the deal: 30 head of cows for $2 a head per month. We returned the same cattle the next day!

We noticed that during the second visit, Mr. Eis' attitude had changed. He seemed more relaxed and talkative than on the prior visit. He told us how his wife, Mary, was still trying to clean every corner of his house and complained that it was hard getting rid of all the chicken feathers. He told us that his teenage son, Jerry Lew, had started school at Miami High School but added, "He won't be much help with the livestock, he just wants to play around."

Lew Eis owned and managed Eisco, a home siding business. He had just started selling additional lines and had hired his brother and another salesman. He was excited as he told us, "I'm going to be rich someday. There are lots of people moving into Colorado Springs. You mark my word!"

"Good." I jokingly added, "Then we'll come to you to borrow money instead of going to the Calhan Bank!" Maybe he wasn't such a bad guy after all.

We had an early winter that year and before long the water in the stock tank froze. Lew Eis broke the ice for the livestock to drink, but he used a heavy bar hitting the bottom of the tank so hard that it made several holes and most of the water leaked out. Mary came over to tell us that there was hardly any water for the cattle and added that Lew thought we should bring one of our own tanks because he was too "busy" with his business to take care of the water. What else could we do? We took our tank over and told Mary that we would chop the ice from now on. I am sure they were pleased.

Soon the Eis' purchased a couple of cows and four calves. Someone gave them a big dog, a Doberman who was a trained attack dog. Next, Lew made a deal with a young man to do chores in exchange for room and board because his son refused to help.

One of the pastures we rented from Lew was directly across from his house on the north side of Jones Road. One day, while checking cattle, Fred found a day-old calf dead with blood still oozing from his neck. We were told by an old-time rancher that coyotes attack calves in the hindquarter first, but dogs kill them in the neck and throat. Fred confronted Lew and told him that his dog must have killed our calf. He quickly replied, "My dog wouldn't do such a thing." It was a few days later that Lew's hired man found this same dog trying to kill one of his four calves. Lew shot the dog the next day. It was years later before he admitted that his dog killed our calf.

I don't know how it happened, but soon Lew was becoming a good friend. His personality was warm and he was concerned and thoughtful of others. He visited us even when he didn't need to borrow anything! He told us about his wild past and laughed at himself and all the crazy things he did in his youth, and for years afterward.

Things didn't go well in Lew and Mary's marriage and soon she divorced him and moved away. Now he was free to enjoy picking up all sorts of 'ladies' in the bars around Colorado Springs. He would often boast that the neighbors around his ranch were perfectly safe and that he would never proposition them. I must say that he was a perfect gentleman every time he picked me up at the bus station, on my return from my dentist in Denver.

Besides loving women, Lew had two other bad habits. He smoked constantly and he drank liquor like a fish. He once told us, while laughing so hard he could hardly control himself, that you could tell where he had driven (while very drunk), simply by looking at the sand in the ditches by the road! Another time, one dark night, he lost control of his car and had an accident. He hurt his neck and holding his head with both hands, walked miles to a farmhouse where the farmer drove him to the Emergency Room at St. Francis Hospital. He had injured his neck so badly that he was out of commission for quite a while. It wasn't long before he bounced right back to his old routine!

Lew came to our place one time and asked to borrow our pickup. He wanted to move several of his calves to another pasture. The next day, Sunday, he took our truck and returned it within an hour. "That was fast work!" Fred complimented. But as he looked at Lew's face, he suspected that something was wrong.

"You got to help me. The cattle are all over the road and they are running in every direction." After Lew calmed down a bit he muttered something about those "wild beasts", six of them, but admitted he didn't close the end gate properly and all the calves jumped out of the pickup while he was driving. Fred, at once, picked up his rope and both drove off. The calves were in two bunches. Fred roped each one and he and Lew dragged them into the truck until the six were reunited and eventually transported to their new venue.

Fred was called upon often to help out with delivering calves and vaccinating Lew's stock. He had about 30 head of cattle now and he often told us how much he learned from Fred.

Some years later, we were alarmed when someone walked into our house around 4 AM, shouting, "Don't shoot. It's me!" It turned out to be a very drunk Lew. I quickly made a pot of coffee and started to pour one cup after another into him, trying to sober him up. After he quieted down, he told us how he had a fight with his girlfriend, Jan, the night before. "She had a gun and was trying to kill me but I wrestled it away from her. I called the cops and they took her away." After all that, he got depressed and started to drink.

It was Sunday morning and Fred had a great idea, "After the chores are done let's go swimming in Prospect Park and take Lew. The cold water should sober him up faster than all that coffee!"

An hour later, as we got into the car ready to drive to the lake in Colorado Springs, Lew gave me a strange look. I was wearing a sleeveless blouse and he pointed to my underarm which I hadn't shaved lately and told me, "How can anybody let herself go like that?" Realizing the source of this remark I didn't need to respond, even though he was partially right. I felt offended to be reprimanded by this man who wasn't so honorable himself!

Apparently, Lew and Jan tried to make up and they lived together for a few months when Fred happened to stop by his house one day. Lew opened the door, bent over, and without fanfare rushed to tell Fred how, "That bitch kicked me in the groin yesterday. I hurt so badly I went to see the doctor this morning. He told me my 'you know what' is broken! All I have to do, he told me, is to keep an icebag on it. It still hurts like hell. She better not come back here. Come in, if you want to, but I got to lie down."

Fred did not stay. He felt empathy for this pitiful-looking human being in front of him while at the same time, he was afraid he would be unable to keep a straight face.

Despite the episode and his threats, he did take Jan back. His 'you know what' healed and soon Jan was pregnant. As the time of delivery neared, both of them came for what I thought was a routine visit. No such luck! In utter disbelief, I heard the father-to-be addressing me with words I never forgot, "You are a nurse. We want you to deliver the baby. Jan doesn't like hospitals."

"No way, Lew!" was my immediate refusal.

"But why not, you're a nurse!" I proceeded to give him all sorts of excuses such as first time babies can give you trouble, the need for a sterile environment, and on and on. Neither of them were happy with my decision.

Not long afterward Jan went into labor which lasted too long. There were complications and the one-month premature baby needed to remain in Intensive Care. The child, a boy, was later adopted by one of Lews' relatives.

Eventually this rocky love affair ended and they separated. But Lew continued to praise her for having been the best bed partner he ever had. And that was quite a statement from a man with his record!

Some time later, perhaps two years, Lew received the news that Jan had died from cancer. She was only 29 years old.

In 1965, Lew put his place up for sale and we bought the 640 acres for $28,800. We saw him occasionally after he moved to a doublewide trailer near Peyton and both our girls worked for him in his office during their summer vacations from college.

Meanwhile Lew had met a delightful young lady and, as he often did, brought his friends over for us to meet. Laura was special. She was from New York and had moved to Colorado to be near her daughter. She was a true lady, outgoing and friendly. Her hair was well coiffed, the skin on her face delicate with a slight amount of rouge. Her features created a pleasant impression of kindness and intelligence. I liked her at once. It seemed that Lew had finally found his right mate. He appeared more relaxed than ever. He resumed his hobby of painting and practicing melodies on his electric organ. Lew and Laura were married.

Years later, we were saddened to find out Lew was suffering from lung cancer due to all the years of heavy smoking. He told Fred with a big grin, "You know I used to tell you I had 1,000 women, but well, there were ONLY 300!"

The saying goes, "A good first impression is very important when you meet someone." Our first impression of Lew was certainly not a good one, but it changed soon. It made us think that people in general are not bad. Perhaps their momentary ill attitude may be triggered by something that we don't know about. Give these people time and space. They just might come around and be the friend that Lew Eis was! 🐏

Queenie

ueenie was a sweet-tempered Guernsey milk cow with a soft caramel colored coat, brown eyes, and long, flirtatious eyelashes—a beautiful specimen who produced gallons of rich milk. She was bred to one of our Hereford bulls and after a gestation period of nine months she was ready to have her calf. Fred always kept a close eye on a "springer," a cow that would calve soon, because occasionally they have problems delivering their offspring and needed our help. Two months before Queenie was supposed to calve she was turned out to pasture and not milked so that she would be in good enough condition to produce a vigorous calf.

It was a cold February day when Fred noticed that Queenie was close to calving. Later in the day, he returned to the pasture and found her in labor. We decided to have a fast supper and then bring Queenie and her new calf back to a warm spot in the barn.

The temperature was below zero and adding to the misery, the wind was starting to blow. It promised to be a nasty night. I quickly added a few chunks of coal to the living room stove and told Tommy and Bonnie to stay home and play with their toys. We wouldn't be gone long.

Fred decided that we should walk out in the pasture to Queenie and that we could take Tommy's red wagon to transport the calf home. After bundling up and kissing the kids goodbye we took off like soldiers going to war. The air was sharp and cold and tiny ice crystals bombarded our faces. A million stars and a bright half moon lit the road. "It sure got dark in a hurry, I hope we can find Queenie," I thought pessimistically, as we trudged on pulling that little red wagon.

"There she is, exactly where I saw her earlier," announced Fred. Queenie was standing up and mooing softly. She looked at us with words written all over her long face, "See what I got!" Now, not all new mother cows are friendly but this was different—this was Queenie and she behaved like royalty. "Hey, look at that, there are two of them—it's our first set of twins!" Fred shouted, waking up sleeping animals all around us.

The calves were small but active and they struggled as Fred loaded them on top of each other into the wagon. We started towards home with me pulling the much-too-small conveyance and Fred trying the keep the calves from falling off as Queenie following us nervously. I wished I'd had a camera!

By the time we arrived home we felt no cold, indeed we were perspiring from all the heavy work. Now, with the light on in the barn, we inspected the babies. They looked just like their mother except they had white faces, inherited from their father, the Hereford. One was a bull calf, the other a heifer. They were small and downright skinny. Queenie licked them, encouraging them to get up and nurse which they did for a few seconds before crashing down onto the bed of straw, extra tired from their ride in the little red wagon!

Upon entering the house we smelled smoke and walked into the living room door where we saw our happy children oblivious to a shroud of blue which engulfed the entire room. Looking at the stove, I noticed that the two-foot stovepipe was red hot and the room was very warm. I couldn't figure out what was going on until our son proudly assured us that he had taken 'care' of things. "I was getting cold and so I put more coal in the stove," he proudly announced. Tommy did not know that you have to open the damper on the stovepipe to let the smoke out and up the chimney. Therefore, all the fumes had been sent directly into the living room and throughout the house.

The incident really scared us. It was another lesson learned! After that, we never left the children alone. Though it made our work take longer, the kids went with us during all the chores, trips to the windmill and every time we had to doctor an animal. They saw it all!

Update of the twin calves. Both died about a month later of pneumonia. Penicillin was not enough, they were too frail...that's life, or maybe they should have spent some time in the warm kitchen! 🐕

Welcome Company From Near and Far

1957 turned out to be another busy year and the summer was especially busy with visitors. Fred taught high school in Ramah in '56-'57 and now was offered a job in Peyton for the following school year. He loved teaching.

For ten years now, Fred had this year-around job teaching 'On the Farm Training', in Colorado's Eastern District of El Paso County. Since he was always so busy everyone in the whole family was called upon to lend a hand in addition to doing our regular 'assigned' chores. My brother Max often joked, "You guys don't have 'hired help', you have 'sired help'!"

It was in July of that year when our good friend, Gret, and daughter, Annie, came for a visit. No sooner had they entered our kitchen when she announced, "I think I'm pregnant!" At once, I burst out laughing. Gret gave me a strange look, not understanding my reaction. She had hoped I would be happy for her. After a moment, I finally managed to squeal, "I think I am, too!" We laughed uncontrollably. But practical people who we were, started to make plans at once. We decided to use the same doctor who had delivered both Bonnie and Susan. I made our first appointments for the following week.

This was a busy year for summer company. As always, we looked forward to entertaining and reminiscing with our friends. First came Mary Ruth Joynton, her husband Harry and their boys. What a good-looking family they were! We first met in New Orleans when we rented rooms from the Dismukes, who were the parents of Rosalind, my former roommate. Mary Ruth was a beautiful blonde, intelligent and polite and we quickly became friends. She had a job as a secretary making $130 per month. Of this, she sent $50 to her widowed mother in southeast Louisiana to supply a simple but comfortable lifestyle. It was her main source of income. Mary Ruth often walked the three blocks to the Baptist Church on St. Charles Avenue after her day's work, to sing in the choir. She was very religious and, to my knowledge, never missed a church service on Sundays.

Several times, Mr. and Mrs. Dismukes invited us on trips to Mississippi to visit friends. I'll never forget the time we were stopped on a gravel road for at least 30 minutes behind what looked like several hundred sheep. I noticed how a couple of well-trained dogs controlled the whole herd while the only man waited, letting his 'helpers' do their job. It was an inspirational sight for me, one I would remember when we owned sheep much later on.

A bit farther down the same road, I saw an outhouse for the first time. A black man was leaving this convenience and was in such a happy mood that he waved to us vigorously. I never imagined that someday I would be using the same kind of establishment!

Years later, Mary Ruth Jordan married Harry and they raised three bright sons. Eventually, the Joyntons moved to a retirement village in Arkansas where they seemed to be quite happy.

After graduating from Touro Infirmary, I was offered a job to work in, what was called T&A (an abbreviation for Tonsils and Adenoids). This actually should have been known as Minor Surgery because we did all sorts of piddly little operations on outpatients. But tonsillectomies were the main procedures and patients stayed overnight. It was in T&A where I worked with my favorite doctor, Dr. McComiskey , an ear, nose and throat specialist. His wife, Donna was his anesthetist. The doctors had two sons, Bobby and Jack, and now, years later, Dr. McComiskey asked us if we would keep the boys for a few weeks. They thought working on a ranch was romantic and fun and he wanted them to realize what it was all about. We agreed, and a month later the boys arrived by train in Colorado Springs. Bobby, 16, was tall and thin while Jack at 14 was quite a bit shorter. On the way to the ranch, they told me that they had orders from their parents to work in every phase of ranch activity. Both were so excited they could hardly wait to get to our place. Earlier, by mail, I had explained and stressed the fact that we had an outhouse and no indoor facilities, there was no telephone, and the water was yellow. On the way home, I reminded them of these facts—they actually loved it, saying, "It's just like being a cowboy in an old western movie!" The lessons started immediately after they arrived. Fred taught them how to milk a cow, ride horseback, and help with all the other chores. It soon became obvious that Jack was more willing and interested than Bobby, a fact that his mother had predicted.

The McComiskey boys. Left: Tommy Bonnie, Fred and Lady.

On the second morning, Bobby came downstairs holding his right arm. He explained that something popped on his shoulder as he turned over in bed. He was sorry, he "just couldn't" work—it hurt too much. Had this happened with one of our children, I'd have said, "Let's see how it feels in a couple of days." But he was a guest. So after Bobby enjoyed a hearty country style breakfast, I took him to Dr. Schwer in Calhan and the doctor give us the diagnosis. "He did pull a muscle. Don't let him lift anything for a few days, give him an aspirin or two for pain, and he'll be fine soon."

When Jack heard this, he mumbled something that ended up with, "...that jerk always gets out of work!"

We took the boys to a Catholic Church every Sunday and afterwards went to North Cheyenne Canyon, west of Colorado Springs, to have a picnic. Their parents arrived a few weeks later to spend a few days exploring Colorado Springs. All four of the McComiskeys stayed in a motel in the city.

The following day, we picked them up and drove them to our favorite area for a "fried chicken with all the trimmings" picnic I had prepared. I'll never forget Dr. McComiskey's

Upper left to right: Fred, Tommy, Dr. McComiskey. Bottom: Bonnie, Donna McComiskey, Me and Susan.

remark as he stood by the gurgling brook, "When I'm back in New Orleans in my busy office, I'm going to close my eyes and imagine being back here." He was really delighted with the scenery and Colorado's cool mountain air.

It was then that he told me how he had gone to the Nursing Office in Touro to ask the director to hire me for the T&A Department after I became a Registered Nurse. After thanking him, we reminisced about working with him as Donna administered anesthesia. After all the operations were done, Dr. M. always rewarded us with cokes and donuts. He was a delight, funny and always pleasant. I was very fond of him. Some of the nurses joked and called me, "The Third Mrs. McComiskey!"—Donna was #2.

We hated so see our helpers go. They were wonderful workers, always polite. They became excellent horseback riders and the fence they built from scratch, north of the house, was a constant reminder of them.

Several years later, Fred and I went to a school board convention in New Orleans. I was anxious to visit Dr. McComiskey and was shocked to see how much he had aged. His face was drawn and pale, his gait unsteady, the twinkle in his eye was gone, and the mood and tone of his voice was somber and sullen. Because he and Donna had divorced several years prior, he complained that all his friends were dead. Although he never mentioned it during my visit, I could tell that he was ready to leave this world. Not long afterward, one of the boys informed us of his death. I shall never forget this special person.

One couple, Sgt. Giles and his wife, usually showed up on weekends to go rabbit hunting. We gave them permission to reduce the enormous number of cottontail and jack rabbits which were mass-producing every summer. One day, the Sgt. proudly showed off his 25 very dead rabbits, saying that his wife would cook one of them the next day and put the rest in their freezer. I suggested that since he was such a successful hunter, he should buy another freezer. It would be filled before long! "Can you imagine if someone were to open it and find nothing but rabbits in it!" I visualized it and shuddered at the thought. The few times we were invited to dinner at their house, we worried about what kind of meat we were going to be served. We shouldn't have because Mrs. G. tactfully chose other menu items instead of rabbit. I was always a bit fearful of eating wild rabbits because some carried diseases.

That summer, Gret and I decided to show our dogs at the Denver Collie Show. She owned a dog called Henry and we had Cindy, one of Lady's daughters. We primped and prepared her by using the family's shampoo to remove the scent of ranch. We left very early, around 6:30 AM, and headed for Denver. "Just be there early so we can clip her for the show" was the plea of the kennel owners.

The show was fun. There were five in Cindy's class and I thought she surely would come in first. The judge however thought differently, explaining that if she hadn't lost some of her coat over her hips by crawling under the barbed wire fences on the ranch, she would have won first prize. I took a plastic 2nd place trophy home and was satisfied.

Henry had more dogs in his class and although he looked handsome and confident, he came in fifth. I felt sorry for Gret. She had high hopes for a better showing. Back home again, we unloaded the dogs from the car and I could imagine what they were thinking, "Let's get out of here and go chase some rabbits!"

The Vorenberg children, Bonnie, Tommy and Susan.

Roy Cross, my sister Anne's stepson, also came for a visit. It was not the best place for him and never felt comfortable with ranch life. His allergies bothered him and he just didn't feel happy. He was such a nice visitor, had great manners, and it was a pity that he decided to leave us earlier than he and his folks had planned.

Meanwhile, the people who bought our house in Ramah were unable to keep up the payments, so it came back to us. Luckily, we found a new buyer with whom we made a contract at the Calhan Bank for $4,000 at 6% interest.

The visitors kept coming! My good friend, Josie, from New Orleans, with whom I worked in surgery at Touro Infirmary, came to visit and brought along her eleven year-old nephew, Junior. We always had fun together and those two weeks were no exception, especially when they were learning how to ride horseback. Besides taking them to a Catholic Church on both Sundays we took them sightseeing and to the State Fair in Pueblo.

But, the best times were spent reminiscing on how we flirted with the medical students, especially Jim who earned extra money doing night duty in the Operating Room. He was a handsome, blond young man attending Tulane Medical School. We would find him napping on one of the operating tables when there was no surgery, but once a call would come in we would compete to see who would wake him up. Jim told us he had a girlfriend in his hometown of Lexington, Kentucky. "Remember the time we decided to make that trip to Kentucky?" Josie quipped and grinned. Oh, how we planned! Of course, Jim was the reason we wanted to go there and meet 'that' person he liked whom we, unseen, disliked.

As nurses who worked in the operating room, we received one month's paid vacation while the floor nurses only got three weeks because they did not have to be on call at nights. So, Josie and I decided to use the last two weeks of our vacation for a trip to Kentucky. I made motel reservations by mail.

It was the first day of our month long vacation. Josie and I played tennis at the Audubon Park and I sprained my ankle. X-rays showed no fracture but I had to use crutches. What a way to start a vacation!

Two weeks later we were scheduled to leave for Kentucky. I arrived at the Greyhound Bus Station at the time we had decided, but Josie never appeared until after our bus had come and gone.

"Don't say anything or I'll go home and I won't go on this trip," she blurted out as she rushed towards a bench. I knew she meant it. This wasn't the first time that her habitual lateness had caused problems. I said nothing though I was boiling inside. I stormed off to Loew's Theatre to see a movie, "Dr. Kildare." When I returned to the bus station I found Josie sitting stiffly on the bench where I had left her. I was still upset. We didn't talk but took a seat by each other on the next bus, three hours later. We arrived at the motel and were placed in the best room because I had misspelled the price of the room by writing "Prize"!

Jim, the medical student, had informed Annie, his girlfriend in Lexington, that we were on our way and when we called her from the motel she said to come to dinner the same evening. What surprised us was that she and her parents were so gracious and hospitable. Actually, we weren't too happy about that—we had hoped Annie would be all bad! The next day, they showed us the Calumet Horse Farm and another where Man O'War was stabled. I must say those stables were cleaner, the doorknobs more highly polished, and the windows more sparkling than most houses people lived in!

Near the end of our vacation, we were getting short of money so Josie suggested that we go to a hospital in Lexington that was run by nuns, arriving around dinnertime. "Maybe if we pretend being interested in a job, the nuns will invite us to a meal." That is exactly what happened! We saved money but Josie always felt guilty that she, a good

Catholic girl, would do such a stunt!

Josie and I were so busy reminiscing that it must have been close to 2 AM before we decided to hit the sack. Those days we were together were wonderful and we hated to see them end. It was a sad day when we took Josie and Junior to the train station in Limon. For us, it felt as though no time had passed.

Upon rereading the diaries we kept since we were married, it continues to surprise me how busy we were. We thought nothing of getting up at 4 AM to do farm work, butcher, or move cattle. Also, it seemed we had constant visitors. Some were salespeople, some wanted to borrow things, and most stayed a while just to visit. Of course, we also had company who came to see us for no particular reason. It was considered 'polite' to exchange views on politics (especially the dirty kind), the low price of cattle, the dry weather, and last years' blizzards. What pessimists we were!

Fall came early that year, Gret and I continued to see Dr. Carpenter, our obstetrician, the leaves changed after the frost, and we began the blizzard season.

I wrote diary-like letters home to my mother in San Francisco. Every day I would describe my new experiences and thoughts and after a week I'd send them off. My mother called my siblings whenever she received a letter and had them come over to read the 'Ranch Report'. After I described a recent blizzard with all its miseries I was quite shocked to read her comments to my letter, "It must be wonderfully cozy during those snowstorms when you are in a warm house, all the family together, while the snow is beating against the windowpanes". By contrast, she obviously had no idea that instead of the Christmas card vision she saw, a rancher and his family spend most of their time outside in the bitter cold taking care of animals. I decided my letters did not clearly convey the situation and that I had to improve my literary descriptions!

No more visitors arrived the rest of the year. The winter continued with a vengeance and it felt as if it would be a long time before the powerful mile high sunshine would return and defrost the Colorado countryside. Meanwhile, we would cope with whatever presented itself while we "poured another cup of hot cocoa!" 🐄

Mr. and Mrs. Fred Varenberg and Tommy, Bonnie and Suzan Ruth visited Varenberg's uncles and aunt in Denver over Christmas. They were gone for t w o days.

Thanksgiving in Denver.

Chapter 6

ONE THING AFTER ANOTHER

Another Winter Blizzard

lizzards in Colorado are frequent. Some bring a lot of snow; others very little—but there are always strong winds. Even the smallest of storms becomes a blizzard. Winter storms produce dry snow while the springtime ones are usually quite wet, and though they are wonderful for the thirsty soil, they are tough on people and animals. Often, radio weathermen predict the storms. When you hear the warning, you immediately begin to prepare by moving the livestock to protected places, making sure the hay and grain is handy and, last but not least, dashing into town to buy food and supplies hoping to be back before the blizzard hits.

The most dangerous storm is the one which appears suddenly and without warning. It bears down with such force that it causes havoc on every living being, also on buildings and brings worry to a person's psyche.

As far as food was concerned, we could have lived for several months on what we had stored. There were many shelves filled with colorful jars of home canned fruits, vegetables and jams, as well as factory canned food along with plenty of frozen and dry storage of food stuff, like frijole beans and rice. Outside, we had supplies of fresh milk, eggs, and, of course, chicken and beef that could have been butchered at a moment's notice.

The main worry was electricity. Very often an outage would occur and last from a few hours to several days. Naturally, everything run by power would then be obsolete including the electric pump which supplied water. You never know how much you miss that precious liquid until there is none. So, whenever there was even a momentary flickering of the lights or even a brief interruption of a radio program, we anticipated an imminent outage and everyone would quickly fetch buckets and other containers and fill them with water.

Without electricity, we depended on kerosene lamps and candles which were always handy. We kept the refrigerator, and especially the freezers, securely closed in order to prevent spoilage. The milking machine became useless. Though all big dairies owned their own generators, we used our hands! And the cows, which were used to the machine, did not like being handled in such a disrespectful manner so they decreased their milk production...which made the IXL Dairy Association decrease our checks!

Using the outside toilet was a terrible ordeal. During one storm, the blowing snow was so intense that I couldn't find the privy. I kept walking, thinking perhaps the wind had blown it away. Finally, I realized I had gone too far and I turned around and slowly, carefully retraced my steps. I became petrified that I might stumble into the awful pit where the outhouse had been. Just then, I saw a shape moving towards me. I froze in panic. It turned out to be Hubby looking for me. I never was so glad to see anyone. I told him, shivering, that the privy had blown away. "No Schlitza, you are standing right next to it!"

Surprised, I urged him to "Wait for me," and I wandered off towards the marvelous convenience. But after I opened the door I couldn't find the darned seat. The entire building, which was quite drafty, was filled with snow. I waited while Fred went for a shovel, then worked for a good 5 minutes during which my poor bladder was extending to somewhere near my chest. He dug until he found the 'throne'! I didn't care anymore. Within seconds I found myself perched on the wooden seat, which was sporting a 1-1/2 inch layer of snow, sitting there with my legs straight out in front of me supported by a thick cushion of snow!

Another major problem which concerned all ranchers and farmers during blizzards was that the roads became impassible due to blowing snow or being covered entirely by massive snowdrifts. In the back of everyone's mind was the constant worry that a personal emergency or accident might happen and the closed roads would keep us from reaching a doctor or hospital in time. The County Road Department did excellent work in their efforts to open and re-open roads, but it was difficult because sometimes, no sooner did they plow the snow to each side of the road when the wind would blow it right back, or new snow would fall.

We tried to be prepared. As soon as the cold weather arrived in the fall, as early as September, we ordered enough coal to heat the house until summer. For cooking and baking we used tanks of bottled propane gas, which John Carner brought throughout the year and we always had a spare bottle.

All these thoughts occupied our minds whenever we heard the word, "blizzard." Country people are resilient and they know how to cope...and so we tried to be tough and learn how to outlast the elements.

Usually, blizzards lasted only a day or two but, of course, there were exceptions. When weatherman Bowman announced that a strong blizzard was on its way and urged everybody to get supplies and then stay at home, as a rule, people heeded his words. One time he was especially insistent. "Get off the streets and find shelter if you can't make it to your house!" he warned. A few minutes later, he returned with the news that Golden, Colorado (30 miles north of Denver) had 100 mile per hour winds and the KOA TV tower had blown down and more snow was predicted. "In Denver," Bowman said, "stalled cars are being pushed by people or pulled by trucks—things are in a turmoil, utter confusion downtown. Please stay off the streets," he urged again.

It wasn't long after this radio transmission that dark clouds appeared on the horizon north of the ranch and soon the wind started to blow—harder, ever harder. We quickly moved the cattle, sheep, chickens and geese to protection and we let the dogs into the house so they would be out of the storm. Before nightfall, the storm was in full force. The wind was tearing at buildings, fences and hurling anything not connected, making them fly erratically towards the south. The snow, which zoomed by horizontally, probably came to rest somewhere in New Mexico! The noise was a constant roar. We were thankful that the family was together and safe.

It was only around 8 o'clock when it happened. There was no warning, no flickering of the lights, the electricity simply went out and didn't come back on. "Let's go to bed," suggested Fred and I thought that was the best idea since sliced bread! Everything was prepared—we had lots of water in different containers, we had extra buckets of coal in the house, and our stomachs were full and so I made hot water bottles, one for each of us, to warm our cold beds and bodies.

The night seemed to last forever. I was restless and could not relax with the clamor from outside! Friend and husband, however, was in dreamland the moment he hit the pillow. He mumbled off and on, threw his arms across my face and didn't even wake up when I accused him of spousal abuse. Sleep finally came to me but it was rudely interrupted by a thunderous bang, even louder than the constant wind outside. I opened my eyes and saw our wind-up alarm clock showing 2:45 AM. I would have to wait until morning to find out what had happened outdoors. Meanwhile Fred slept, snored, mumbled and yelled, "Push that cow out of there!"

There was no use getting up at our usual 5:30 to 6:00 hour. We still had no power, the house was freezing cold, the blizzard continued to roar, and no human being would dare venture outdoors. For a rancher to stay in bed until 7AM was definitely considered immoral, a sin you had better not mention, even to your best friend. But this miserable display of Mother Nature's anger made everything different. Even the children, who usually were up early, remained in their warm and cozy beds.

We were fortunate that a friend had given Tommy a small battery-run radio which we used to listen to newscasts, our only link to the world. It was breakfast time, "Let's hear about the storm" was Fred's remark, muffled somewhat by a mouthful of beef sausage, as he turned on the small transistor radio.

"No change in the weather," Bowman said, "Wyoming is still getting it, all the lines are down. It's the worst storm in twenty years!"

"Well," we figured, "with Wyoming in such bad shape, we'll probably have some time before it gets better here."

Now that it was daylight, we could see what had happened during the night. A power line was lying on the ground, draped over a three-foot snowdrift. We found what made all the racket the night before; there was a window screen dangling by one corner of its frame as it rose and fell with each wind gust. The wind also blew off several boards from the windbreak north of the house and the six-foot extension pipe which drained water from the sink to the outside was frozen solid.

Wintertime horror stories were familiar to ranchers. The tales told about brave farmers who, in a blizzard, went to care for their animals or to do a chore only to become lost between the house and the barn. They were found frozen to death just a few yards from safety. After hearing the stories over and over again many ranch folks, including us, would tie a rope from the house to the barn or wherever you wanted to go so you could find your way back.

Periodically, the howling wind seemed to lessen and we became optimistic expecting relief from the icy blast. But the thought had no sooner crossed our minds, when it started all over again. We became hermits for the day and it seemed strange. The living room which was dark even on a bright sunshiny day, looked like it was nighttime and the kerosene lantern did little to drive out the gloom. The temperature in the kitchen was below freezing and the windows all rattled in unison as if Arturo Toscanini from the New York Philharmonic Orchestra was directing his musicians. We played Chinese checkers and wrote a couple of letters while periodically checking the weather. Nothing changed. The wind gusts continued, but were less frequent.

The meals I made during blizzards were always very simple: split pea soup or lentil soup, both fortified with potatoes, onions and finally a ring bologna. The oil stove in the kitchen always blew out whenever there was even a whisper of wind, so it felt like you were outdoors. My cooking attire during storms was a heavy winter coat plus a woolen cap and gloves. We ate our meals in the living room by a roaring fire and when it came time to clear the table I donned my woollies and braved the kitchen with a load of dirty dishes. I became the fastest dishwasher west of the Mississippi!

Towards evening, Fred tried to make it to the barns to check on the livestock but returned only minutes later. It was not worth risking life and limb. So—to bed early again, hoping and praying for a better day.

And it was! The wind was down to a soft breeze, the sky was blue and the sun was laughing. We expected to see snowdrifts but we were not prepared for the unbelievable sight which unfolded before our eyes. Part of the north barn was almost completely hidden by the white stuff and you could walk right up to the roof. All the gates and corral fences were covered but in the center of the corrals was bare ground, evidence of the force of the winds whirling the snow about. The south barn was filled with several feet of snow on the inside. To the east of it was the windbreak where we kept the cattle that didn't fit into either barn. These poor cows were a pitiful sight, standing so very quietly and still as if their feet were anchored to the ground. They were thin from lack of food and water and had a blanket of snow on their backs. The animals' tails were ice encrusted and urine stained, hanging limply all the way to the fringes and looking like frozen strands of necklaces. When these brave warriors saw us they gave a soft mooing sound as if to say, "Give us something to eat!" Fred understood 'cow talk' and at once started hauling several bales of hay, throwing them over the corral fence. I expected a mad rush, but instead the cows slowly ambled towards the feed while their heavy tails clinked with each step, like wind chimes on a porch.

That afternoon the electricity was turned on again and everyone was overjoyed. But as abruptly as it had come on, it went off again after only an hour. During this brief time we rushed to replenish the water supply and did jobs like re-lighting the ugly oil stove in the kitchen. Hoping the power would remain, I anticipated an evening in a cozy, warm house lit by incandescent lamps instead of the filthy kerosene ones. I switched on the radio hoping for some news about the weather, etc. Here he was again, good old Ed Bowman who never slept during a storm, was telling us that huge numbers of power lines and poles were down. "Don't expect any juice," his expression for electricity, "for at least 24-48 hours or more, depending where you live." All the linemen were scheduled to work throughout the next few nights. No sooner was I getting comfortable when the lights flickered and my delicious 'hour with power' was gone!

It was now the fourth day since the storm started. The weather was pleasant, the sun continued to shine onto a white world and small puddles appeared from melted snow in a few places, only to freeze again during the night.

The children, all bundled up, were playing in the snow when Tommy came storming into the house, "I think the snowplow is coming!" Sure enough, a few minutes later there was the bright orange machine opening up Jones Road followed by a big truck from the Mountain View Electric Company. What a wonderful sight!

Two linemen jumped off their vehicle and in no time our downed electric wire was firmly back on the pole. Before they finished the job I asked when we could expect to have electricity.

He answered, "I have no idea, Ma'am, perhaps tomorrow, perhaps a week from today."

I did neither want nor deserve such an answer. I was discouraged enough, but I thanked him anyway and they were off following the snowplow down the road to the Farrells.

Another day went by and I was getting sick of the cold kitchen, worried about the desperately low water supply, and frustrated with the meager light from the kerosene lamp. My frustration didn't help me, but finally common sense ruled and gave me strength and willpower as I decided to attack a couple of jobs with gusto. First, I melted mountains of clean snow for drinking and boiled it thoroughly. Next, I attempted to clean the living room floor which had become filled with sand, dirt and piles of ashes from the coal stove. I thought of cooking a great meal but decided against it. I didn't really want to dirty more dishes. That was my best excuse ever—save the water!

Towards evening, two more snowplows moved slowly past our place and we felt waves of relief. The road finally was open and suddenly we felt free. The cloistered, hemmed-in feeling was gone. On each side of the road were mountains of snow up to 12 feet deep and the view of Pikes Peak appeared when we stood in the middle of the road. Things were looking up!

We slept better that night and got up refreshed and eager to find out what the day would bring. There was no wind and it looked like another beautiful Colorado winter day. The snowdrifts around the ranch were now hard and crusty from the frosty nights and they crunched when we walked on them. We figured it would take a long time for the ten feet and larger drifts to melt away—a big job for the weak winter sun! To the children the many 'snow mountains' became adventure lands and only reluctantly did they stop playing and come into the house to eat.

The whole family was outdoors when suddenly we heard loud music coming from the kitchen. We all raced back to the house. The radio, which had not been turned off when we lost power, was blaring as Bing Crosby welcomed us with, of all things, "Sleigh bells ringing, are you listening" and finally the last part of the song, "Walking in a winter wonderland." We laughed, we danced, and we hugged each other. We checked the lights, I opened the fridge, and everything was back to normal!

Fred Wagoner came by the house the following day with an armload full of letters plus a free sample of Colgate toothpaste. Since our mailbox was under what seemed like tons of the white stuff, he almost embarrassed and shyly, asked us if we could possibly dig it out soon. I put it on the husband's list of things to do!

Milk cows need to be milked twice a day or else they quit producing, so when the milk truck could not negotiate the roads we were forced to dump many full cans onto the ground. Fred encouraged us to drink as much as possible of the 'cow juice' and so we spoiled the cats, chickens, and any other thirsty animals with gallons of the precious liquid. I made butter and froze it, cottage cheese ended up in a cloth bag on the clothesline to drip, and we ate 'sour milk' sprinkled with sugar and cinnamon. Surprisingly, we never got tired of milk and its products.

Miraculously, the storm only caused two cows to get a slight case of pneumonia which we treated immediately with penicillin. They always said that aspirin was the true wonder drug. No way! In those days, penicillin took that honor due to the many cattle—and of course, people—who were saved by it, thanks to Dr. Fleming, the founder of this great medication!

Life was back to normal, now, but winter was not over. There would be several more blizzards in the season and hundreds more for us. We enjoyed each day until Mr. Bowman would once again warn us with the word, "Blizzard!" 🐴

A Baby With Colic

For the last seven months, both Gret and I had monthly appointments with our obstetrician, Dr. Carpenter, in Colorado Springs. We made this 'our' day eating lunch in a restaurant and doing some leisurely shopping, unencumbered with children and husbands. "Any day now," guessed Dr. Carpenter, "and we'll be seeing both of you in the hospital."

We didn't plan it, but we figured we got pregnant the same week. It surely made things interesting. "Wouldn't it be funny if we were in the hospital sharing a room together!" Gret and I laughed.

Mary Stouffer was born first—on February 10th. She was a chubby baby—7 lbs.12 oz. and the nurse said that she looked like a girl from China because her eyes were slightly slanted. Fred and I visited Gret and I "pledged" to join her in the hospital soon.

As "promised," I was admitted to Penrose Hospital on February 14th, ready to deliver. All at once my contractions quit. Gret asked one of the nurses whether there was anyone in the Labor Room.

Her answer was, "Yes, somebody from the country, and she is doing nothing."

My good friend marched right over to the Labor Room and visited me. "Elizabeth, today is Valentine's Day and dinner will be great. I know, I filled out my meal ticket yesterday."

Taking her advice, I ordered my holiday meal. Usually, patients who are ready to deliver are not given any food but the nurses thought I would be 'messing around' for a while so they let me eat every bite. How wrong they were!

Jack Allan was born just 30 minutes after I finished the last piece of fiery-red cherry pie. He was small but healthy, weighing only 5 lbs. 2 oz. Fred was elated and he walked all around the hospital, talking to everybody, and swinging his bolo tie in continual circles. Best yet, Gret and I ended up having adjoining rooms. Once again the luxury of food being served to me, clear water for drinking and bathing, plus a flush toilet were almost too much for me. As the saying goes, "I thought I had died and gone to Heaven!"

I remained an additional week because Dr. Carpenter's brother, a surgeon, wanted to strip my veins. I had been having a lot of trouble with varicose veins, swollen veins in my legs, and this was a perfect time to do the surgery. There were twelve incisions. Apparently, all those worm-like things in the specimen pan caused one of the doctors to ask the other one, "Want to go fishing? This would make great bait!"

Naturally, Gret and I took the babies to their pediatrician on the same day. At one month, Mary weighed 8-lbs.12 oz while Jack weighed 7-lbs.10 oz. All of us were pleased the babies gained so beautifully. Gret and I celebrated by eating a fattening meal at one of the nicer restaurants, the Village Inn.

While I was in the hospital, the cattle prices went up by a few cents and all the ranchers breathed a sigh of relief. Steers now brought 30-35 cents per pound, heifers 20-30 cents a pound, cows 19-20 cents a pound and bulls 24 cents. When I heard this, I jokingly told Fred that, "We should have a baby every year!"

But my 'never-understanding-jokes-husband' replied, "No, we have enough kids now, two boys and two girls. That's enough!"

My mother and three siblings were constantly urging me to visit them in California. When we decided that I would go in late June, Susan got excited, "I want to go, too!" So, she, 4-month old Jack and I caught the train in Limon. In Denver, we transferred to the California Zephyr. It was a classy train and special waiters delivered meals to our roomette. Susan loved going through the many tunnels in the Western Colorado Rockies

Four kids, a dog and a sling.

but the plains in Wyoming became monotonous and she did art work with the crayons she brought along. It was a long trip, lasting two days and one night before we finally arrived in San Francisco where the family awaited us.

For Jack, the trip was downright miserable as the poor baby was plagued by almost constant colic. My pediatrician had given us some liquid seconal to keep him quiet and sleepy but as sometimes happens with babies and older patients, sedatives have the opposite effect—they make the patient tense. The roomette was small but I managed to walk Jack up a few yards and down a few yards while I had the radio playing music, loud music. Sometimes this actually worked and he rested—as did I. The day after we arrived, I took him to Children's Hospital where x-rays proved nothing wrong except air (colic) in his intestines and they prescribed different medication to relieve his suffering.

The week went by fast. It was wonderful to be with the family and they showed us the entire city of San Francisco, the beautiful and extensive museums, rocky coastline, seals and we ate at the best restaurants. I especially enjoyed, once again, tasting my mother's cooking and finding an adult camaraderie I hadn't known before. I was pleased to see that she enjoyed living in San Francisco and, especially, that she looked and felt so well.

Max, Anne and Martin were happy. All had good jobs—Max worked for an import/export business, Anne had a job as an R.N. in a hospital and Martin was employed as a tailor in a major clothing store. They were glad to have moved away from Denvers' snowstorms. I thought I was used to frigid weather, but in San Francisco the continual cold, moist breeze chilled me to the bone. Here it was the middle of summer and the grass was brown! I believe it was Mark Twain who said something like, "I spent the coldest day of summer in San Francisco!" I was ready and anxious to head for home where summer was summer.

Back on the Zephyr, the return trip was pleasant. Susan was extremely sweet and well behaved and Jack slept almost continually, lulled by the steady and sometimes jerky motion of the train, helped by the new medication.

In Denver, we had a 1-1/2 hour layover before the Rock Island Railroad would take us to Colorado Springs. Aunt Blanche and Uncle Herman came to the station to see us and we planned to eat at the restaurant in the station. However, Aunt Blanche told me that there was an earlier train leaving right away. I was all in favor of getting home sooner because we were really tired. I asked the station supervisor if we could catch the train which was leaving in one minute. He told me to rush to the other track and he would hold the train for us.

No sooner did we step inside the door and the train was on its way. We arrived in Colorado Springs 1-1/2 hour earlier than expected, so naturally, no one was there to greet us. Susan sat on the one suitcase, while I walked my restless four-month old up and down the station platform.

An hour later, Fred arrived, all smiles, not anticipating the mood I was in. I was exhausted and the wait had only added to my fatigue. Fred gave me a welcome-home kiss and I became angry because his breath smelled of beer. "If you had come here earlier and not stopped for that drink we would be home by now!" Later, I apologized for my explosive attitude.

Earlier, Fred and our good friend and neighbor, Mr. Cottrell, had cleaned the house and afterward they stopped at a bar to have a hamburger and a beer. After all, they were over an hour early. I felt embarrassed that I made a scene. Fred never spent time drinking away from home and though we always had a few beers in the fridge, he never drank much. After I recuperated a bit, I realized that my remark was totally unreasonable and I again apologized.

During the 45-minute drive to the ranch, Fred told me how Bonnie had an accident. Our new male sheep, a ram, cornered her inside the garage and butted her, making her fall with all her weight onto her left arm. When she complained of pain, Fred applied Horse Liniment to the area. Next he fashioned a sling for her arm. The cattle needed checking so he took her along in the jeep for what must have been both a bumpy and painful ride.

The next day, Fred explained that he took Bonnie to the folks on their ranch near Castle Rock where she was to spend a few days. Aunt Blanche saw the injury and insisted on taking Bonnie to the local doctor. After taking an x-ray, the doctor pointed out a slight fracture. He didn't think a cast was necessary, all she needed was a sling. After all, Fred had done the right thing and Bonnie was thrilled to spend several days at the folks' ranch.

Fred then told me how lightening killed three steers and how lucky we were to have insurance. "You could see a streak all the way down their legs where the hair was burned."

"Got any more 'good' news?" I quipped sarcastically.

"No, that's all and I'm sure glad you're home!" So was I. It was a fun trip while it lasted but our less than modest and humble home was a warm, comfortable, and, most of all, welcome sight! 🐎

Susan and Bonnie relax in the warm spring sun.

Mumps and Me

Children should be taught to share, but certain things like colds, should be excluded. Somehow, Tommy constantly caught them from other children at school and would bring the germs home where he spread them evenly among everyone in the family.

It happened more than once that Fred would wake up very early in the morning speaking with a nasal, gurgling sound, "'I'b' sick. I can't work today—you'll have to do 'by' chores." I would get up, throw on my robe, and go after my thermometer to take his temperature. It often had 'soared' all the way to 99 degrees! I would flood him with gallons of orange juice and water, making him need to get up and go to the outhouse every ten minutes or so. Finally he came to the conclusion, "I 'bight' as well stay up." Then a hearty breakfast would convince him he was not ready for the deathbed so he could trudge outdoors to do his chores. The rest of the day I pretended how sorry and concerned I was for hubby's illness but deep down I chuckled, "I won again!" The trick had worked.

Two days later, it was my turn. I sneezed and blew my swollen nose until Fred woke up. Bless his heart, he got up and brought me a tall glass of orange juice. I really felt like staying in bed but I couldn't allow myself that privilege. Thinking back to when I was a child, I didn't remember the 'common cold' making me feel so miserable.

The same year, Tommy was sent home from school because he felt sick. It turned out to be measles which he again shared with the rest of the children, especially Susan who became sicker than the others. I rocked her for most of a Sunday as she was quite listless, refusing food and drink, speaking little, and dozing continually. I knew I could handle childhood diseases like measles but I thought I had better take her to the pediatrician the next morning. I got up during the night to check on her. No change. At 6 AM her temperature was normal and she asked for something to eat. There was no need to go to the doctor!

Fred turned to teaching to balance the uncertain ranching income. He secured a job teaching algebra, chemistry, and woodworking at the high school in Ramah. He loved it. The following year he transferred to Peyton where he taught English, Spanish, and soil conservation. Both positions paid $3,600 per year.

The teaching money came in handy because the cattle prices were unusually low. We needed rain badly as the pastures continued to get drier and the grass was withering away. It seemed this was happening almost every year. Such hardships! Sometimes I slumped into depressions so deep I felt like I was covered with a sodden comforter. Little things like admiring nature or the children's antics always helped to pull me up out of my despair.

One day, Fred came home from school later than usual. He had stopped at the Calhan doctor because he had been exposed to mumps and wondered if something could be done to prevent the disease developing in him, perhaps a gamma globulin shot. Unfortunately, the doctor told him there was nothing to do. Two weeks afterward, almost like clockwork, Fred developed diarrhea and a neck so swollen he looked like a fat pig ready for slaughter! He had the mumps in both parotid glands. A few days later, Tommy and Bonnie woke up with the same disease. The house took on the look of an infirmary and I spent my time between patients and the livestock. I preferred the latter!

To add to the turmoil, it was calving season and I needed to watch the cows to make sure they calved successfully. Three times a day I loaded little Susan, who was still in good health, into the Jeep along with a rope, a bottle of tincture of iodine, strings, a bottle of penicillin and a syringe. We were off to the 'maternity pasture.' Though we had to search through the large pasture, the cows usually were in one protected area. They were calving with regularity, producing two or three calves a day who received our usual routine for all newborns—a Penicillin shot plus tying off the umbilical cord and pouring iodine over it to prevent infection. This task alone took almost an hour each day. In some cases, I had to pull the calf with the help of a tool called a 'calf puller', a contraption with a pulley and a chain. I had to place the chain onto the calf's front legs which normally, and hopefully, appeared first, then I would ratchet the pulley and pull out the calf. It was heavy, grueling work—definitely not women's work, but I persevered and often used strength I didn't know I had.

Back home again, I gave my three grotesque-looking patients food and drink after which I would do several more hours of outdoor chores. This miserable, strenuous, challenging routine went on for days as the children got better and Fred got worse. After one particularly rough day, I walked home and into the 'Shop of Horrors' to be greeted by good ole' Fred who quipped, "Tonight I want to have a <u>good</u> dinner!" True, I hadn't done much cooking those past few days but neither did I need, nor deserve, this additional demand. I was angry and I decided that I would take Fred to the doctor's office and hopefully to the hospital the very next day. I fed everybody and soon thereafter, dropped onto the living room couch where I fell asleep and did not wake up until the next morning.

Early the following day I did a quick set of chores—I was getting good at that—and loaded all the kids and Fred into the car and headed for Colorado Springs. Next, I called our doctor from a store and told him of Fred's problem. Over the phone he diagnosed pancreatitis and told me to take him straight to Penrose Hospital. Hallelujah!

Hours later, driving back to the ranch was a rejuvenation process for me. I felt free as if a yoke had been removed. The chores somehow became lighter and the cows were calving without trouble.

After eight days, Fred returned home from the hospital. Eventually, he became a diabetic because his pancreas was unable to produce insulin due to the infection. He was on a strict diabetic diet—no carbohydrates (sugars or starches) and had to take Diabenese tablets daily. Just as fast as he became sick, his body started to fight the illness and after a year he was cured. No more diabetes. We celebrated with a home-cooked 'blue plate special' which consisted of a bottle of Rhine wine and everything he'd been denied in the past year, including his favorite—chocolate cake.

The summer of 1956 remained dry and the cattle prices kept going down. Many cattle were sold as ranchers ran out of grass. By fall, we needed to sell our young livestock and

Uncle Herman was willing to buy ours. He looked them over and chose 29 head for his ranch. He offered 17-1/2 cents per pound for the steers and 14 cents for the heifers. We also had some thin cows which needed to be culled from the herd, so we took them to a livestock sale and received a measly 8 cents a pound for them. The total came to $2,650.88, not much money for a year's work considering our investment in the ranch plus interest on our outstanding debt.

It was a tough time. The Calhan Bank decided to help out ranchers in financial trouble and loaned us just enough to pay Mr. Kline for the mortgage on our ranch, plus the cost of living. However, they refused to loan us the money we needed for livestock so we were forced to approach a short-term loan company in Colorado Springs who were willing to help us buy cattle the following spring. It was to be our last year with our local bank.

The Rains Finally Come

Just as 1955 was one of the worst years, 1958 was among the best. Not only were we blessed with a lot of moisture, but good things happened as well. Of course, It started out with the birth of our son, Jack, a sweet but sickly child.

Next, the second birth was when our quarter horse, Socks, had a beautiful pinto colt, white with large brown spots, whom we named Cochise. We discovered first hand that mares are not in labor as long as cows. In fact, you hardly ever see a colt born unless you just happen to be there. Lucky mares!

We started training Cochise by putting a halter on him and leading him around so he would get used to people. Only a day-old, Mother and son galloped across the pasture and it seemed as if their feet barely touched the ground, the new colt keeping up with his mother's gallop. It was a heartwarming sight. Watching those magnificent animals travel at high speeds across the green pasture reminded me of Pegasus, the mythical winged horse. Cochise already showed the spirit of a reliable cowman's horse who would only quit when the rider did.

The third birth happened when Lady, our collie, had a litter of five pups during the summer. We gave Uncle Herman and Aunt Blanche one of the males whom they named

Training Chochise begins early.

"Boy," who was later returned to us when they sold their ranch. By then, he was a gorgeous dog, tall with a full coat, typical of his breed with a loving disposition. We laughed when he would circle around a mud puddle, wary of messing up his white feet.

We were glad when Mr. Cottrell offered to do some of our farming. It was a time-consuming job but he felt that "sitting on a tractor and pulling farm machinery was the most relaxing thing in the world!" He stayed with us during much of the summer and fall, except on weekends when he was with, as he would say, "the ole lady!"

The rains continued throughout the early spring season and everybody hoped for a few dry days. They eventually came and Fred hurried to plant the sorghum seed. The field was north of the house so I could watch the planting through the kitchen windows. Luck was not with us. After a couple of weeks, a violent rainstorm pelted the field and washed out three-fourths of the seedlings. Small rivulets formed into rushing streams which eventually made several large lakes in the fields.

We didn't know what to do. Should we let the remaining seedlings grow to maturity or start all over again? My suggestion was immediate, "Leave it alone! The rains might come again." Since I was raised in the city and didn't have farming know-how, my good husband found it imperative to consult others who recommended that we "plow the entire field again and drill another batch of sorghum seed into it!" So, Mr. Cottrell and Fred spent the next few weeks doing just that. Though gentle rains interrupted the procedure off and on, the job was finally finished. Both were no sooner proud of their job well done, when another furious storm came and ruined not only the entire field but also both their pride. To this day, Fred concluded, "I should have listened to you instead of all those other 'people.' It turned out to be a costly deal!"

I felt like saying, "We city folks don't know much about farming but we do have common sense." I didn't speak those words, Fred was suffering enough.

We needed a new car and Mr. Lasky's son, Frank, worked at the Chevrolet dealership in Colorado Springs. So Fred stopped by and asked to see the best used car he had. Frank told him, "I've got a honey of a car for you. It's a '58 and only has 11,000 miles on it." Fred liked what he saw. The price was right—$3,000. He had already talked to the banker who said they'd loan us the money. The following day he hitched a ride to Colorado Springs with a neighbor and bought the car.

I was anxiously awaiting the new vehicle when a beautiful station wagon pulled up. Out jumped Fred just as I leaped out of the kitchen door. "What do you think?" Fred asked me. I was speechless. There stood a huge car, two-toned beige and light brown, beige upholstery that looked like leather, and white walled tires. Not a scratch anywhere. "Can we afford this?" was all I could say.

After he reassured me, he added, "I'll put it in the garage and then let's eat."

"That man! All he can think of is FOOD," I thought. The garage was barely big enough to house the car. After dinner, the whole family jumped into the 'wagon' and showed it off to the neighbors. There was so much room inside and it rode so smoothly. I loved it.

Fred gave me a Toni Home Permanent every six months. It took hours and left me with kinky curls all over my head. I never liked them, but my rancher/farmer/hairdresser thought they looked better each time he produced such a mop! First, he took a handful of hair and with several big 'bites' of the scissors, bingo—I had a "haircut," he proudly announced! Next he pulled the hair around rollers, added the evil smelling solution, and we sat and waited for the juice to work while the constantly dripping liquid stung my eyes. Bonnie startled us with her remark, "Daddy, you made Mommy look like Queen Elizabeth." Oh, what horror I paid for beauty!

On Monday morning, Mr. Cottrell came around 7 AM and told us that his son, Jake, was in town and that they wanted us to go with them for a drive up Pikes Peak the next day. None of us had ever been there and the best part—it meant a day off!

The following day was warm, promising a clear summer day. We left Susan and Jack with Mrs. Cottrell in Colorado Springs while the rest of us climbed into Jake's station wagon for the climb up the 14,000-foot mountain that we looked at every day. Surprisingly, Mr. Cottrell, his son Jake, and his 12-year old grandson, plus the four of us all fit comfortably. Before long we were climbing up the mountainous gravel hairpin curves when Jake pulled off to the side and announced that he "needed to ask another traveler something." Later we figured out that he had to go to the bathroom! He parked the car at the extreme outer edge of the road so close that we overlooked the timberline and the city far below. The minute Jake left, the kid climbed into the driver's seat and started moving the gearshift, pressing buttons, and tugging at the steering wheel. He pushed and pulled on all the buttons on the dashboard. Mr. Cottrell told him to "leave things alone." But he didn't. Suddenly, the car began inching forward. Then it stopped. We all yelled at the punk, fearful of certain death by tumbling down the mountain only to be stopped by the trees. The kid thought it was funny because he had never seen grown-ups so scared. Still, he didn't stop. Instead he resumed his maneuvers. Fred, who was in the middle of the back seat, grabbed him by his collar and tried to pull him away from the steering wheel but he wouldn't let go. Again, the car jumped forward, helped by a sudden wind gust. Luckily it stopped. There in front of us was our lifesaver: a good-sized rock. Just as Fred was yelling at the brat, Jake returned.

Jake backed up and resumed the climb to the top of the mountain. When we arrived, a thick fog spread its opaque wings over the one and only building which housed a small restaurant. The constant wind beat against our faces. We walked briskly to a lookout tower and climbed about 20 steps, hoping to be rewarded with a view of the countryside and our ranch far below. But it was not to be, for the fog had now engulfed the entire area. We rushed into the restaurant to wait for the haze to lift, get out of the wind, and warm ourselves. But soon we decided to leave because it looked like it would be a while before the weather would clear. Going downhill was slow since most of the tourists had the same idea and were squeamish driving around the many curves. Looking back, you could see the thick fog clinging tightly to the peak. Though everyone felt disoriented because of the high altitude, Tommy and I developed a headache and Bonnie was nauseated from the thin air. Only the 'brat' felt great—too bad!!

The intermittent rains continued throughout the summer. The pastures were a lush green, the garden produced copious amounts of vegetables, and the cattle sported shiny coats—each exhibiting a picture of health. But most importantly, the prices for yearlings were constant and high. The cattlemen's future looked bright.

One day, Fred received an invitation from CSU in Fort Collins to come to his 10-year reunion. He was so excited! But he felt equally guilty when he asked me, "You don't mind staying here and taking care of everything, do you?" I assured him I didn't mind and I

Susan and friend.

promised the children that for the next three days we would eat 'bad' food, no balanced meals, and all the candy we wanted! When Fred returned, he couldn't stop talking of the many classmates, professors, and friends he saw. He even received an honor, a can of furniture polish for being the 'Most Polished Gentleman!'

I was told that it was the duty of a ranch wife to can enough preserves to last for one winter. Being sick, pregnant, or not in the mood was no excuse. So at canning time, we bought a case of half gallon Kerr jars because with our growing family, quarts just didn't 'make it' anymore. Fruit coming from Colorado's western slope was plentiful and delicious and before long the shelves in the cellar groaned from the weight of the filled jars.

Fall had arrived with all its beauty. The air was fresh, the rains had just about stopped, daytime temperatures were pleasant and the nights were delightfully cool, making it necessary to use a blanket on the bed. There were no thunderheads on the dark blue sky, only an occasional soft white fluffy cloud.

The aspens were showing off their golden leaves which twinkled in the soft breeze.

Over the radio we heard the announcer tell all listeners to drive to Cripple Creek, which used to be a busy gold mining town, and drink in the breathtaking beauty of the aspens. Knowing that this golden opportunity would only last until the first frost, the roads were filled with cars, tour busses, and bike riders all heading for the foothills. How lucky we were to live in Colorado and be surrounded by so much beauty. If we could only do away with the blizzards this would be a superb and almost-perfect place to live.

Our financial situation was in a state of hold since the Calhan Bank could not, or would not, handle our livestock operation anymore. We applied to a loan company in Colorado Springs and they finally approved our request. We had asked for $25,000, of which $8,000 would be used to purchase 50 yearlings. Our family expenses were $200 a month which closely matched Fred's income from GI teaching at $191 a month. But, we still had to pay a debt to the Calhan Bank of $12,630 and we owed Mr. Kline $9,250 for the ranch. Each year we paid him $1,000 plus interest. We were overjoyed with the new loan and we immediately zipped into town before, as Fred said, "they changed their mind!"

A friendly group of people introduced themselves to us and assured us full cooperation in all our dealings. We felt comfortable talking with Carl, the man in charge of our loan. He suddenly got off his comfortable armchair and excused himself. He returned soon after, loaded down with papers, more than it took for the Trump prenuptial agreement! We read everything, including the fine print and signed our names until our hands cramped. Carl finally told us that an inspector would look at our place sometime that week and concluded saying, "It's good doing business with you!" We shook hands and he showed us out.

The inspector came to the ranch and estimated that we were worth $40,000 which he reported to his boss at the loan company. Apparently, his boss was not the only one informed because quite a few neighbors came forward and, jokingly, asked Fred for a loan! "Good to have a rich guy in the neighborhood," they teased.

We felt far from rich living in a place like this, without a bathroom and yellow water, and we were getting very tired of the inconveniences! We thought about building a house by the good well, west of the house. We discussed it with a contractor and became so excited that we thought of nothing else.

At about the same time we heard that Mr. Buckner was interested in selling his ranch. Both he and his wife were not in good health anymore and they wanted to move to the city. "Let's see how much he is asking for his place. They have a modern house with a bathroom, a telephone and clear water, lots of it. Besides we need more land for all of our cattle," Fred encouraged.

We visited the Buckners and inquired about the ranch deal. They were anxious to sell their 1,600 acres with the house, milk barn, two sheds and a chicken house, all in good shape. The asking price was $50,000. We had to find out from our newly acquired loan company if they would be willing to carry us.

We needn't have worried. They agreed to guarantee the loan and in a matter of days the four of us, the Buckners, Fred and I, found ourselves at the Calhan Bank signing papers for the sale of an additional ranch. The date was November 20, 1958. We now owned 3,040 acres of land and could move in during March, 1959.

The weather was extremely cold most of November. Frost was everywhere, on the bare branches of the trees, on fences, on roofs of the house and barns, and even the cattle showed some white on their faces. Some of their backs had streaks of frost running from the neck to the tail.

On one particular day all the cattle were completely silent, no mooing, even at the welcome sight of the cottonseed cake which was the extra protein supplement they received daily. Something was not right.

Usually, when cattle see the pickup they anticipate the cake and run towards it, kicking up their heels and making all sorts of happy noises. They seemed to crave it, and would eat it all regardless of how much they found. Too much of it would make them sick, so we had to be careful to distribute the correct amount.

Fred counted the yearlings and found several missing. He 'caked' the ones that were there and then saddled Topsey and rode off into the white and still world, searching for the 'no shows.' He kept riding south, then west before he found three yearlings. They were lying down, completely covered with frost and hard to notice. As he got closer Fred wondered what made them sick. Then he saw it. They were not sick, they were dead!

Fred continued to search for ten more missing yearlings and finally found all of them standing close to one another, huddled together absorbing each other's warmth. Steam rose from their nostrils. A cloud of fog embraced them and it was a wonder that Fred saw them at all. He then tried to move them home but they refused to walk.

"I got to get help," Fred thought as he galloped home. The wind started to blow a little and by the time he reached the house his eyebrows were frozen and his face was a fiery red. "There's something wrong, I found three dead and ten sick ones. We got to get them home. Please go call Dr. Henry. Tell him that this is an emergency and see if he can come out today. Ask Bill (Farrell) to bring his horse and help me," Fred shouted as he tied up the horse and entered the house.

I threw on my warm coat, the one I bought in England, drove the mile to the neighbor who at once got off the couch, not too happily, and went outside while I called the Vet.

During that time Fred made himself his favorite drink, a cup of cocoa, and soon stomped outside just as a horseback rider entered our driveway. "Hi Bill!" Fred shouted, and then on closer look, he realized it wasn't Bill after all, but instead his 13-year old son!! It took them an hour to bring the obviously sick animals home and into the barn.

"The Vet will be here tomorrow morning." I informed Fred. My message, short and to the point, didn't make him happy. He had hoped the Vet could come right away. Now, instead, our job was to put most of the yearlings into the two barns and the rest behind windbreaks in the corrals. The night was supposed to be a fiercely cold night according to Weatherman Bowman, so we hoped the yearlings would keep each other warm. I felt so sorry for them.

The family before moving from the old place.

The next morning, around 7 AM Dr. Henry drove up and brought along two of his sons. The Vet, a big hulk of a man, stood close to seven feet tall and must have weighed 250 pounds. The two teenagers were equally hefty and quite tall for their ages. And they were so polite it was a pleasure to talk with them!

The men, including the two boys and Tommy, checked the yearlings and diagnosed Shipping Fever and signs of pneumonia. After only a brief analysis the Vet told us, "That bunch of cattle you just bought at the auction were already sick. They, in turn, infected your herd. We have to give all of them a shot of serum—today. Let's get started."

Luckily, the Vet had all the supplies with him. They worked fast and furiously injecting as many as possible before dinner, which is served at noon in the country. I prepared and served a huge meal, knowing those big boys and the Vet were not used to small helpings.

The cattle work was finished and all the guys came into the warm kitchen late in the afternoon. "It is brutal out there," one of the boys said while his teeth chattered like castanets. It was only 4 PM and it looked as if the day was coming to an end already.

Before the Vet left, he gave us our instructions, "Let all the cattle out, leave only the very sick ones in the barns. This disease spreads from one animal to another if they are kept close together. You might still lose a couple more." And so they left. We hoped for the best. We faced the next morning with concern, but were relieved when only one more yearling died during the night. The rest survived and thrived.

Thanksgiving was coming and we were invited to the folks in Denver. But, the weather was not cooperative and another blizzard tormented every living being. We were forced to stay at home. Since we had no turkey for the traditional meal, we substituted a freshly butchered chicken and I fried tons of potato pancakes. Home canned applesauce spruced up the latter. The family enjoyed this simple meal so much that Bonnie remarked, "We should have a blizzard every Thanksgiving"! I gave them the biggest smile I could muster...it was like receiving the 'Good Housekeeping Seal of Approval'!

Susan was an exceptionally good four-year old. Only once do I remember that she lied and I gave her a pat on the behind. The indignation was too great—she cried. I always stressed to the children the importance of honesty. I'll never forget my mother's remark she made when I was a youngster, "The best thing about telling the truth is that you don't have to remember what you said." Makes sense.

With Thanksgiving out of the way the next project was to make cookies and fruit cakes for the upcoming holidays. I had plenty of help from the girls and by afternoon the entire kitchen table was covered with oatmeal cookies, ginger snaps, sand tarts, and pecan cookies.

A few days later, the three of us measured and mixed ingredients and greased pans to bake our traditional fruit cakes and date/nut loaves. Later, we made candy. Peanut brittle was the children's favorite, then truffles and fudge. We didn't have much money but we surely ate well.

There were two more things to be done before the year ended. One was to have John Snider spray our cattle for lice and grubs. He was an outgoing, friendly person who always seemed to be in a good mood and never complained about anything or anybody. We only saw him a couple of times a year and when he said he would be at the ranch at 7 AM, he was there at 7 sharp. Fred, always a stickler for punctuality, too, and always had gathered the cattle hours before John was expected.

When the green, rattly, old Ford truck pulled up at our place John would get out to make sure he had enough water in the tank in back of his truck. He used a strong solution of DDT to mix with the water. In later years, government regulations ordered him to use something else. He would then drive up to the corral and unfold several yards of hose with a spray handle on the end to control the flow of the spray. The cattle loved the cool water on their hot bodies in the summer, but in the winter they tried to avoid it, but couldn't because we used a small corral with gates tightly closed so they couldn't escape.

Several times I rode with John in his truck to the next location where another bunch of our cattle was waiting for the wet treatment. Getting into the truck on the rider's side took some time. Poor messy John cleared an area which was covered with rags, papers, small empty boxes, small full boxes, and tools. Eventually, and after he exclaimed, "Gee, I've been looking for this," there was a space a few inches wide, showing a light grey seat cover. I weighed slightly more than 100 pounds and fit perfectly into the niche.

One time, while Fred was making out his check, John told us, "You know, I never have any trouble collecting from ranchers, but it is different when I spray trees for the Broadmoor crowd. They are so rich they don't realize I need the money."

Country people had a good reputation. On one particular shopping trip to J.C. Penney's in Colorado Springs I bought six pairs of socks and handed my check to the clerk who was being trained by her supervisor. The trainee asked for an ID but before I had a chance to retrieve my driver's license, the supervisor interrupted saying, "Let me see the check," and immediately added, "anybody from the country is OK. You don't need to ask for an ID." I was proud that I belonged to such a highly respected group.

The second job to be done before the end of the year was to butcher chickens. In one day, we slaughtered ten hens and twenty-five roosters which were taken to the Calhan freezer locker. The house smelled of wet chickens for days and occasionally, a feather or two powered by a sudden draft would flutter around as if it were alive. It descended soon to another place unless a certain housewife would snatch it in midair and dispose of it.

It had been a good year and we were grateful that ranch life had been so satisfying!

Chapter 7

OUR SECOND RANCH

The Vorenberg Ranch

March 1959 was here and we finally were moving onto our new ranch. The 'Old Place' cost us $28,000 plus $2,000 for oil rights and was a total of 1,440 acres. By contrast, the Buckner Ranch cost us $50,000 for 1,600 acres, making us the proud owners of 3,040 acres. It was 2-1/2 miles between the houses and we were ll-1/2 miles from Calhan, and on the southern most border of the Calhan School District. A school bus would pick up the children and take them to school in Calhan.

Moving into our new place was work but it was also joyful. Friends helped us with the heavy items and before long we sat down to a meatloaf dinner I had prepared the day before. By late afternoon everything was in place, beds were made and we could relax a bit. The kids were excited, running in and out of their rooms. Everyone was talking and telling of what they liked best. Nobody asked me so I volunteered, "I like the clean, WHITE water!!"

"Now, for the first time we can wear white clothes!" was Bonnie's quick reply. How true!

The new house was made of cement blocks covered with plaster and painted white with green wooden shingles on the roof. The large windows were trimmed in green. There was an enclosed porch onto which we put our dependable Maytag washer. The kitchen had plenty of cupboards and storage spaces and the living room was quite large. There were three bedrooms and, best of all, a bathroom. What luxury!

A few days after we moved, we received a $10 check from Aunt Blanche who wanted it to be used for an 'occasional chair for our new house.' At once, I knew how to use the money. I'd buy the dreamy, black, pearl-like toilet seat I'd recently seen in J.C. Penney's. So, a few days later Fred ceremoniously ripped off the old white one and put on my beautiful 'occasional chair.' I treated it with great respect and, like a full-fledged idiot, I showed it off to everyone who came to visit. They probably thought I was totally deranged!

We cherished our new telephone. Calls to Calhan were free, but our nearby neighbors in Rush and Yoder were considered 'long distance.' The phone was on a party line which we shared with five other customers. The lines were strung between wooden poles alongside the roads and during storms they would produce loud static noises or be blown down altogether. Several years later, the lines were buried underground which solved the problem. To us, it didn't matter, at least, because we now had a phone!

From the porch, steps led down to a full unfinished basement with a cement floor. In its southeast corner was a crudely partitioned area where a coal furnace was located with large ducts to deliver heat to the rooms, a most welcome feeling during Colorado's fierce winter weather. Close by the furnace was a place for the coal. Above this bin was a

155

window through which the black lumps were dumped. In those days, when coal was in demand, a ton would only cost $20, delivered! On the west side of the basement were plenty of shelves which stood empty, waiting for summer and fall when fruit and vegetables would be canned.

Very early the first morning in the new house a horrible noise ripped me from a state of unconsciousness. "What in the world—and it's only 5 AM. Where is that racket coming from?" Now, fully awake, I realized Fred was not in bed. I threw on my robe and ventured carefully out of the bedroom. This event of uncertainty and fear reduced me to a quivering mass of Jell-O. And suddenly there was the same noise, but now I realized it came from the basement. I rushed down the steps and found Fred roughly pulling the shaker back and forth to clean out the furnace of yesterday's burned coal.

"What are you doing up so early?" asked my surprised husband, "I was going to let you sleep late this morning." 'Sleeping late' meant 6 AM! Without another word, I turned and retraced my steps back to the still warm bed, snuggled into a fetal position and daydreamed of a world where well dressed servants tended to my every wish, money was never heard of and the weather was always gorgeous. The house, with many bathrooms, was located in a pristine forest and surrounded by plenty of obedient dogs.

Ring!!! Darn that alarm clock! It must be 6 AM and my wonderful dream, yet unfinished, was rudely interrupted by an inanimate, unfeeling black object ticking happily away, much too close to my head. It seemed to reprimand me with each tick, "Get up you lazy thing, you wanted to be a rancher's wife, didn't you?"

The house was warm now thanks to the coal furnace and my ambitious husband. I stepped outside. The cool air caressed my cheeks. It was still quite chilly at nights even though it was spring. The animals didn't seem to mind, but once the sun appeared they would lie down and stretch their limbs while gazing into the bright rays. A soft breeze danced about making the view towards Pikes Peak so clear, you could almost count the spruce trees. This was Colorado, the state I fell in love with. The state, I swore, I would never leave after I arrived here in 1946.

Later that day I decided to explore the surroundings of our new home. Immediately north of the house was a dilapidated root cellar. It must have been 6 x 6 x 6 and was covered with a heavy wooden lid. It had been used to store potatoes, carrots and other root crops. As it turned out, I never once went down into that dark hole!

Farther north was a large two-car garage and chicken house, both made of cement blocks and wood shingled roofs. They were painted white and green to match the house and barns. The garage was large enough for two vehicles and a place for tools of different sizes. The chicken house had plenty of windows to the south. Small boards against one wall served as a resting/sleeping area where chickens would balance themselves on one leg while the other one was drawn up against their warm body. Eight empty boxes were nailed against another wall for the birds to deposit their eggs.

To the west of the garage was the outhouse in the same color scheme. Though we had a bathroom in the house, this privy came in mighty handy for our large family who was by now all too comfortable with outdoor accommodations. This outhouse was not as

Our new, modern, ranch house.

architecturally interesting as the one on the Old Place, but it served its purpose. It was pitch-dark inside because no one had bothered to carve a half moon into the door.

Right behind the privy was what we called, 'the forest,' an acre full of trees, bushes, and shrubs. In this lush expanse of different shades of green were cottonwood trees, lilac trees, crabapple trees, and many choke cherry bushes. Years later, the children earned money by picking the fruit. They were paid all of a penny and way up to 5 cents for a gallon of the small berries. Some of the trees welcomed us, their new owners, with full bloom, while others had already leafed out. We also noticed wild onions, garlic, and asparagus peeping up among the tree trunks. In one corner, stood a lone apricot tree which showed tiny green fruit. During all the years we lived on this ranch we were able to harvest lovely, sweet fruit only three times. It seemed, while in full bloom, a strong cold wind or a snowstorm would interrupt the growth and thus end my longing for home grown apricots for yet another year.

My 'inspection' led me towards a feed storage shed north of the house, to a large two-story barn, and east of the house to another large barn, painted white with the same green wood shingles. It was an eight-cow milk barn and a feed room—all nice and clean. Between the latter and the house stood a windmill. By turning a couple of valves it would pump water either into an underground cistern for house use or to the tanks in the corrals for the animals.

To the south of the house was a cement porch along with several wild yellow roses and a large cottonwood tree in an area which would become our front yard. Beyond it was a gravel road which soon became known as the Vorenberg Road.

We all felt we had moved up by owning this new ranch and we deeply appreciated the differences between the primitive 'Old Place' and the more sophisticated new one. I used to say that "we really started at the bottom" and that as a city person I survived through some extremely tough, challenging years. We felt it would be easier from then on. After all, we had a decent house, a bathroom and lots of clear, white water. Life was getting better! 🐂

My Mother, Melanie, visits to see the new ranch.

Getting Settled On Our New Ranch

Living on this new ranch was good for our psyche—at least mine. No longer did we have to explain to visitors that not having a phone was all right when we had neighbors who let us use theirs. As far as the outdoor john, the pride of the Old Place was concerned, well, I didn't mind accompanying some people after dark to the mystical 'abode' even when the flashlight I was carrying attracted all sorts of flying insects. I had to assure my frightened and squealing visitors that in all those years we had endured and survived attacks of flies, gnats, mosquitoes, millers, and other moths. All this talk didn't help the by now frightened company, but it surely sped up the duration and lessened the frequency of the outhouse visitations. No longer was this necessary. This was past history and nobody enjoyed these improvements more than I did.

We did need a few things for the dining/living room, so the same week of our move we took off for Colorado Springs and a store known for their inexpensive furniture.

Since we had put about 100 acres of farmland into the Soil Bank program we had some extra cash. Actually, we received $1,398.75 per year for ten years. The government wanted to take cropland out of production and thus rewarded farmers with hard cash. A lot of city people were against this, stating, "The U.S. pays farmers to do nothing!"

Anyway, we arrived at the Chicago Factory Outlet Store, a huge Quonset building away from downtown in an area near a creek and surrounded by huge cottonwood trees.

As we entered we not only noticed furniture, but dishes, utensils, even televisions. There seemed to be no limit on their selection. Everything in stock was new merchandise. The salesperson explained that things could be bought any time, but once a week certain items would go on auction. We stored this information in our memory and planned to return on some Wednesday, the magic day, should we need something again. But for now we purchased a beige Naugahyde couch which could be opened up into a regular-sized double bed. When used as a couch, the backrest sported an imprint of a proud looking Indian head surrounded by a half dozen feathers.

Next, we bought a soft brown rocking chair, also Naugahyde, a brown table and six matching chairs with yellow plastic seats for the dinning room. Also, three small side tables, and finally four pairs of paper drapes at 98 cents each for the living room windows. Those had pictures of green temples from somewhere in Asia, on white background. At the time I thought they were quite pretty! The sales ticket for these items came to $268.26 and included delivery to the ranch thirty-five miles away.

The delivery was made a couple of days later. Gone was the memory of that ugly and dark living room on the Old Place. Now, the huge windows invited light and sun to cheer us. It seemed as if invisible chains had suddenly disappeared and a sense of freedom enveloped our very being.

Next, we needed a pick-up truck, something we should have had a long time ago. Since the jalopy (Chevy coupe) had a huge trunk we transported all sorts of items in it, even an occasional baby calf. But the necessity for a pickup was definitely increasing and Fred found an old one for sale. Soon, my proud husband drove up in the rickety vehicle grinning from ear to ear, "I'm just trying it out. It's cheap. I'll probably buy it, you can't get a pickup for less money." It cost $200 and was ten years old.

I looked at it, disappointed that Fred thought so much of this 'thing' which grunted and groaned while idling. But it was its color which really turned me against it. Purple, honest-to-goodness purple! Not knowing anything about cars or trucks, I offered no advice and instead christened that machine 'Purple passion.' I knew Fred was going to buy this historical masterpiece because the price and the word "cheap" were classical music to my man's ears.

The time came when we were discussing buying a clothes dryer for the coming winter. The four clothes lines north of the house were fine and I used them regularly but in cold weather the minute I would hang things on those lines, they would freeze into grotesque shapes only to defrost after spreading them out around the furnace in the basement. And now, we were on the Vorenberg ranch and we hoped for something better—a dryer.

We noticed when we bought our furniture at the Chicago Factory Outlet that the price of dryers was as reasonable as everything else they sold. "Why don't you go to town and buy a dryer, today." I was shocked when I heard this question/demand. I did not like making purchases like that by myself. My normally low self-esteem would not allow me to make decisions of this caliber, and before I could answer, I heard in disbelief, "And you can pick up a couple of baby calves at the Sales Barn on Nob Hill." Today is sales day.

A deep breath—or was it a sigh—was followed by several more and slowly I decided what I had heard myself thinking so often in the past: you married a rancher! It was time for me to realize as his wife, my obligations were not only to run a decent household but also to help out in the business of ranching whenever a need or emergency arose. The wife's duty, according to some of my neighbors, also included having his babies, preferably boys, and keeping him happy—in bed and out.

"And while you are at the store, see if they sell paint. I need five gallons of white outdoor."

"Anything else?" I asked sarcastically disbelieving that I actually agreed to all of this.

"No, you go alone, I'll take care of the kids. I'll gas up the pickup for you." I felt like saying, 'Let's not go overboard with kindness,' but I said nothing, changed into clean jeans and a T-shirt, made sure I had my checkbook and driver's license and was off.

The 'Purple Passion' did not let me down even though it made unpleasant noises. I parked close to the store, entered full of confidence and strode towards the clothes dryer and washing machine department. There was only one (large) dryer. "Goody," I thought, "I won't have to make any decision here which one to choose!" I asked the salesman all sorts of unimportant questions trying to impress him with make-believe intelligence and in less than ten minutes, I was making out the check. There was no, "Let me see some I.D., a driver's license, or whatever proof you have that you are honest and have money in the bank." People trusted people. They loaded up the Norge and the paint and I headed for the Sales Barn.

Never before had I bought calves on my own, so this was scary. I hoped I would understand the auctioneer and that I would stop bidding when the price got too high. I was really scared. "I'd rather give a patient an enema than do this. At least I would know what to do," I kept telling myself as I entered the noisy, smelly, and very crowded building.

Finding an empty place next to some guy who was guzzling a Coke, I tried to act like just another female cattle buyer. The man started a conversation but before he finished his sentence a pipe-organ-like belch came from his bearded mouth, hitting my face with such force that droplets of Coke landed onto it. He did not apologize, only said, "Every time I drink Coke this happens."

Luckily, the sale progressed. They just finished auctioning off a saddle and some tack. Then, a couple of goats entered the ring. Next it was time for calves. I knew Fred wanted Holstein bull calves, so I sweated while they brought in some white face calves and a white shorthorn. Eventually, a young cowboy pushed in a lone calf, the kind I hoped to buy, and I bid on him. I wasn't even sure whether I bought him but the auctioneer soon asked for my name. The next calf entered and I also bid on him. I had my two calves, I paid, and a man loaded them into the Purple Passion behind the Norge and the paint. I felt proud of my accomplishment. Much later, about a week or so, a neighbor of ours who had seen me reported to Fred what a professional cattle buyer I was and how proud he must be of me! Actually I felt quite proud of myself that day.

I left the Sales Barn and headed towards Highway 24 when the police suddenly began stopping all the cars. I tried to figure out what was going on. Imagine my surprise when a fancy black limousine with two small U.S. flags on its front fenders slowly entered the intersection. In the back seat sat a person whom I recognized as President Eisenhower. At once, for some reason, I waved to him and he waved back to me giving me the biggest grin only this President could produce. Several other cars followed him and then they were gone. I found out later that they had arrived at Peterson Fields military airport and were on their way to the graduation at the Air Force Academy, north of Colorado Springs.

This turned out to be an all-around exciting day for me. I learned a lot, conquered a great fear and was rewarded. I was one step closer to being a real ranch wife. 🐎

Memorial Hospital

The cattle business was calamitous one year, and our bank, the Cattleman's Credit Association, was downright uncooperative. Ranchers and farmers tried different ways to keep their heads above water. This remark is a joke in a way, for a very severe drought had hit us. In fact the pastures never even greened up in the spring. Some people thought the grass was dead. Grama grass, a drought resistant plant, was the grass of choice in these parts of east central Colorado. It had a reputation of unbelievable survival. A few drops of moisture was all it needed to return it to vigorous growth and bright green color.

Another problem with the persistent dry weather was the many cacti which suddenly appeared like magic from out of nowhere, showing off their beautiful blossoms of soft, waxy, yellow and purple. They crowded out the grass so nobody wanted them in their pasture.

These were the times when ranchers needed to feed their livestock hay, an added expense. We turned once again to farmers on the Western Slope of Colorado who supplied us with their expensive feed. They always seemed to have a bumper crop due to their very snowy winters.

Instead of buying feed, some ranchers, opted to sell all or part of their livestock herds. Others got jobs in the city and some even sold their ranches. The banks wanted their money and their demands were draconian.

We were no different. We decided I should get a nursing job in Colorado Springs. I went to Memorial Hospital and was hired on the spot for an opening in Geriatrics. I was pleased with the assignment.

The next day, after a restless night, I was full of excitement and happy anticipation as I put on my uniform from years ago. Nursing was in my blood, I always loved it. In fact, whenever I would dress in duty clothes, my whole attitude changed. I became outgoing, fully assure of myself. A friend of mine once told me, "You have more hang ups than a walk-in closet." Well, there were no hang-ups now, and I felt great.

Once at the hospital, it was 6:35 AM, things looked and smelled familiar. We had the morning report from the night nurse and I realized soon that the patients still were the same while the medications and treatments had drastically changed. I had to learn a lot in a hurry. I was assigned four patients, ending a twelve-year absence from my beloved profession.

One morning, I arrived at the usual time, 6:45 AM and saw one of my patients walking the hall. I approached her, saying, "Mrs. Smith (not her real name) you look lovely this morning." And before I knew it, a swift blow from her right hand struck the right side of my face, sending my white, starched nurse's cap onto the floor.

Before continuing down the hall, she said, loud enough for all to hear, "You liar, you know I look awful!"

I knew better than to get angry at her, knowing that she had psychological problems and had outbursts with other nurses before, I took it in stride and dismissed the whole event.

When her doctor arrived that morning I jokingly told him what had happened earlier, at which time he replied, "Let's send her back to her nursing home, she's well enough to go." She returned to the home that afternoon. I kind of missed her as she really was a sweet lady when she was in a better mood.

Weeks later, the head nurse called me to the telephone. It was Fred. He was in Colorado Springs, at the doctor's office. "What happened?" I inquired anxiously. "I'll tell you about it later. Don't worry. I have Jack with me. We are both okay."

The two words: "Don't worry," means nothing when it concerns a visit to a doctor by your husband and 1-1/2 half year-old son. I worried all afternoon.

When I got home at 4:15 PM, I found Fred with his left thumb in a splint. Then he told me, "I was milking the cow when she got restless and started jumping around. I grabbed the milk bucket. She slipped and fell and my thumb got caught between the handle and the bucket. I knew right away it was broken and I also knew I had better see an orthopedist. So, I went to the house, changed clothes and put a fresh diaper on Jack. Something upset the baby and he cried, even after we got into the pick up. By the time I drove to Ellicott he hadn't stopped fussing. I then asked the lady who worked in the grocery store to figure out what could be causing his continuous wails. She looked him over and immediately noticed the problem. "You pinned the diaper to his skin!" The lady then re-pinned it and the boy stopped crying. I felt really guilty. My thumb hurt and it bled through the make shift bandage. I'm okay now, got to go back and see the Doc in a week. That's all." Everything eventually turned out well—at least, until sometime the following winter when more excitement happened.

After a busy day at the hospital, I did some fast grocery shopping and headed for home. It started snowing just outside of Colorado Springs and I wondered how the weather was at home. I decided to take a chance instead of staying at the Nurses Home.

By the time I arrived in Ellicott, the highway looked like Upper Siberia and felt just as cold. I stopped at our friend's house, the Dickinsons, to call Fred so he could be on the lookout for me. He told me, "I'll be at the corner with the jeep. We can leave the car there overnight. All the roads are closing up with snowdrifts. See you later, alligator!"

Fred was in a good mood. I felt differently but drove off into the snowy night feeling hopeful. Snowflakes danced violently in front of the headlights. It almost made me dizzy.

After driving about thirty miles an hour, I arrived on our corner and reliable Fred was there in the jeep. We transferred all the food I had bought earlier. Next, we piled into the jeep, my white stockinged legs stiff from the cold. A few moments later, we were at the house unloading groceries. It was now 6 PM.

The wind blew all night long but every time we checked the snow had quit. Lucky for me, I thought, I had to go to work soon.

The next morning came much too soon. I was dead tired, the wind had stopped and it was dark as any night might be. The stars were out, winking mischievously at us while Fred tried to start the jeep. The darned engine refused to turn over despite Fred's cajoling and cursing.

"Look what I found in the jeep," he called to me, carrying a ten pound sack of potatoes. "I bet they are frozen. We didn't see them last night when we emptied the jeep. By the way, the only way you can get to the car is by horseback."

This was not the first time I had to opt for four-legged transportation. I returned to the bedroom and put on thermal underwear bottoms. I folded my uniform, put my white shoes and purse into a backpack and mounted the horse who was not too crazy about taking an old lady down a snow packed country road. Fred rode his horse and together we arrived at the corner where the car was parked.

Fred awaits with my ever-dependable taxi for my commute to work.

It was now sunrise and what we saw in front of us nearly scared us to death. By the car was an area about a foot wide of bright red snow. "Something must have bled here, a rabbit or something. Maybe we ran over an animal last night." And then we noticed it—a broken glass bottle, originally filled with ketchup, which must have dropped out of a damp paper sack. A hearty laugh did us good! I got in the car which started at once, and was off while Fred rode home leading my horse.

A few weeks later I was transferred to the Intensive Care Unit which was open only on weekdays, giving me the weekends off. A nice change. The winter had been so miserable that the hospital president offered me lodging in the Nurses Home for a fee of $10 per week and Fred and I agreed to accept this. Traveling was often difficult and the hospital wanted to be certain that they could depend on my being on duty.

One Friday, Fred called me at work, "I got two sick kids and I'm coming into town in the Jeep. Both Susan and Jack have earaches. I'll meet you at the hospital after the doctor sees the kids."

It had been a light day with few patients as most surgeons performed their operations in the beginning of the week. Patients would spend some time in Intensive Care until they recovered from the anesthesia and were stable. Then they would be returned to their rooms.

It was close to quitting time, 3 PM. The last patient had been moved to his room. I counted the narcotic pills and wrote the report which had to be delivered to the nursing office. With all my tasks done, I was ready to leave for the weekend.

My family was waiting for me downstairs at the main entrance. The children didn't seem too sick but Fred looked terribly tired. It was then when I found out that the two little ones cried most of the night with earaches and Fred took them both to bed with him. The doctor had given them something to feel better and Fred had already picked up their prescriptions at the drugstore. "Let's go home," I said, and everybody agreed. "Who wants to ride with me in the car?" Susan and Jack came with me; Tommy and Bonnie went with Fred.

The trip on Highway 94 was uneventful but when we turned north onto Calhan Highway things changed drastically. Even though the snowplow had moved the snow to each side of the road, the wind had blown most of it back to the center again. When Fred had left earlier that day he had to drive through the pasture and it looked like we would have to do it again.

At the four mile corner on Calhan Highway, Tommy opened two wire gates and closed them both after the car and the jeep were inside the pasture. Fred decided to drive the car and Tommy got the honor of driving the jeep. A few minutes later the car got stuck in a hole filled with snow. Regardless what Fred did, he could not move it. Meanwhile, Tommy with his only passenger, Bonnie, was driving along over bumps at a pretty good clip, neither giving us a second thought nor a quick look to see whether we were coming. Here we sat, in the middle of a pasture, the weather turning sour again. Fog was now spreading its misty white wings like a blanket over the entire neighborhood. Somebody said, "Let's get out and walk home, it can't be that far!"

"No way," I remarked in a hurry. "They'll come back when they realize we weren't following them."

It was a little scary. We turned on the headlights of the car so our rescuers could see us as the fog and snow became thicker.

"I think I see something," both Fred and I blurted out at the same time. The two kids in the jeep were searching for us and Fred started honking the horn. "Push that sucker some more," I encouraged Fred, and he did. They heard us.

The jeep stopped, Tommy's head popped through the open door. "Do you want me to pull your car?"

Fred's answer was quick and emphatic, "No we are all getting into the jeep with you. The weather is getting worse by the minute."

So all six of us squeezed into the vehicle while Tommy did the driving. He felt important having rescued his family. The ride was uncomfortable—everybody sat on somebody's lap—but we arrived safely at home.

We made no attempt to get the car before Sunday when the weather cleared up enough so we could see where we were driving. It was easy to attach a long chain between the jeep and the car. One hard pull and the car was out of the hole and now Fred was able to drive the rest of the way home.

The two patients, Susan and Jack, recovered fast. Our road was opened by the county's snowplow, Sunday night. And Monday morning at six o'clock sharp, I was heading back to Colorado Springs and Memorial Hospital until Friday when I would return home for another weekend.

Smart or Dumb

When people found out that we owned a ranch, they would often ask which animals were the smartest and which were the dumbest. Being an animal lover, this was a difficult question to answer. I told them about the intelligent things my dogs did, how Topsey used her 'horse sense', and how often the cows showed their intuition. Even though I've heard tales of dumb sheep, I found it just 'ain't so.' After we had accumulated a band of different breeds, our sheep often showed more common sense than some people. The animals became my friends and sometimes I would just spend time with them in their corral and shed. I delivered many lambs and cared for them and their mother's health. Sheep became my favorite ranch animals. They seemed to know what I was thinking and feeling. They anticipated the weather better than any of our other animals and seemed to have a sense of compassion for each other, for the dogs, and for me. They were far from dumb!

As far as smart animals were concerned, ranchers felt that burros were the winners. Our good friend and neighbor, Gret, owned a couple of them. She told us that when a donkey, or burro gets tired it would stop and nothing can move it. Compared to the horse—who will work, even when tired, until it drops. Gret said that her burros would not venture far from their shed when there was an approaching storm—snow or rain.

One afternoon, during the summer, the whole family was outdoors playing ball. Even Lady, our lovely collie dog, was enjoying herself trying to steal the ball away. She was successful at times and would take off, the ball firmly between her teeth. The kids would chase behind her and eventually she would drop it and her game was over—until the next time.

Lady was protective with all the children. She didn't like for them to fight whether make-believe or real. One memorable day, as it happens with children, there was a disagreement and Tommy uttered some 'choice' words. Fred heard it and warned him, but he continued. With more speed than I had seen Fred use in some time, he started after him, intent to impress on his bottom that such words were not allowed in our family. He never made it—Lady jumped on Fred's back forcing him to stop the pursuit. A mighty surprised father just stood there and laughed as did the children. Yes, Lady had again stopped a fight, not realizing or caring whether it was real or make-believe.

In the bird population there also were degrees of smart and dumb. The sad thing is that they all are the owners of 'bird brains!' Chickens, for example, seemed to have a hard time recognizing their owners. We would enter their chicken house and even though we would be in the chicken house several times a day, they would fly around, hitting the windows, running into corners and screaming what sounded like sounds of their impending death! They never learned that we really only wanted their eggs!

The geese, at a young age, became our pseudo-watchdogs and I was their 'Mother Goose'. They followed me everywhere and would often snuggle up to me. This was indeed a sure sign of intelligence! Then, of course, they enjoyed chasing everybody else, including Fred, whom they never recognized as part of the family!

The champions of all the 'bird brains' were the turkeys. The poor things come into this world with absolute zero, zilch, nada of brains. It is a wonder they grew up at all! We decided to raise turkeys one year because, after all, they are delicious when you pull them out of the oven, producing "oh's and ah's" from the guests as they grace the Thanksgiving table. We bought ten 2-day old turkeys, called poults, for $1 apiece. I placed them in a box with a light bulb above, to supply warmth and light. The moment it got dark the poults, as do all chicks, crowded into a corner to sleep. They had to be encouraged to eat and drink and only take short naps. We placed special feed into an easily reached dish into which we placed a couple of shiny marbles. Turkey poults like bright objects. They will pick at them and 'accidentally' get a beakful of grain. You had to try different tricks to teach them to eat.

Lady adopts a new friend.

Next, we also added a couple of baby food cans filled with water. To give them special care, we brought them into the living room so we could keep an eye on them during the night and listen to their happy sing-song. I got ready for bed and returned to the box about ten minutes later for a final good night. To my horror, one poult had already drowned. There he was with his head in the can of water and his fanny facing the ceiling! That never happened when we raised baby chicks. The next day, we rushed out and bought a special water dish just for turkey chicks so this couldn't happen again.

Poults apparently love to die and a few months later, only six remained. It was summertime and they were allowed to run outdoors during the day so they spent a great deal of time chasing after what must be a delicacy to turkeys, grasshoppers. One particular day, we were doing the neighbors' chores when a sudden thunderstorm surprised us and dumped at least a half inch of wonderful rain into the ever-dry soil. When we returned home, we were startled to find our six turkeys completely soaked to the skin and looking miserable. They stood humped over in the middle of the driveway. Why these 'bird brains' never ran for shelter, of which there was plenty, was something we never figured out. After toweling each one dry and rubbing their chilled bodies, they recuperated and to my amazement, thrived, and grew strong and big.

Whether smart or dumb, animals can't do anything about it. They cope and do the best they can with what they have. People are here to care for them and animals, in turn, show friendship and devotion far beyond their brain power.

Picnic

e always enjoyed picnics with our friends and relatives. Eating a meal outdoors is invigorating and stimulating and regardless where we happened to have the picnic and with whom, it put everyone in a relaxed and pleasant mood.

Soon, after we moved to the main ranch, Fred built a long picnic table with two equally long benches. I painted them a bright green and purchased an oil cloth with red and white checks to make everything look cheerful.

The yard was delightful for picnics. We placed the table and benches under a big cottonwood tree. On each side were lilac bushes and several pine trees. Facing the house, you could see flower beds overflowing with marigolds, zinnias, and hollyhocks highlighting the four steps up to the house. The last two weeks of unseasonable warm weather had brought the flowers to full bloom.

Our first picnic guests were the Fred Goldsmiths. I had met him after I moved to Denver and we dated quite a few times, going to movies and even ice skating at City Park. It was through this Fred that I met 'my' Fred who became my husband nine months later. Imagine my surprise when I found out that both Freds came from the same area in Germany and knew each other there! Fred Goldsmith married Bernice, a Chicagoan. I liked her right away. They eventually became the parents of two daughters.

The day was perfect for a picnic. It was unusually warm. The kids wore their shorts for the first time this season. They were excited and kept looking down the road in hopes of seeing our friends' car. Our guests arrived and it was good to see them again. Bernice helped me carry out the food and we all sat down on the hard benches. The sun trickled through the leaves and onto us. It felt good to be having a picnic this early in the year, knowing there were yet quite a few chilly days coming.

The meal was tasty: fried chicken, potato salad, sliced tomatoes on a bed of lettuce, and fire-engine-red Jell-O with peaches. For drinks, there was a choice of iced tea and red Kool-Aid. To make it easy for myself, I served the food on paper plates and cups.

Everyone's plate was filled with the colorful food when, a sudden, strong gust of wind, came out of the west and blew with such force that Bernice's plate was upended, landing on her chest and falling into her lap. What a calamity! I expected to see her very annoyed and upset because her white blouse had turned into one with a red design and was dripping strawberry Kool-Aid. Instead, Bernice sat there laughing so hard she almost cried! What a wonderful attitude! Her reaction was contagious and none of us could keep a straight face while I helped our guest scrape off the food, most of which by now had accumulated in her lap. We both went in the house, where I planned to loan her one of my blouses. Jokingly, Bernice asked for a red one, just in case it would get windy again! When we returned to the table I noticed that everybody was holding onto their plates, just in case.

We laughed because we always seemed to have food problems whenever we got together. The last time the Goldsmiths invited us to their home Bernice had offered us a cup of coffee. Imagine everyone's surprise when only boiling water poured from the percolator. Yes, she had forgotten to add the coffee. We always laughed about it.

It was during that visit when the Goldsmiths had shown us their new Sunbeam electric blanket, told us how it worked, and raved about its warmth. We were convinced and we bought our own a few weeks afterward. As far as I am concerned, an electric blanket is the best invention since the wheel. There is nothing my cold feet appreciate more! I have been known to take it on all my trips, much to Fred's chagrin.

Meanwhile, the food on the table began to disappear and as a host you like to see guests enjoy your cuisine. The conversation never seemed to slow down and we laughed a lot. You couldn't help it. Bernice was such an effervescent person. After the picnic, they asked to see the sheep, of which I was especially proud. Here it was late spring and all our ewes had their lambs. Most of which were twins and one set of triplets. Since sheep only have two faucets, as the kids called them, the weakest or smallest of the three were pushed away from the udder and would have starved had it not been fed separately. Therefore, the littlest lamb got his milk from a baby bottle every few hours, day and night.

While our city friends were looking at the sheep they noticed a baby lamb nursing a ewe. "What's the matter with that baby's wool?" I explained that we were trying to have the ewe adopt this lamb. Hers had died at birth, so we cut off its hide and slipped it over the healthy one's body. Our hope was that when the mother checked the scent of her lamb to make sure it is hers, she would get fooled and accept the lamb as her own. After a few days the hide would be removed and, hopefully, the ewe and lamb will have bonded. This old trick was used on many different kinds of animals and it worked almost every time.

As we left the sheep pen we went for a short walk and later sat around visiting. The Goldsmiths returned numerous times.

The Colorado summers do not last long and you must make the best of them so we had many more picnics, with or without company. September is the cut-off date for picnics. The entertainment moves inside, but it can't hold a candle to a good picnic. 🐴

The King Of Implements

On everyone's ranch, baling wire has the distinction of being 'King.' There is no way of running the business without it. I learned this soon after I became a ranch wife when my first, and only, husband asked me to get some wire so he could tighten a fence. I had no idea what he was talking about. In my prior city life, wire hardly ever crossed my path and when it did, I didn't pay any attention to it.

A combine, a clumsy machine which picks up mowed hay in the field, squashes it, and presses it into a cylinder, uses baling wire. Two wires come from within the machine, wrap themselves around each bunch of hay and—voila—a bale, 60 pounds or more, is tightly secured and ready to be picked up by a gloved hand. Bales are gathered and placed in large stacks in locations near corrals. At feeding time, the hay bales are taken down and thrown into feeders as a whole or are divided into flakes and fed separately to cattle, sheep, and horses.

After its duty with hay is completed, every strand of wire is recycled because it then takes on its role as an 'implement' which Webster Dictionary calls "a tool, essential to the performance or execution of something." Indeed, baling wire is a farm 'implement' as important as any tractor! On a ranch, not a day goes by when baling wire is not called into service for some unique task.

The 'King of the Implements' can withstand rain, snow, frost, and heat, stays fairly pliable in all kinds of weather and has dependable strength. But it does rust.

The storage and care of baling wire has no set rules. As the wires are removed from the bales some folks, especially the ones in a hurry, simply toss the loose strands towards any designated resting place, while the rest of the ranchers fold each one into a neat 'package'. Then they throw them into a large and always unruly pile often located in a corner outside a barn or in abandoned root cellars, empty drums, or barrels. Wherever the wires are assembled, they are ready for their next job, that of repairing or temporarily holding together anything that has come apart.

One time in the midst of a heavy snowstorm, Fred asked me to help separating some calves in the big corral. He wanted the younger ones in a more protected area and he yelled for me to open the north gate. I ran there, following the boss' order, and found that the top hook on the gate was missing. In its place was, you guessed it, baling wire. Though I tugged, pulled, and attempted to un-twist it, nothing would budge. I was wearing men's work gloves that were several sizes too big for my hands and my fingers were stiff from the cold, so despite my intense will power and clumsy efforts, I was unable to move the unattractive fastener.

Fred's impatience got the better of him and he shouted, "What's the problem?" He at once came running and with his bare hands removed the wire telling me, "The hook fell off the other day and I haven't had time to fix it. The wire will work for now."

To which I answered, "I hate this inefficiency!"—Not the first, nor the last time I used this exclamation.

I am also certain there are many more uses of bailing wire not yet invented—always coming in handy and able to save the day! Yes indeed, the implement survives.
Long live the King! 🐎

Chapter 8

NEVER A DULL MOMENT

It's A Strange World: Satan?

Both the journalists and the neighbors snickered at the news. They didn't believe it. We didn't either. Satanism? Oh, come on now!

Why were bright lights seen in area pastures? Why was blood spilled on the ground with the nearby cattle dead, their sex organs severed? What was going on? So many questions...What was the reason for this strange phenomenon? Was it a cult? Were we being visited by a spaceship?

Nobody had answers. Some folks believed that the deaths were due to Satan worship. Others tried to forget about it, but couldn't. No sooner had things calmed down, when one animal after another met the same bloody end. This was getting very serious—not only the untimeliness, but also the gruesome and severely painful deaths the cattle were dealt.

People were nervous, worried, and on constant watch for any kind of strange happenings. But, just like a watched pot on the stove, nothing happened. The slaughter continued intermittently, then moved miles away, then suddenly stopped. It was spooky. A few months later, the strange devastating business resumed its dirty work again in both El Paso and Lincoln Counties. Articles appeared in newspapers and people spoke of the devil. Everybody who owned a ranch checked their livestock more than usual, but nobody could find a definite cause. While these strange occurrences went on, the regular work had to be continued—Satan or no Satan! And thus we continued our daily routine of checking the cattle.

There were two large pastures close to the Old Place where cows who were ready to have their calves were kept. It was around 10 AM one morning when we noticed a cow calving. As she saw us getting out of the pickup, she stood up and raced towards Fred and me with the intention of destroying us. Indeed, she was a nasty piece of work. We could be very swift when we needed and this was one time. Rather than antagonize the old girl, we decided to leave her alone for a while.

Two hours later, we returned to find a new, little white-face baby calf walking around its mother. Correction—he was anything but a little calf, weighing over 100 pounds. The cow was lying on her side, still keeping a vigilant eye on us. She was not getting up. Fred slowly eased out of the pickup, hoping she would move towards her baby. She tried a couple of times but always fell back onto her side. Her eyes looked wild and she gave a shrill bawl of disapproval but was unable to move. I felt so sorry for her—all she wanted was to be left in peace. "Go home and leave my baby and me alone," she begged. So we did, hoping baby and mom would be all right.

Just before dark, we returned expecting both of them to have wandered back to the herd. No such luck. The cow was still in the same position, paralyzed from the hard birth. The hungry baby now searched for his mother's udder which was caught under the cow's body. He needed help so we took him home and fed him on the bottle while we brought feed and water to the cow in hopes that she was only weak, not permanently disabled.

When we returned to the cow the next morning, she still had not moved. For the next week we took feed and water to her. She just lay there, eating a little and drinking only when very thirsty and cussing us out a lot! We hoped she wouldn't get pneumonia, a frequent development in similar cases.

The second week, she made a little progress. She still shook her head menacingly while she glared at us with contempt but otherwise she could not move. Yet, her appetite grew and every day she improved. One day, after a solid month of 'breakfast in bed,' she pulled herself up and chased us back to the truck. We knew she was on the road to recovery!

The next day she was able to join her much friendlier sisters in the pasture while she continued to recuperate. The calf grew and became a wonderful steer. But we never forgot his mother. If she hadn't been so mean, she probably wouldn't have recovered. A calm and decent milk cow would never have survived the ordeal.

Meanwhile, the occasional slaughter and dissection of organs by Satan or whatever abruptly stopped. We thought about these episodes often. Luckily, we didn't lose any livestock to 'Satan', but it did make us nervous. We never discovered the cause. 🐎

Improvements

A few years after we bought and moved onto our second ranch, we decided to modernize it. While it was quite an improvement from the Old Place we realized that it would be nice to add another bathroom to the house. Bonnie and Susan were growing up and both seemed to spend more and more time primping in front of the bathroom mirror. We hired a carpenter by the name of Al, chose the bathroom and shower equipment, and within a month a small part of the living room was cut out to serve as the second bathroom by the master bedroom. We enjoyed the added convenience.

Next, we wanted to surround the entire house with siding from Lew Eis. We decided on the best material that he had to offer: steel. I preferred a light blue color but Fred liked white—so it was white steel—and it looked great. When it was finished, I agreed with Fred's choice.

Next, the roof started to shed its wood shingles. We had a couple of roofers tear off the whole business. As these guys ripped off the old shingles, they had earlier fashioned a sort of funnel through which most of the rubble landed in their truck. Trouble developed when a lot of nails and staples missed the proper channel and instead fell into the driveway. The tires of our vehicles knew exactly where they were and picked them up regularly. Flats became routine for a while. It was worth all the trouble because the new green roof and the white siding looked beautiful.

Compared to the pretty house, the large garage/shop, now didn't look so great anymore, so friend-husband bought paint to be used on the wood shingles of the roof which were still in good shape, but had lost their color. I had hoped he would get the same shade of green as the ones of the house. But no—there was a sale on a hideous color, kind of chartreuse, which made me gasp. No wonder it was on sale!! It clashed with the other green but Fred insisted on using it. And guess who was elected to paint that roof! Fred does not like heights and I was stupid enough to admit that I didn't mind climbing up to do the job.

We also wanted a new barn across the road from the house. We decided on a cinderblock shed that opened to the south. We called on the same carpenter who built our second bathroom. He suggested that we hire a cement truck and Fred being stingy, or to use a nicer word, frugal, told him that we'd hire someone to mix the cement by hand.

"Schlitza," that's my name my mother had coined for me years ago, "go to Colorado Springs to the Unemployment Office and find someone who wants a job!" Obedient as I was, I soon found myself in the office and staring at about twenty men sitting on benches along one wall. Most of them were dressed shabbily, had several days' growth of a beard and were either smoking or chewing something.

I told the receptionist what I wanted. She, obligingly, went directly to the 'ambitious' looking men on the benches and said: "Is there someone who wants to go to the country and help build a barn?" I expected a mad rush, but no one budged. They just sat there as if

Cattle enoying breakfast of hay in the new shed.

no one had spoken and probably reasoned that getting a welfare or unemployment check was more pleasant than working.

I knew I had failed my boss and hated to face him after I returned, but he understood. "Well, we just have to do it ourselves!"

"Did that include me?" I wondered.

The cinderblocks, what looked like millions of them, were delivered, as were hundreds of cement sacks. Fred shoveled a pickup load of sand from a dry creek bed and parked it next to a large square tub that he borrowed from a neighbor. This tub was going to be used for mixing cement.

Soon Al came and started lining up the foundation and laying in the steel reinforcement rods which were put in the cement through the holes in the cinderblocks, parallel to the ground. It had to rest for three days.

Fred was there mixing cement, sand, and water with a hoe. He filled buckets and carried them to Al who was laying the cinderblocks. It was a tedious job but he didn't complain. Al was a fast worker and before long he was waiting for Fred to finish mixing the 'mud' as he called it.

They had been working since 7 AM and it was 9 AM when I went across the road to see how they were progressing. "Bring us some sandwiches and beer," they begged. I returned to the house, made four bologna sandwiches and took them, along with a couple of cans of beer and delivered the 'order.' Both dove into the 9:10 AM meal as if they hadn't eaten for days.

The shed construction was moving along so slowly that we knew things had to change. It looked as if this job wouldn't be finished before the first snowfall. Finally, Fred hired a guy from the neighborhood and on Al's repeated suggestion, ordered a cement mixer truck.

Now, things sped up considerably. "Give them plenty of good food and keep them happy with lots of beer," was the boss' order, which I fulfilled to the letter: Beer every two hours and food every four.

"Do you also want me to bring in dancing girls?" This question was answered with stoic silence, of course, knowing Fred.

At the end of the day when they had worked almost twelve hours, I invited them to

*The Vorenberg Ranch looking west with Pikes Peak & the
Rocky Mountains in the background.*

dinner and asked where they had put the empty beer cans. "Oh, we stuck them inside the blocks." I laughed at the thought that some day, many years hence, someone might wonder why and or what reason there was to embellish so many blocks with aluminum cans.

Despite its slow beginning the shed was soon finished, its shiny metal roof proudly protecting some of our livestock.

Next on the agenda of improvements was building a new corral, also across the road from the house and, believe it or not, another open shed. It looked like Fred just could not stop the building mania, but as long as the money held out who was I to complain?

Waiting to be fed.

Everytime something needed painting, like buildings or wooden fences, my man would approach me with: "A paintbrush never fit my hands!" Which meant, "Schlitza, you do it!" Actually, I love to paint, and after a while, the buildings or corral fences glowed with fresh coats of white.

There were many more improvements which Fred told me, "All these things we did improved the value of the ranch by $100,000. Later, we added more land. We bought the Marshall place of 80 acres for $3,000 and the Eis ranch of 640 acres for $28,000.

Adding the improvements to the ranch made us feel that we were growing and succeeding. As it grew, so did our confidence. We prospered and became more established as 'real' ranchers. 🐂

What Was That Noise?

The last part of the evening chores in the winter months included filling up the back of the pickup with bales of hay to be fed first thing the next morning. We usually drove it into the garage unless spring was on its way, then we parked the truck close to the house.

So far April had been lovely, at least the first week, but the nights remained quite cold. No snow, no rain.

It was still dark one morning while we were having our eggs and steak breakfast. Our main conversation dealt with a tough math test Tommy was taking that day. How I remember my math tests in Germany! It was my weakest subject and when my grade was a C, I was satisfied, but a B would actually thrill me beyond words. I might add that this did not happen often! I was glad that Fred could help the children with their homework.

Just then a horn sounded in front of the house. Tommy ran to the window and looked in both directions, "Nobody's here!" A few moments later—there it was again!

"You eat, I'll check," I volunteered to greet the early morning visitor. "I don't see anybody, either." By now I was getting a bit disgusted and hoped the person would come to the door and knock. I hate people to blow the horn. On second thought, perhaps we were all hallucinating!

No, this was real—the horn again! Now, Fred became curious as to what was going on outside. He scraped the chair over the linoleum in a great big hurry and rushed to the window and, with the biggest belly laugh he ever mustered in his life, he yelled to us to come and look.

By the time we rushed over to him, the hysterical sight had disappeared. But it did not go unnoticed by Fred. "The gray cat is jumping around in the cab of the pickup. When he accidentally landed on the steering wheel horn, the noise scared him. That's why you didn't see him. Poor thing, he's been in there all night long!"

Without even putting on a jacket, Fred went out, opened the pickup door, and without saying, "Thanks, kiss my foot," or whatever a cat might say, he leaped out as if chased. From that day on, he never again lingered around the truck!

Another time, one Saturday morning, Fred took Tommy and Bonnie to livestock judging try-outs. They were supposed to go to different ranches, to judge milk cows. The kids were excited and Bonnie talked a mile a minute. It reminded me of when she was little we used to call her "Walkie-Talkie" for obvious reasons.

The three returned home very soon after they left. Fred told me that when he got away from home and for roughly six miles, he thought he heard a noise. Then again he begged Bonnie to be still a moment and, sure enough, there was a scratchy noise somewhere.

He stopped the pickup, listened and walked toward the front. Suddenly, a sweet little meow came from beneath the hood. There was one of our kittens sitting on top of the battery looking at Fred innocently and scared, but happy to see us.

The kids cuddled the kitten and they drove back to the ranch where they dropped it off and headed back to the judging.

From that day on the kitten had a name: The Battery Cat!

And just like people learn from a bad experience, the kitten never repeated this event. It had learned its lesson.

The Texans Among Us

Frank and Ronda Dickinson lived in Ellicott, a farming community 24 miles east of Colorado Springs on Highway 94, also known as Farmer's Highway. As you approached the sign indicating Ellicott, it would take no longer than 60 seconds before you were through the so called, 'town'. On the north side of Ellicott there was a filling station, an auto repair shop, and a small grocery store all of which were operated by the same family. Next to these establishments was a fire station and the United Methodist Church. On the south side was a blacksmith shop and a small residence with a large garden. This was Ellicott proper.

Only a few folks lived in the tiny town. Most of them lived away from the highway. There were numerous cattle ranches, dairies and farms growing corn and other feeds for livestock. This was strictly an agricultural district where people made a decent living. None were rich, none had fancy homes, but they were content.

The Dickinson's came from Johnson County, Texas in 1955 after Frank suffered a severe heatstroke and his doctor advised him to move to a cooler climate. After investigating several areas, they selected Ellicott. At that time, eighteen people lived within half a mile of the tiny town.

Meanwhile, they packed all their necessities into a big homemade trailer along with the children, Vicky (4 years old) and Darol (12 years old) who were excited and thrilled with the brand new experience. Twelve dairy cows and two horses also made their way to Colorado.

They were settled in their new place in Ellicott almost at once. After fixing up the barns and house (notice that the barns always have priority over the house!), Frank and Ronda turned their attention to the 97-student school about half a mile away. It was a small building with a coal stove in each room and no indoor plumbing. Soon, they added a kitchen and Ronda cooked and worked as a room mother. With Frank's strong sense of community, they donated land so the school could be torn down and a new one built in 1974.

Frank later got interested in raising higher quality Quarter Horses. One particular stallion, Silky Fox, of whom he was especially fond and proud, and a mare, were Grand Champions at the National Western Stock Show in Denver. He developed them and many other horses, not only by proper feedings but also by exercising them daily on a round walker and a treadmill. He was a man who really knew horses.

Frank and Ronda ran their dairy of twenty cows with perfection which rewarded them by producing high quality and considerable quantity of milk. The Texas cows and eight Colorado cows gave the family a decent income month after month.

Ronda was especially gifted in sewing and created beautiful dresses and men's western shirts. Also, there seemed to be nothing she couldnít do when it came to art or interior decorating.

As the children were growing up they became interested in horseback riding, especially Vicky. She entered numerous Quarter horse contests such as barrel racing and won many awards. Darol's heart was not quite in that sport, but he had apparently inherited his mother's gift for art. He was still in high school when the teacher noticed his drawings were quickly becoming quite artistic. Before long he began taking drawing, oil painting, and photography classes. His camera became his constant companion. Soon, the word spread and owners of prize cattle and horses wanted a painting of their animals. They hired Darol to first photograph them, then develop the film. If the picture was satisfactory, he would paint the fine animal in his neat and well-lit studio next to Frank's dairy barn.

Eventually, Vicky graduated, married, and moved to Washington where she raised her family. Darol married a local girl and they became very active with the Baptist Church in Ellicott and were instrumental in developing and opening the Baptist School in 1974. Both the school and the church were built on land again donated by Frank and Ronda. They started raising Texas Longhorn cattle as well as other exotic breeds which they exhibited at Denver's National Western Stock Show. Soon, they were well established and bought land across from Frank's on the south side of Highway 94, also in Ellicott.

The National Western Stock show opened in Denver on one of the typical icy cold winter days with which this show seems to be associated. Frank and Darol stopped by our house after returning from there. We were always very happy to see them. This time they

*Frank Dickinson winning Grand Champion Quarter Horse
with Silky Fox at the National Western Stock Show.*

brought disturbing news. Some wealthy Texas cattlemen whom Frank knew went broke! How could that be? This was quite a shock because we never suspected anything like that from such successful operators.

Much too soon, rumors—or were they?—of a pessimistic future for the cattleman began to echo from different parts of the nation. The news media blared out reports of ranchers losing their homesteads and turmoil ensued in the whole industry. Bankers were telling their borrowers to 'tighten their belts.' When we heard this, Fred said to me, "This is nothing new, I've been told this ever since we borrowed money from our bank. Don't know how much tighter I can make the belt!" We both grinned, but it was no joking matter.

We faithfully listened to the cattle market report, even before the latest problem arrived. One day, we heard what was going on, and now we knew the cause of all the trouble. The United States was importing huge amounts of beef from foreign countries. The meat was flooding the American market, driving down the price of domestic livestock.

It didn't take an Albert Einstein to figure out why the rancher's future looked bleak. The cost of raising a steer, for example, remained the same while the selling price was significantly lower. Is it any wonder that ranchers went broke even if their places were paid for? Many of us were shackled by a mortgage and we hoped our bankers would stay with us and show much needed compassion.

The dilemma caused many folks to sell all or part of their ranches. Real estate folks were busy convincing these same people to cut up their land into small parcels. This was especially noticeable in the Ellicott region where, as time went by, fenced lots with a mobile home or a modest house, sprang up. It seemed living in the country was in vogue. I often wondered why these city folks preferred a long ride in all kinds of weather to their jobs in town. I guess they saw in the country the peaceful environment, clean air, and water and the best place to raise a family—the same things we did.

With the population increase Ellicott needed additional services. Close to the blacksmith shop on the south side of the highway a small strip mall was built which included a most welcome restaurant and a laundromat. A few months later a grocery store opened, giving the one across the street some needed competition.

Ellicott could no longer be called a 'little country school,' instead it was a fine looking building serving almost 600 students. An energetic superintendent plus a great teacher saw to it that the English Department was tops and many young people earned honors in Public Speaking, a fact I witnessed when judging the district contest.

As the Ellicott population continued to grow, they decided a small park was needed. Soon picnic tables and benches painted a glistening white were in place as well as swings for the kids. On every Fourth of July a marvelous display of fireworks from the park thrilled the many on-lookers.

Occasionally, Darol Dickinson would instigate cattle drives and would offer city slickers a chance to get a taste and a thrill of what we did for a living. The local press printed some colorful stories and hoped that this event would be repeated often.

Frank and Ronda were great citizens who did a lot for the town and were very respected. We were pleased to have them in our neighborhood.

Ice Skating

Unusually cold days reminded me of how I loved to skate when I lived in Germany. During the winters, you could always find me on a lake in the Kurpark. For ten cents, I could skate all day if I wanted to.

School during the winter lasted until noon. I would rush home, eat a bite, and don several sweaters, extra heavy socks, wool cap, and mittens. Even on the coldest day, I was on my way with ice skates in hand and the all-important key on a string around my neck to fasten my skates to the heavy boy shoes I always wore.

There were no lessons for me but I could skate faster than my friends could. Often some boys would encourage me to "crack the whip" with them. There were eight or ten of them—only boys—with me at the end, the only girl. How I loved it! When I finally let go, I would skate at top speed to the length of the lake. I bet the boys hoped that I would fall but I never gave them the satisfaction!

When we moved to Denver the first thing I bought in the beginning of that winter was a pair of white skates. Impatiently, I waited for a solid freeze. Later that year, I resumed my beloved sport together with my boyfriend, Fred Goldsmith, at the lake in City Park. I was horrified when the realization set in that I was scared of falling and quite unsteady on my wonderful figure skates. What happened? Eventually, I felt more comfortable, but not to where I had been so many years earlier.

Years later, on the Old Place, I wanted to skate at the Ice Arena in Colorado Springs. It was where many Olympic hopefuls practiced. Maybe some of their talent would rub off on me.

"They charge too much and it's too far to go. Why don't you skate on one of the ponds?" said my frugal (frugal—no, cheap—yes) husband. Why not, I thought, and the whole family could come along to watch me make a fool of myself.

The ice along the edge of the pond in the north pasture was rough but the center was smooth. I carefully moved away from the frozen ripples the wind had caused and became brave in front of all the eyes riveted on the 'ole lady. It didn't take long before I fell on my derriere, then on my knees and many other places. It was no use pretending I was a skater. I tried to blame my pitiful exhibition on the uneven ice and the leaves and dirt on the frozen surface.

On the way home, one of my smart-assed kids asked, "Mom, when you fell where did it hurt the most, was it on your knees?" Actually, that's the place it hurt the least. The coolness of the ice, which penetrated my jeans, felt pleasant and it dulled the pain.

The next day, my body reminded me of where I had been the day before. Every muscle ached, my knees looked swollen and I swallowed my pride, "I know I am not the athlete I used to be. I guess I'm getting old." I had hoped at least one person would disagree with my statement but nobody did. Needless to say, that particular pond in the pasture defeated me and I did not return to try skating on it again.

It was the following year when I decided to take one more try, not on the pond, but at the perfectly manicured Ice Arena of the Broadmoor Hotel in Colorado Springs. This time I wanted to be alone, no familiar eyes staring at me, wondering how long I might be hospitalized with a fractured hip.

The place was filled with people of all ages, some were great skaters but most were mediocre, like me. Some were practicing all sorts of jumps, not always landing on their skates, while a few were hanging onto the rail around the arena.

I finally got courage and glided right through the center of the arena. I didn't fall. I was having the time of my life! Just then some guy racing in my direction failed to turn away and slammed into me knocking me down while he continued on his merry way. Some young kids skated to me and helped me up. They were concerned and I assured them that I was not hurt. I returned to the arena a couple of more times. No more mishaps. It was fun.

What a Life! Never a Dull Moment

Before Jack was thirteen years old it was time to make plans for his Bar Mitzvah. At that particular time a student rabbi was in charge of the Jewish community of Colorado Springs. Jack's progress of learning Hebrew was slow, so I asked the rabbi for a textbook in order to teach him myself. This proved to be the right thing. Jack learned and at the same time I got a great refresher course. Next came the speech, and again, no help from the man who was our religious leader.

A bright idea entered Fred's mind, "Let's write to Rabbi Bergman who was so helpful with Tommy's Bar Mitzvah, and ask him for a tape so we could learn all the blessings and prayers."

In a few weeks the tape arrived and, now, with a small portable recorder, we learned to chant even when we were driving. Soon Jack became fluent in all phases of his education. It was a pleasure to be involved and I was proud that I had learned it almost as fluently as he had!

A week before Jack's Bar Mitzvah, Fred became sick. His ankles and legs were very swollen. He gained eighteen pounds in a matter of days and our Doctor admitted him to the hospital. He needed tests and a thorough kidney check-up as only this particular doctor could do. He left nothing unturned and was the most thorough physician I ever met. Naturally, we had a lot of faith in him.

A Happy Jack and a sickly Fred.

The night of the Bar Mitzvah arrived and Fred was still in Memorial Hospital. He was allowed to leave for three hours. When I picked him up he was extremely weak and I hoped he would last through the ceremony and the excitement without fainting. (Fred has always been an expert when it came to this. A bad cold, a case of diarrhea, a sharp pain somewhere, anything could precipitate a fainting spell.)

Tommy, about to graduate from Northern Colorado University in Greeley, came home for the weekend. Annette, my brother Max's daughter, came from Denver to attend. There were many of Jack's classmates, several teachers, and quite a few of our friends.

Jack performed beautifully in English as well as Hebrew. His handsome face beamed a smile as wide as the Grand Canyon. We were proud that Jack had done so well and that Fred did not faint! The refreshments were catered because I didn't have time for baking—I was running a ranch! Fred's three-hour pass ended and we delivered an exhausted but happy patient back to his hospital bed. We relaxed, recovering from the euphoria of the very successful event.

Back at the ranch, it didn't take long for life to fall back into the old routine. Jack wrote his Thank You notes to folks who showered him with lovely gifts, Tommy returned to Greeley from where he would be graduating within a week, and Fred finally was dismissed from Memorial Hospital. His final diagnosis was kidney failure due to overwork. It was ten days before his strength returned and my workload finally returned to normal.

A few days after Jack's Bar Mitzvah, a 4-H Square Dance Contest was to be held at 7 PM and both he and Bonnie were going to compete. While we were there, a reporter from the Colorado Springs Gazette Telegraph was taking a picture of Jack's recent ceremony to accompany a story he was writing. Afterward, we stopped at Bonnie's ballet studio to pick up the tutu and wig for her upcoming recital.

We had just enough time to eat a hamburger before driving to the auditorium and parking the station wagon about a block away. A neighbor offered to take the children home but I wanted to see how they did as I always loved music and dance. I decided to stay.

The hall was filled with many 4-H club teams and soon the music started for warm-ups, followed by the actual contest. The judges, six of them—three men and three women—sat in a row, stern faced and silent, each checking evaluation forms and adding personal comments. Our club performed beautifully, swinging those puffy skirts and shuffling in time to the country tunes as the caller guided them through complicated routines. They got a red ribbon.

It was around 10:30 PM when the three of us, anxious to get home, walked to the car. At once we noticed the broken vent window on the driver's side and looked inside to discover that it was completely empty. Gone were Jack's beautiful suit, shirt, tie, and shoes, Bonnies tutu, wig, and toe shoes, and a library book I had planned to return the next day. Terribly upset, we walked to the police department near our pillaged car and excitedly explained our situation to the only officer on duty. He took fingerprints off our car door but told us that they most probably would not find the culprit. "If there had been an assault or a murder we'd put a bunch of investigators on the case, this just isn't that urgent or important enough!" To us, it was important and naturally we were very upset. The trip home seemed longer than usual. Bonnie cried, "Now I can't be in the recital." I tried unsuccessfully to calm things down.

It was close to midnight when we entered the front door of the house. Fred had been asleep. When he heard the gruesome story, he became extremely angry and scolded me for not letting the neighbor bring the children home. Eventually, he calmed down and we managed to get a few hours of sleep.

Warren Garage fixed the broken vent window. Co-owner, Charlie volunteered, "That's the trouble with station wagons, you can't hide anything. Thieves can see everything through the windows." We decided, then and there, that our next car would have a trunk. No more station wagons!

Not winning a contest and having unexpected problems is 'life.' Though they are difficult to endure as a child, I actually think those situations help prepare a young person for their future. ♞

Flood

To ranchers and farmers, the radio is extremely important, more so than for city dwellers. Several times during the day, right after the news, came the cattle market reports from the Denver Stockyards. They updated us about how many cows, bulls, sheep, hogs, and other animals had been sold and what they brought. The weather report followed. Nobody in their right mind who made their living from the soil would skip this vital information whether it was summer or winter.

One summer day in 1965, the weatherman announced that a major cloudburst had pummeled a large area around Denver. We were not too concerned because downpours happened often. The dry creeks would collect the run off, swell up like a river for a few hours and usually, the next day everything was back to normal.

We were not anxious; after all, Denver was 90 miles away from our ranch. All afternoon, the local newscaster from the KOA station kept interrupting the programming and reporting how the rain was causing severe flooding. People were being rescued from low-lying homes and cars were floating down the streets. Some motorists abandoned their vehicles while other brave souls stubbornly remained in them, hoping for a piece of luck to come their way so they would be saved.

Around midnight the news got worse. Trains were not traveling between Colorado Springs and Denver as large holes had developed beneath the tracks, washing them out. Interstate 25 was closed. The Highway Department issued warnings of treacherous areas. About the same time the rains moved into the Castle Rock area, some 30 miles south of Denver. Residents who kept calling and informing KOA reported more destruction. Parts of hills and low mountains became barren as trees, bushes, large rocks and mounds of soil were washed onto other people's property. Since Uncle Herman's ranch was in that area we began to get concerned. "Let's call them in the morning and find out what happened to them."

Since we did not have a radio by our bed, I was awakened during the night as Fred was stumbling into the living room to get news about the flood which seemed to be racing south leaving behind so much misery. "There's no change, but it really sounds pitiful. Go back to sleep."

In the morning, we discovered that the low mountain range just north of Colorado Springs, called the Black Forest, had received several inches of rain during the night. This was getting close! Our area was not known for big floods, but this was a lot of rain to come all at once.

We were still concerned about Uncle Herman and his Castle Rock ranch so we called the foreman, Miguel. He told us how most of the fences had been washed out and all the cattle in the area had swum to higher ground. The Plum Creek, which ran through their property as a slow and lazy provider of water for the animals had mushroomed into a fury of water. In addition, the drinking water in the well was brown, there were small trees on the ground, and rocks had washed down from the steep hills that surrounded the property. They were completely isolated. This was indeed a bad report and we wondered what would be next.

Fred called some of our neighbors who told him that they had neither rain nor flooding. "Aren't we lucky to live on a hill," we reassured each other. I wondered how our friends in Ellicott were doing.

The next day, the sun was making the world a friendly place. But the news kept everybody on edge. The flood even made the national news.

Later in the afternoon, Frank Dickinson visited us on his way to Calhan to purchase some feed. He told us how a wall of water had reached the Ellicott valley, washing out the main bridge on Highway 94. A motorist, who was trying to get home, drove onto the bridge and fell through a hole and into what had become a raging and angry river. Neighbors tried to rescue him but the water was so strong they feared for their lives. Two days later, and several miles downstream, another neighbor noticed a car sitting on dry pasture where the water had been. The unfortunate motorist, still in his car, had drowned.

News of the destruction travelled fast. Cattle drifted for miles since the fences were washed out. Animals drowned, basements filled with water and both Highways 24 and 94 were closed for some time. Repair crews were everywhere. For many weeks, the Army from Fort Carson helped ranchers with repairs. The Ellicott folks were immensely grateful and appreciative of the willing helpers who gave them a hand in their hour of need.

The flood of '65 won't be forgotten. People who live by the soil are used to problems but nature has a way of testing their character and will power. Love of the land keeps them going, and in no time at all, they gather strength and enthusiasm to prepare for what nature will hand them next. 🐎

Maximilian Von Rolf

There I stood looking at the name on the registration form: Maximilian Von Rolf. It had the sound of something special. Gret was there with a friend in hopes that we would want to buy a dog. Then the kitchen door opened and in walked a very handsome animal, with purebred written all over him. He was nine months old, supposedly good with children, a fine watch dog and in good health. But he seemed far from being trained and his current owner held him using all his strength applied to a heavy chain. Immediately the dog and I meshed, and I secretly told myself, "I've got to have him!" I remembered all the times in Germany when I had wanted to have a German Shepherd. Now was my chance. All they wanted was $35 so they could finish paying for him. I thought, "what else could I ask for?" We did need a dog. Boy, a collie, had died a couple of months earlier and all we had left was another aging collie, named Pete. Surprisingly, Fred agreed to the sale fairly easily, deferring to my opinion. Dogs were my department—cattle, his.

Max had fairly good manners, could sit up and beg, and sometimes came when he was called. Other than that, I could see he needed a lot of work to become a well-trained dog. Because this type of dog has strong shepherding instinct, I was afraid to teach him around our cattle and sheep. "What if he takes it on his own and he might even injure some animals? I better just leave him by the house and make a nice watchdog and companion out of him." That was my plan, not his!

None of our dogs were chained or even wore collars. So now, that Max was one of us— so to speak—off went the heavy collar and he was free to roam the premises. Max attempted to make friends with dear old Pete but was rejected, with looks of disgust from the older dog. I bet if Pete could have talked he would have said, "Do I have to put up with another kid?"

Max couldn't care less. He took off exploring the ranch, staring at the livestock and all the other animals. Then he noticed a hen minding her own business. Soon, the race was on. He ran quickly and caught the bird only to let her go seconds later. Not one feather was out of place, but you could see her little heart going lickety split! Ranch dogs must be obedient and never, never chase anything. "If he kills a chicken, he'll have to go," was the ultimatum I heard from Fred. I immediately was on the dog's side explaining to him how the dog had "never seen ranch animals before" and how "I would start teaching him right away."

There were quite a few wild animals around our ranch and to me the most fascinating ones were the coyotes. In fact, Max looked a little like them. Every so often, I would watch a single coyote approach the sheep pen, checking them out one by one, and he wondered just when we would let them out to graze...I swear you could almost see him licking his chops. During early evenings and into the night you could hear coyotes howling from many corners of our neighborhood. It seemed that once one would start, they all would answer in their high pitched voices. It was full concert sound that could last as long as 20 minutes.

While riding horseback, Fred once noticed a whole family of coyotes sunning themselves just outside their den. After they saw the horse coming, it took only a split second for them to disappear down through the entrance and to safety. "We don't need more of these pests around here," said Fred who promptly called the Wildlife Department. The next day, two uniformed men came to the ranch. Using shovels they dug a hole into the coyote den and pulled out six of the most beautiful shepherd-like animals. They barely had their eyes open and when I reached over to pet them, they started to snarl at me, demanding my poor hand for dinner. Innocently, I asked, "What's going to happen to them? Are you going to take them to a zoo or someplace?"

"No," one of them answered. "Zoos don't want them. We are going to clobber them over the head and kill 'em." My whole day was ruined and I could not get this terrible thought out of my mind. Ranch life could be cruel.

One day, after returning from Colorado Springs to do some shopping Pete and Max greeted us with great enthusiasm, just like normal. We sent out Tommy to bring in the sheep so they would be safe from predators during the vulnerable nighttime hours. When he returned, Tommy announced that one was missing!

Maximilian Von Rolf.

This was unusual because sheep always stay close together, in fact they move over hills and down valleys all at the same time. Something must have happened. Though I tried reasoning with myself by saying, "Perhaps it was a hungry coyote," I had a sick feeling that my new dog had done something very bad. After a while we found the dead sheep with a small part of it missing. I concluded that our well-fed Max would never stoop so low as to eat part of his catch! This remarkable statement made sense to Fred and he, more or less, apologized to Max. Lucky for him; lucky for me!

Unfortunately the incidents didn't stop. Things started to heat up when we found a young bull calf dead, close to the house. There was swelling on his neck with some blood that had trickled down on one side. The wildlife people had told us that dogs kill animals by biting them in the back of the neck, while coyotes go right for the throat and then drag the carcass to a hiding place. If this was true, Max was guilty and we would have to tie him up whenever we left the ranch. Obviously, he was bored and just wanted to have fun! The subject of 'getting rid of him' never came up because Fred had grown to like this energetic pup.

Soon after this episode we found a dead chicken close by Max's doghouse. I had read somewhere that when this happens and you suspect the dog, you should tie the dead bird around his neck and leave it there for a day or two. The article said how the dog would become so disgusted from the weight and discomfort that he would realize his mistake and never repeat the bad habit. The insult and punishment of having to carry a dead chicken around his neck ended all the killings and Max finally realized that he better grow up and do what his mistress was trying to teach him. He was cured.

During the winter, the cattle needed to be fed extra protein because the grass and the hay did not contain as much as it does when the pastures are green. So it was necessary to feed supplemental cottonseed cake which comes in hard two-inch pieces. The cattle crave the extra feed and they will gallop for a great distance when they hear or see the truck, knowing it is loaded with 'goodies.' The whole herd would be on the run because first come, first served. In the depth of winter the young steers and heifers were kept overnight in corrals so if a storm would blow in during the night, they could go into the open sheds for protection. They also would be fed from the back of the pickup.

Before school one of the kids would drive the truck into the pastures or corrals with either Fred or Tom in back. They would first feed the sacks of cottonseed cake and afterwards, the bundles of hay. The cattle were hungry so they crowded all around the entire pickup just as bees might swarm around sweet nectar. The driver of the pickup had to move the truck through the throng at a crawl to avoid running over the hungry critters. Even yelling and honking would have little or no impact on them.

All of a sudden, something stirred in Max's head. He had been in the back of the pickup with Fred when he suddenly jumped off and gingerly walked to the front of the vehicle and continued, very slowly, to clear the path to make room for the driver to continue. Max had just created his newest job. Every morning he would stand at the kitchen door, whining, as Fred put on his shoes so he could go to work. Fred's pride for this dog was growing and all the mischief from the past was not only forgiven, but also forgotten. Here was a deed which was not learned or copied, it was a natural thing, the instinct to herd gently.

Max continued to develop his job description! Several times a year you need to treat cattle by branding, vaccinating, eartagging, or testing for diseases. It required that they be moved into a series of ever-smaller corrals, which eventually becomes a narrow lane and could only accommodate one animal. The cattle were pushed down this lane and towards a contraption, called a chute. Once inside, the back gate of the machine was closed. One person would then push in the sides to narrow the chute so the animal could be held completely still.

Max noticed that some cattle were too frightened to go through the lane and into the chute. He figured out that if he would reach between the boards and nip them on their heels, they would be more 'willing' to go forward in order to get away from the 'pesky' dog. It worked. Then, as soon as one animal was in the chute and the back door slammed shut, Max would turn to fetch the next animal. He became a valuable helper, willing and happy to perform—all he asked for was a diet of Purina Dog Chow and love from his human family.

Time passed quickly, one season melted into the next. Holidays came and went and it was another New Year's Eve. The day had started as usual, another sunshiny day with the temperature struggling to reach 32 degrees. The main task we had planned for the afternoon was to take one of our Hereford bulls to a pasture to breed heifers, which are young females who haven't yet had their first calf.

It was not often that the ranch work decreased to the point where you could get a spare minute to read a book while the sun was still up, but that was exactly what I was doing that day. My brother, Martin, had sent us a subscription to "Reader's Digest" the year before, and Fred and I loved it. When the chores were done and supper was over, you were usually too tired from all the physical exertion to read. Watching our favorite shows on television like "I Love Lucy" and "The Carol Burnett Show" was all you would be capable of. So there I was curled up reading—during the day—on the rocker next to the coal stove when Susan came in, "Mom, you got to come out and look at Max. He's hurt." I was not thrilled to be interrupted and I answered, "Bring him in and I'll check him out in here."

"I can't," she answered, "he's bleeding an awful lot."

As if I were shot out of a cannon, I raced to the poor dog and found him in terrible shape, bleeding from his mouth, with his head hanging close to the ground. When I took a closer look I noticed his lower jaw was in an abnormal position. All I could think was, "It must be broken."

The children stood by Max with concern etched onto their young faces. They explained how Fred had wanted to load one of the bulls into the trailer to take him to the heifer pasture.

Trailers come in different sizes and ours had two compartments which were divided by a gate. When animals were loaded, the heaviest ones would go into the front compartment with the lighter ones in the rear. If you transported only a few head of cattle, they had to be in the front of the trailer to prevent the trailer from jack-knifing and causing a serious accident.

The children continued to explain just what had happened: Tommy had backed the trailer up to the loading chute. The back gate of the trailer was opened for the bull who entered the lane but refused to load into the trailer. Max 'encouraged' the big Hereford by nipping him on his heels which did the trick and he leaped forward.

But something was wrong. Nobody had opened the dividing gate within the trailer. The bull immediately realized he could exit, so he quickly turned around and ran back down the lane where he spied Max who was ready to nip him on his heels again, his head reaching between the boards. The bull had other things on his mind. With his massive head he angrily attacked Max' head ramming the dog's head up into the boards.

Now, everybody was in a tizzy. Fred got the bull reloaded and transported to the heifers. Meanwhile, we prepared Tom and Bonnie and the jeep for the trip to the veterinarian whom I had called, so he would be expecting them. Max was too proud to show signs of pain and defeat. He was a soldier. It only took Fred 10 minutes to return and he and the two kids headed west towards Colorado Springs while the rest of us finished the evening chores.

The vet was waiting. He decided that it was not a bad fracture and that it would heal without doing much to it. All he needed to do was pull one of Max' canine teeth, the long one on one side, so he could close his mouth. The vet sprinkled some ether onto a cloth, placing it over his nose and soon the patient was peacefully asleep only to awaken later with more discomfort from the hole left by his tooth than from the fractured jaw.

When the Jeep pulled up in front of the house, I swear I could smell the ether almost before I closed the kitchen door behind me. Things looked encouraging. Max was semi-conscious from the anesthesia so Fred carried him into the kitchen. He 'ate up' all the attention he was getting and you could almost hear him say, "It was all worth it". Finally, he gave in and went to sleep. It was New Year's Eve and fortunately, we had no plans so we could stay home to be with the patient.

It was 9 PM when someone drove up and we, always anxious for company, were excited to see who it was. Imagine my surprise when the local Baptist preacher, the Reverend John Mullingham, greeted us and presented us with some fruit. He made a habit to come for a visit perhaps once a month during which time he stayed...and stayed...while enjoying coffee and cookies. "I want to visit my good Jewish friends and spend the last day of the year with you. Is that all right? Are you going to stay up until midnight tonight?" Without waiting to see whether it really was all right or not, he entered. We were glad he did, as it was a good distraction. Usually we would ask him to sit at the kitchen table but this time we led him into the living room to munch on Christmas cookies and drink several cups of coffee. Fred likes to talk religion with the Reverend but I don't. I left to check on Max. The kids wondered if they should feed him, after all, it had been hours since the tooth extraction. "Go ahead," I encouraged them. They fixed his dog food, softened it with water until it became a mush, but he wouldn't touch it. Eventually one of the children put some of it onto Max's tongue and only then did he swallow it. This was encouraging and before long the bowl was empty.

Meanwhile, back in the living room, the Reverend John Mullingham stretched, made himself more comfortable, if this was possible, and uttered something like, "I'm having such an enjoyable time with you, I should come more often!" All I could think of was,

"Please don't."

"Mom, he's walking...Max is up and walking," came the joyful announcement and almost at once, here came a wobbly dog, so unsteady on his feet that it looked like he might fall down any minute. I grimaced to hold back tears, seeing my lovely dog in so much pain. He walked towards the Reverend, wagged his tail a couple of times and with no apparent effort, vomited all over the poor man's trousers and shoes. I rushed to get a paper towel and tried to get most of the smelly, gooey stuff off his clothes. I never saw anybody get off a couch so fast, run through the kitchen, and out of the door. We followed him to his car apologizing copiously. I don't know whether he heard anything, but he took off, as they say, "like a bat out of hell."

Our daughter Susan with Max.

Sharp Teeth, Gentle Bite

ne day the telephone rang and Uncle Herman wanted to know if we would like visitors. Aunt Blanche, whom the children adored, wondered if she could spend a few days with us during Susan's graduation. What a question! "Of course," I answered. "When will you be coming?"

"Tomorrow, if that's all right with you," Herman said excitedly.

Whenever the folks from Denver came for a visit, it reminded me of when they came to see us in Ramah and how they were on the doorstep when I uttered the now-infamous remark, "We better hurry up with this, because the Vorenbergs always come too early!"

All sorts of plans had to be made for Aunt Blanche's visit, and there was not much time. Important things had to be done. First planning meals. Next a couple of haircuts. I had become quite experienced and Fred was proud of me because we saved a lot of money! The 4-H cattle were brushed and the house was cleaned. Fred hurried off to dehorn some calves for our neighbors, Bob and Helen Wilson, who lived about three and a half miles, as the crow flies, north from our place. By evening, things were well organized and we went to bed dead tired, but glad we had accomplished what we had planned for the day.

The next morning was gorgeous, a typical Colorado summer day. Blue sky, accentuated by white lacework of thin clouds covering the entire firmament. Pikes Peak and the whole mountain range looked so near it seemed you could just walk right up to it.

The folks got to our ranch loaded down with an oval shaped basket filled with the usual goodies and snacks, plus a few toys and dog biscuits for Max, our loveable dog. After unpacking the treats, Uncle Herman went with Fred to finish the morning chores. It was a pleasure for Herman as the 'cattle person' emerged and his love of them made for a pleasant trip through the chores. Aunt Blanche visited with the children and me. She was always in a good mood, a really lovely lady who regularly complimented me, often on things undeserved.

After the men returned, Uncle Herman told us he couldn't stay because he was going to help Miguel on the Castle Rock ranch. They were getting two truckloads of steers and heifers from New Mexico and they needed his help. An hour later, he excused himself and said good bye to Blanche and the rest of us.

The girls gave up their room so that Aunt Blanche could sleep comfortably with privacy. She was hanging up her clothes in the tiny closet while talking to Max. She was as much a dog lover as I was—another reason we got along so well.

When there was no school, we had our big meal at noon. It must have been 1 PM when we were sitting in the kitchen finishing a piece of apple pie and some good hot coffee. Suddenly we heard strange noises like the sound of dice rolling around in someone's hand. "What in the world is that?" I asked, when I noticed that the door to Aunt Blanche's room was slightly ajar. I went in and to my horror there was Max with Aunt Blanche's upper set of dentures in his mouth. He was, no doubt, enjoying the flavor of her toothpaste. I took

LEONARD TARPENNING, President
DOROTHY ANNE PIEPER, Secretary
PHYLLIS KELLY, Treasurer

MANFRED VORENBERG, Vice President
ROBERT HAVER, Director
RALPH K. CALABRESE, Superintendent

CALHAN PUBLIC SCHOOL
DISTRICT NO. R JT. 1
P. O. Box 21   Phone 347-2335
CALHAN, COLORADO   **80808**

Calhan School had Fred's name on its stationery during his 20 years on the School Board!

the false teeth out of his mouth expecting to find some of them missing, but to my relief, all were there and there was not one scratch on the dentures!

I wondered what Aunt Blanche would say now about this 'wonderful' dog after I told her what I found. I waited in silent anticipation for her reaction. Quietly, she rose from her chair, ambling into her room. I handed her the false teeth, which she put in one corner of her suitcase, closed and locked it! "He's not going to get to them any more," she said laughing all the while! Only a real dog lover would forgive Max. She later told us how the dentures had been hurting her and how she was taking them out to eat. Max had easily retrieved them from her opened suitcase. It is hard to believe that his teeth left no imprint, no scratch.

The next day was Susan's graduation from High School and Fred was the School Board member scheduled to hand out diplomas. He was so proud. Aunt Blanche had brought one of her best outfits to wear for the occasion. In fact, we all dressed up and it felt good wearing a dress for once.

Soon afterward, we were bird sitting for our neighbor, Lew Eis, who was away on a business trip. He had asked us to keep his parakeet, Stinker, for a week. Of course, we promised to take good care of him. I always have loved birds since we had a canary when I was growing up in Germany. I had no experience with parakeets "But, what's the difference," I thought. Well, the difference was Lew let Stinker have the run of the house and rarely confined him in the cage.

But now that the bird was with us, things had to change. I was careful that when Max was in the house I would make sure Stinker was behind bars. But every time I put him there he would make the most awful noises, screeching and cussing me out at the same time. In order to make peace with Stinker I could only do one thing and that was to send Max outdoors so the bird could fly to his favorite curtain rod.

Then it happened. Stinker was out of his cage and someone opened the kitchen door. Max walked in, happy to be with his mistress when all of a sudden, there was this outburst of energy as the dog spied the bird, ran over to the curtain, clawing at it and barking furiously.

Before long, feathers were flying in all directions as Stinker flew from one side of the room to the other with Max in hot pursuit. Eventually, the poor thing just gave up and landed on the floor, completely spent. Max pounced on it, picked it up ever so gently and carried it into the kitchen where I was watching in horror. He then set the bird down and licked it a couple of times before simply turning and walking away.

Naturally, I was scared to death and I expected the worst. Here was a German Shepherd, whose breed is known for being aggressive and mean, but in this case he simply wanted to ask, as Mr. Rogers does on television, "Will you be my neighbor?"

Lew returned from his trip and I washed all the curtains in the living room! Stinker was happy to see Lew, (I think) and vice versa. But I was the one who was most relieved. I was glad to see the bird go to its home. The curtains needed to be washed anyway, even before Stinker abused them!!

When Max was only ten, he developed severe arthritis in his hips. He could hardly climb the two steps into the house. He spent all his time in the warm living room on his rug. Sometimes I could hear him whimper but when I talked to him all the pain was forgotten and he tried to be with me whenever he could. Medication did not help. One evening I told Fred, "One of us has to take Max to the vet so he can be put to sleep. We got to do it before it gets cold. I dread doing it. Will you?"

"How about doing it tomorrow because we are supposed to have our first storm of the season in a couple of days," was Fred's reply. As an afterthought, he continued, "I'd be more than willing to do it for you but you'll have to bring in all the cattle and take them to the barns before sundown. It's supposed to be a nasty storm." Not wishing to ride horseback by myself all day long, I decided to give him the 'honor' of doing that job while I tried to be strong for the other, more distasteful task.

The next morning, Fred gassed up the Jeep for me. I lifted Max onto the seat of the Jeep along with my coat, purse, shopping list, and everything else I needed for the trip. I arrived at the vet clinic but the doctor was on an emergency call and I would have to leave Max in one of the small kennels. I declined. Instead, I did the shopping. I had to put several sacks of food around Max because there was so little room in the jeep and I told him not to touch or even sniff anything. Then, I pulled out a box of vanilla wafers and told him he could have the whole box right now. He ate every cookie, every crumb. I returned to the vet hospital and walked him slowly to the waiting vet who ended his suffering with an injection of a sedative. My wonderful dog was gone. I drove home, alone, and utterly devastated. My eyes overflowed with tears over the loss, the suffering and the untimely death of this magnificent animal, my pal, Max.

A heart-to-heart with Max.

Chapter 9

JOIE DE VIVRE

Glenwood Springs

The only time we ever took off from work was when company came and we wanted to show them the beautiful state of Colorado. You didn't have to go far to be surrounded by nature's splendor. Those were lovely hours and despite the fact that we had seen many of the sights before, we continued to enjoy them.

But these were brief visits because we never could stay away from the animals for several nights in a row. It was a pleasant thought when our good friend and former neighbor, Mr. Cottrell, suggested and then convinced us to get away for a weekend. "I'll take care of your chores, don't worry," he promised.

We had heard so much about Glenwood Springs on the Western Slope. It had a swimming pool as big as a city block. Both Fred and I loved swimming and our minds were made up to make this our short vacation spot.

A few days later we bought swimwear for all of us and our excitement grew steadily until Friday when we planned to leave. I had packed all necessities into individual cases. Fred's and my things were together in a suitcase while each child had his or her own large paper sack with the name printed on the outside. I thought this was a fine and clever arrangement.

The happy day arrived and so did Mr. Cottrell. Fred left the poor man with so many instructions, both written and oral ones, that nobody could possibly remember them all.

Finally, we drove away. It was a beautiful summer day and the kids were excited. Fred had placed a mattress in the back of the station wagon and the children played, sang and slept there.

We stopped for hamburgers, for restrooms, for advertised scenic sights. The landscape changed continually and the farther we drove the larger the blue spruces grew. We planned to stay overnight in Leadville, the silver mining town whose mines made many prospectors wealthy.

After arriving there, we walked through the town and admired the old Victorian homes, and looked at all the old silver mines, including the one owned by the famous Tabor family. It was a neat town but it had almost no trees except for a few occasional pines because it was almost at timberline. Museums and restaurants were everywhere, along with saloons. Occasionally you would see a pickup or a car with an out of state license plate. Dogs were everywhere and a few burros walked the streets by themselves.

Around 5 PM, we decided to go to a restaurant to eat and to find a hotel of which there seemed plenty. A couple of cowboys complete with boots, shiny buckles on their belts, ten gallon cowboy hats stomped into the restaurant, sat down at the table next to us and hollered to the waitress, "Bring us the coldest beer you got!"

Fred likes to talk to people and soon we learned where they lived, where they came from, why they liked Leadville, what their wives' names were, how many children they had, and on and on. I expected any moment they would tell us of their secret sex lives and direct us to the nearest whorehouse. They guzzled their beer as if it had been water. One last question from Fred was "How far is it to Glenwood Springs?"

"You can make it in a couple of hours!" And they were gone with their spurs clinking on their boots.

"You know what I'm thinking of, we could go on to Glenwood, now, instead of staying overnight here. What do you think?" Fred's idea was great and we all agreed. "OK, everybody go to the bathroom and hurry up." I learned a long time ago, you never leave on any trip without sending the kids to the john.

We had been on the road for an hour and the sun was still up as we entered a canyon with a rushing creek below. Fred drove very slowly and almost too carefully. The constant winding highway with its perpetual traffic hugged the sides of a mountain one moment, and the next zooming precariously along the edge of an enormous drop into the creek below made Fred quite nervous. He wanted to stop somewhere just to catch his breath but there was no chance, no place safe enough to recuperate, so he persevered.

People continued to pass us constantly and I asked Fred if he could try to go with the flow but all he said was, "it wasn't safe."

By now, the sun had set, the remnant of a delightful orange sky was there to bid us farewell. I marveled at how quickly the horizon turned a dark blue and stars made their appearance.

"What did those cowboys tell us—two hours? To Glenwood? Incredible! These aren't 'hairpin curves,' they are 'bobby pin curves' our driver joked! Was Fred getting funny, is he getting a sense of humor? I thought, "This could be serious!"

All of a sudden we found ourselves out of the canyon and in the midst of a street with houses on each side. A pungent odor like sulfur permeated the air. Next, we saw to our left a huge swimming pool, so large and lit so brightly that it seemed like daytime. People were everywhere.

We made it! We were in Glenwood Springs. "Let's get a motel quickly." Good idea. It was late, after 10 PM and all of us were tired, most of all Fred. He was exhausted.

Someone directed us to the motels and we drove across the railroad tracks to a street lined with motor courts and trailer parks. Signs in front of the offices said "No Vacancy" as we moseyed along from one to the next. This was getting serious. We stopped at one of the last motels and asked the man where we might find lodging. He directed us to the "Red Mountain Motel." We retraced our route all the way back to the railroad crossing and another mile north.

We arrived at the motel and its sign said "Open"! There were two adjoining rooms to be had and we felt lucky even though they were small and quite stark. We were carrying in our belongings when we noticed that there was only one big paper sack. Oh no! We forgot to load the other three! This meant that we had to buy three swimsuits in the morning.

We went to bed right away because the next day would be a busy one. Three of the children had no pajamas, they were in the sacks back on the ranch, but sleeping in their underwear was no big deal to them.

If it hadn't been for the loud locomotive whistle and the plaintive noise which woke me up and made me sit up straight in bed several times that night, it would have been a restful night. I was the only one who was bothered by the train!

Saturday morning was here. Though we were anxious to get to the pool, first we had to eat breakfast. The motel owner told us to "go to the Dinner Bell for good food." Boy, did those waffles ever taste good—it was another meal I didn't have to cook!!

After breakfast, we bought swimsuits and trunks and then were off to the pool. The dressing rooms and showers were immaculate. Very few people were around and hardly any children.

I felt terribly conspicuous in my swimsuit and imagined the whole world was looking at me. I felt fat even though I weighed no more than 105 pounds at five foot three inches.

The whole family enjoying our first vacation.

One lady approached me and told me that there was a baby pool and an attendant to watch the little ones. Jack was certainly a candidate—he was two years old and having someone to watch him was perfect. We went there and found a cute-looking teenager, who was already watching a couple of older children, so the rest of us now could enjoy the water.

It was hot in the smaller of the two pools. There were cement benches all around the four sides and some older folks were soaking up the soothing effect of the hot sulfur water on their arthritis. I couldn't stay long in the therapeutic pool; it was so hot it made me weak. The other pool was cooler, yet still wonderfully warm. We were told that the water coming out from the rocks was so hot that they needed to cool it considerably before it flowed into the pools.

We spent a lot of time swimming and when we returned to pick up Jack, we found him sound asleep in the arms of the attendant. Some young guys were standing around flirting with the girl and making remarks about her motherly instincts.

The next two days were delightful. Becoming lazy was wonderful and the time off recharged our batteries. We all got sunburned faces but that didn't bother us.

As I mentioned earlier, Fred is a very friendly and outgoing person, so it was no surprise when he told me that he met a couple watching the swimmers from outside the pool building. "They are going to come and visit us on the ranch. I gave them our telephone number and address. They have a couple of lovely German Shepherds." That was all I needed to hear—people with my favorite breed of dogs couldn't be anything but great!

We left Glenwood Springs on Monday, reluctantly. We learned several things: make reservations in the motel, especially if you go on weekends, bring enough skin protection as the sun is strong, and don't forget the large paper sacks with the clothing for the kids!

When we arrived home everything seemed OK except that one of our bottle lambs was dead. According to Mr. Cottrell she was sleeping in the shade of the pickup and he didn't see her there. As he started off, he felt a bump, got out to see what happened and then realized that he had run over the lamb.

There was no reason to get upset. Of course, all of us were saddened, but we had such a glorious weekend and didn't want anything to dampen our thoughts of those memorable days. Only for one moment did I wonder whether all of us were getting a bit blasé about the loss of an animal but quickly brushed the thought aside. Blame it on the moment; blame it on the circumstances. No, we never took such things lightly, not one of us.

Being mentally and psychologically refreshed we dove into our responsibilities with gusto. We realized the importance and value of planning a hiatus every so often and promised one another to keep this on our calendar.

Willie, Ilse and Two Dogs

e couldn't forget the Immerlings whom we met in Glenwood Springs along with their two gorgeous German Shepherds. Willy was tall, close to six feet and slightly overweight. His hair was black, he had a healthy complexion from his many outdoor activities. His nose seemed too large for his narrow face but there was a twinkle in his blue eyes that said, "All is right with the world." His wife, Ilse, was a stunning beauty. Her long blond hair framed a face with perfect features and no apparent make-up. Her 5'6" height was well proportioned and she spoke with a distinct German accent. We had such a pleasant conversation about the ranch that it was obvious that they wanted to spend some time with us, in the country.

Three weeks after returning from Glenwood Springs, the telephone rang and the voice on the other end said, "This is Willy from Denver calling. Remember you met us in Glenwood?" Of course we remembered him. He then asked whether they could come to visit next weekend.

"This is going to be fun, they plan to bring their dogs, too," I tried to get Fred excited. Actually, he was uneasy about having two huge canines share our house.

I cleaned the house until it sparkled, made up the bed, even put a bouquet of sunflowers on the dresser for them the day before they arrived.

Early the next morning a white van drove up and out sprang a couple of huge dogs, and then Ilse. Much later, Willy emerged carrying a box into the house just as we opened the door to welcome them. The dogs zipped past us and inspected all the rooms while we, the people, became reacquainted. I made a quick cup of instant coffee for everyone and we settled down at the kitchen table.

It was then when we learned of their plan. They proudly explained that they were going to put up a tent and live in it for the seven days they hoped to be with us. They added that they had cots to sleep on, a kerosene lantern, and a cook stove.

Then Willy told me that the box he had brought from Denver was for me and I should open it. It was closed with large staples, and after struggling a while with it, Willy reached into his pants pocket and withdrew a pair of pliers. "Here, let me help you," he plucked out the staples and the rest was easy. I next retrieved, one by one, a set of dinnerware, blue and white with a Chinese design. I thanked them copiously.

I still had not fully recovered from the shock of their camping and I wondered where they were going to keep the food and whether they brought any at all. They soon stood up and told us that they would look for a good place to erect the tent. Behind the house were lots of trees and they chose a couple of enormous cottonwoods.

When dinnertime came along, we always had our main meal at noon during the summer, I thought I would invite them at least for the first meal. Since they had a cook stove, I presumed they would do their own cooking after that. How wrong I was!

"What time do you want us for supper?" was the question put to us after they consumed a fair amount of fried chicken. Perplexed, almost speechless, we told them: "Six o'clock, and breakfast is at 7 AM," realizing that they had no intention of using their cookstove!

*Years later with the sign
Willy made for us.*

In between meals, both Willy and Ilse came to the house just to visit. They were fun and we laughed a lot.

After the seven days were up, the tent came down and in no time the van was loaded. The only edible thing they had brought was a case of beer which we kept cool for them. The remainder of the brew went back to Denver with them. And they were off. We, again, were on our own and it felt good. But Fred complained, "At least, they could have given us the beer!"

A few days later, Ilse called us. She wanted to invite us to dinner at their house in Denver. Happily we accepted. "See you before noon next Sunday, okay?" Yippee, I didn't have to cook on that day. I never really liked cooking. It is just one of those things a housewife has to do and Fred loves to eat!

Sunday, we rushed through the outside chores and the housework, got the kids ready and we were on our way. There was not much traffic all the way to Denver, even within the city. We got lost several times but eventually arrived at their house around 11 AM.

We rang the bell several times—no answer. "Maybe they are out or at a neighbor's. We'll just have to wait in the car."

Nobody came. It was now 11:55 AM and Fred went back to ring the bell again. This time Ilse came to the door in her nightie, looking very sleepy. "Come in, we are just getting up, sit down in the living room."

Fred called to us and we all sat there very quietly and embarrassed, not knowing what to do. We felt like going home—and maybe we should have. Instead, we continued to sit there like dummies while our hostess got dressed and then started dinner. Did they forget we were coming? Why were they so late? They never offered any explanation.

Ilse cooked an authentic and delicious German dinner—or was it tasty simply because we didn't eat until 2 PM.

About two years later Ilse called again, "We're on our way to Kansas City, may we stop by your place?"

"Of course, stay for lunch, all right?"

And so I prepared lunch for two extras. Imagine my surprise when six people emerged from their station wagon, all women and one child.

"Where's Willy?" I asked.

"Oh, we got divorced a year ago."

Fred stood there like a deer caught in the headlights of a car. Suddenly all these people collected in our living/dining room. I fed them what I had prepared, then asked Bonnie to make a tuna fish casserole mixture. When everyone's appetite was satisfied, they continued on their trip. There had been so much confusion that we never found out who all the guests were except for Ilse and her daughter.

We never again heard from them.

It was a disappointing time almost from the beginning of our acquaintance with these folks. We had hoped for friendship but it didn't materialize and we felt used. However, this new experience did not discolor our attitude towards strangers. After all, we are all people with different likes, dislikes, and habits—good and bad. None of us is perfect.

Guests on New Year's Day

On a ranch there is so much work to do, one day looks a lot like the next one. Cattle need to be fed, they get sick and need to be treated, and ice that has accumulated on water tanks and ponds needs to be chopped so the animals can drink the water. So it goes until you have spent most of the day going from chore to chore. As if this weren't enough, people also get sick and you begin to almost anticipate emergencies to arrive and always at the worst time. Often, however, unexpected, nice things do happen and that was always a special treat!

Living so far away from people, it was always a delight to have company, especially when they brought kids with them. So this year, my brother Max and his family from Denver were coming to the ranch on New Years' Day to stay for a couple of days. We were thrilled!

Hurray, company! That, of course, meant planning the meals and beginning to prepare what could be done the day before. Jack, ever helpful, had a great suggestion for dessert, "Why not have watermelon?" I explained that this was winter and they weren't in season. Whereupon he asked, "Are strawberries in 'heat' now?" Living on a ranch, Jack was learning the facts of life early!

It was New Year's Eve, the weather was cold but delightfully clear and sunshiny. By afternoon I had a couple of pies, apple and cherry, cooling on the kitchen table along with a big bowl of still-warm potatoes for my special German potato salad. In the fridge I had strawberry Jell-O and cranberry sauce. Later that day, Fred promised to kill a chicken for tomorrow's dinner. Having finished all the food preparation I realized that there was only one big job left to do—cleaning the house. Reinforced by Bonnie's severe remark, "This place looks like a "Schweinestall," the German word for pig stye, she then added, "I'll help you clean it up."

It was late afternoon before the house was presentable, the food prepared, and I had sunk into the old wooden rocker by the coal stove to relax. No sooner did I close my eyes when another neighbor drove up in a noisy, old blue pickup and announced that one of our cows had a bucket stuck on her head. We had rented a pasture for 50 cows and had just moved them there two weeks ago, and here, we already had a problem!

"Let's go, there's not much daylight left," Fred said in a frenzy. The whole family put on warm jackets and raced for the Jeep. Arriving at the rented pasture, about 12 miles from the ranch, we saw a cow with what looked like a huge head, walking and tripping. As we approached, we noticed that the poor thing couldn't see because her entire head was stuck in an old rusty bucket which probably had been lying around in the pasture for years. She tried in vain to get rid of that annoying thing but couldn't because the handle rested on her neck. The only way to solve the problem was to rope the cow then throw her to the ground and remove the adornment.

It was not an easy job. When the cow heard us approaching she became more nervous and ran in all directions and by accident stumbled into a nearby pond. Actually, that was helpful to us because she could not move very fast in the water and Fred, great with handling a rope, was able to swing a huge loop around her head, bucket and all. Everybody pulled on the rope until she was out of the water. Fred removed the bucket after which that darned cow simply walked away, drank gallons of water from the pond and proceeded to join the rest of the herd. No "thank you"—no nothing! Yet another emergency resolved.

Once we arrived home, it was already dark and we all had to go outside to begin the evening chores. They consisted of milking the cows, feeding the six calves on the nurse cow, feeding the chickens and collecting their eggs, haying the sheep and locking their corral before doing a final evening check of the expectant cows. Though it seemed like a lot to do, we were still excited because we were looking forward to the yearly display of fireworks from the very top of Pikes Peak which started at midnight every New Year's Eve. Since it was a cloudless night, we enjoyed another marvelous show for about 30 minutes and we didn't even have to leave the ranch!

Still tired from a short night, we awoke early to a cold clear day, excited because the company was due to arrive soon. We put on nicer clothes than on regular days and we were ready. Soon a white Chevy drove up. "Here they are," screamed Bonnie and everyone ran outside to greet the anticipated company. The kids, Annette and Steve, were the first ones out of the car followed by Pedro, the Chihuahua dog, and finally Amy and Max.

By now, we were through kissing and embracing each other and everybody entered the house. Pedro was in the lead, ran through all the rooms and discovered our beloved Chanukah bush. The holiday had just passed and since Jewish folks don't think a Christmas tree is proper, some people, including us, find a nice round tumbleweed or a yucca bush, decorate it with colored lights, and place a few gifts beneath the scratchy branches. It made everything quite festive and we enjoyed one just about every year. Pedro liked it too! He quickly raised his hind leg and relieved himself. We were all watching in shock, but Amy burst out laughing, "He is blessing the bush—isn't that cute?"

Dinner was served at 12:00 noon, sharp. Everybody was ready at the table, hungry eyes all around, when I noticed something moving on Amy's chest. Imagine my surprise when Pedro's head suddenly appeared from between her ample breasts and he stretched his neck to survey all the good smells coming from the table. Fred, still not a dog lover, almost got sick while the rest of us laughed hilariously at the display!

Dinner over, Fred wanted to show off our new well which was in the northwest pasture, about 10 miles away, so all of us piled into Max's car for a jaunt along the gravel roads. We left Pedro in the house. Along the way we answered many questions from our city cousins, laughed and enjoyed the carefree atmosphere. After riding for a while, I felt the need to return home to straighten out the kitchen and Max drove me home after which the rest of them continued on their ride to other places of interest. I opened the kitchen door and there was Pedro snarling at me. The little dog came after me and would not let me into my own house. He barked viciously with all of his 8 pounds and promised to eat me alive unless I left the house which he had now decided to protect and claim as 'his'. It was some time before everyone returned, Pedro was released from his duty as security guard and I could safely enter and work in my own kitchen! I never liked Pedro after that.

The two-day visit went by very quickly. We saddled horses and the kids rode in the corrals, they played in the hay barns, were delighted by the four new baby kittens, and there were numerous games of Kick the Can. For the final night, Bonnie had written a play which was performed by her and her siblings for the guests. It was presented in the basement, complete with programs, scenery, chairs for the audience, lights, and curtains. Bonnie introduced the show and made a special announcement, asking the audience to "Please give us clap." After an awkward pause and some hushed giggles, the audience figured out that she meant "applause!"

It was the next morning when, with a sigh of resignation and the need to return to our daily routine, that we said goodbye and wished our company a good trip home. For us, the work and preparation was worth the excitement and fun of showing off our way of life to others. It refreshed our routine, lessened the feeling of isolation, and renewed our enthusiasm for ranch life. 🐎

Max, Annette & Susan on horses with
Jack, Bonnie, Steve, and Fred.

Movie

"This is Paramount Studios in Hollywood calling. I want to speak with Mr. Vorenberg." That's what the man on the other end of the line said to me. "What in the world is that all about," I thought. "Is Fred being asked to be a movie star?" Handing the phone to him I heard him saying a lot of "Yes's" and "No's". I couldn't figure out what the man was saying by Fred's response. Finally the conversation ended with, "OK, I'll wait to hear from you, tomorrow."

"Tell me, Tell me!" was my impatient urging.

"Paramount wants to use a bunch of our cattle for 'The Lawyer', a movie they're going to shoot on the Calhan Fairgrounds," Fred announced.

"And I thought they wanted <u>you</u> in the movies!" was my immediate, somewhat sarcastic reply.

Indeed, Paramount Studios somehow found Calhan! The town clerk told them who the large cattle ranches in the area were. Fred didn't know what to do about the deal with Paramount, so he got together with some townspeople to discuss the proposal. It would be great to have our animals in the movies, but they all agreed that the price offered was just not enough. The movie folks didn't realize that the cattle would either have to be trucked or driven by horseback twelve miles to the County Fair Grounds. Then they would have to stand all day in the blistering heat of summer before returning them home again. They all agreed that the amount of money offered didn't cover the cost.

As promised, Paramount called the next day and Fred was ready. He explained how the cattle would lose weight during the filming and why we needed more money for our 'actors.' "We can't give you more money so I guess there won't be a deal," the casting agent said. Two days later, he called again, "Have you changed your mind?"

"I'm afraid not," was Fred's immediate answer.

A couple of weeks later, the motion picture crew arrived in Calhan to inspect the setting. They talked with the Mayor about changing some names of several stores because the film was set in a town called Baker. Eventually, they did find a rancher who was willing to supply the cattle—their chance to be in a movie. Other filming would take place in Colorado Springs where the Penrose Public Library became the "County Courthouse" of Baker.

It was a hot day when Paramount announced via television and newspapers that extras were needed to fill the grandstands for the movie. "Anyone interested in being in 'The Lawyer' should be at the County Fairgrounds at 8 AM on Friday. Be sure to bring ID and your Social Security Number. The Paramount Studios will be paying the normal salary for extras."

Talk about excitement! The whole town showed up. By the time the Vorenberg family succumbed to the temptation and arrived at the fairgrounds, there was a line snaking around several buildings. People were in a holiday mood. We stood in a slow moving line with the early, but strong, summer sun beating down on us causing failure of the antiperspirant we had applied earlier. Nobody complained. People laughed and someone joked about getting his star in front of Grauman's Chinese Theatre.

Finally all the Calhan 'movie stars' were assembled in the grandstands. I wore a hot pink, sleeveless blouse I had recently purchased and a pair of old jeans, like everybody else, dressed up hoping to be noticed. The film director kept looking over the crowd and rearranging the seating. We couldn't figure out his reasoning. Then, one of the guys called out to another one. "Move that pink lady towards the stairs." They were talking about me! So I, in my new, hot pink blouse, moved next to the stairs. It did the trick for when the filming finally started, the main actor came down the stairs and...bingo...filmed me sitting there just as he passed by me. Hurrah! I was in the movies—Hollywood had a new actress!

RECOGNIZE ANYONE?—Except for star Barry Newman, standing, the cast in this scene from the movie, "The Lawyer," which has just opened at the Ute 70 Theatre, is made up of residents of the Pikes Peak Region. This part of the movie was shot on location at the El Paso County Fairgrounds in Calhan.

There I am—in the movie and the newspaper!

It was interesting to watch the process of filming and of observing the 'real' actors but it was getting hot and we started to wonder just how much longer we would have to be 'on the set.' Some smart people had brought water to drink and they didn't mind 'hanging around.' We were dismissed after several takes. Incidentally, the other guy's cattle stood around in the arena most of the day, panting and looking hot. We were glad that we had left our livestock at home.

Months later, 'The Lawyer' opened in many of the movie houses in Colorado Springs. Most of us Calhanites went to see it, mainly to watch for familiar faces. Remembering how long we sat there in the grandstands made us think we would have plenty of time to look over all the faces on the screen. Nothing doing! A split second of the crowd—and the camera zoomed to other areas. But that short time was enough for me to shine in my hot pink blouse. The movie was very good and a few years later, was regularly aired on T.V.

Calhan, oh excuse me, Baker was now on the map and we were proud of it. Maybe next time Hollywood would return and let us keep our small town's name.

County Fair

The children weren't the only ones who loved and participated in the County Fair which, conveniently for us, was held in Calhan. Colorado Springs is also in El Paso County, which naturally brought in many participants and visitors to the yearly event.

I have always been proud of my garden. It supplied us with many different types of vegetables. We never tired of mounds of leaf lettuce at every meal. I tried raising new things every year. I was especially proud of my brussels sprouts because my father had been so successful with them in Germany. The best part was that they needed a frost to bring out their certain sweetness, therefore they could be harvested after everything else was done for the season.

Someone gave us rhubarb plants and I found it necessary to bake rhubarb meringue pies at every opportunity and which luckily everybody in the family loved. We also bought strawberry plants eventually producing gorgeous sweet fruit which I froze along with everything else.

But squash—summer and winter varieties—filled a huge part of my garden. This plant probably was my most prolific vegetable. These creeping plants tried to invade the whole garden and I found myself moving their several feet long branches back into their reserved area.

Every spring, Fred would dump truckfuls of manure onto the garden. To my chagrin, he dropped the load in one place and I had to spread it evenly over the plot. I developed gorgeous biceps from this job! When you are a rancher's wife there is no need to belong to a gym. You get all the exercise you need if you have a garden because it is usually considered the 'little woman's' job.

The yearly date of the El Paso County Fair was suddenly moved ahead four weeks and this made it too early to exhibit any produce except my yellow squash. There must have been at least twenty-five ready to be picked and the yellow blossoms would not quit. Every day I checked those plants looking for three perfect squashes. They had to be the right size, a good color, and no blemishes. That would be easy and I planned to pick them early in the morning on the day of the fair, as the judging would start at 9 AM. This indeed looked like a bumper crop.

The day before the fair was always the busiest of the year. The children's livestock was readied, their record books were checked, and additions made. The baked goods were lined up in boxes to be loaded the following morning. Months of planning, of practicing, and of decision making accumulated on this day before the fair. Even though nerves were on edge it was a happy time as every one of us hoped for a ribbon, preferably a blue one for first prize.

That afternoon, as happens so often in the summertime, gray clouds moved in, shutting off the sun. A thunderclap alerted everyone to stay indoors and then it came. I couldn't believe my eyes when instead of the usual rain, a barrage of hail, the size of ping-pong balls pounded everything in sight. The sound of the hail hitting windowpanes, the roof of the house, and the pickup outdoors was deafening. Leaves from the trees were strewn everywhere while the bare branches waved in the wind as if they were startled by the violent activity around them.

In times like these, in order to feel better, one always says, "At least we are safe and together." We thought it often that afternoon as more and more lightening bolts passed in front of our eyes, immediately followed by monstrous thunder. It was easy to imagine Thor, the God of Thunder driving by us in his chariot while whirling his horsewhip.

All of a sudden, the storm left as quickly as it came. The sun was back peeking between a few left over clouds and trying to tell the world that everything was fine. It moved east and was busy doing its damage there. I thought of my garden and also of the poor farmers who grew crops in their fields. They probably had nothing left. This had been a severe hailstorm and my thoughts also went to the livestock out in the pastures who took the brunt of the hailstones. How that must have hurt on their faces and backs!

Carefully, I decided to inspect the garden, expecting to find nothing and prepared to view total disaster. In order to get there, however, I was faced with what looked like a winter scene. The ground was white and in places the accumulation of the hail was over a foot deep.

When I got to the garden gate one look said it all. The leaves of my beautiful squash plants were ripped to pieces, most of them dismembered, lying partially covered with hailstones. It was silly of me to go inside the garden and check if anything was left. My thoughts of finding three beautiful yellow squash for tomorrow dropped to zero. Yet, I went in anyway.

I fought back tears as I went from plant to plant only to find squash which looked as if someone had used them for target practice. I turned and went to get a bucket which I started filling with usable vegetable for our consumption. And then, I found one perfect sample. Excitement and hope energized me — "Could there possibly be two more?" I continued in my search and to my biggest surprise, I found two more equally perfect specimens.

The following morning was the first day of the County Fair and we were excited. Fred was the Superintendent of the Agriculture Department and I always helped out with the paperwork. We met the farmers who entered their produce and grains and registered them for the contest. It was great fun as you saw everyone in the neighborhood and from miles away. We had some friends whom we only saw during the Fair! The judges arrived and soon they were looking, smelling, touching, and turning over the produce as they struggled with their decisions.

There must have been close to a dozen entries of bush green beans and an equal amount of pole beans. After a while, I announced that the judging would begin for summer squash, and all the entries were brought to the table. They all looked shiny and perfect. I watched my courageous squash sitting bravely on a paper plate along with their

30 competitors—It always was the category with the most entries. I could only wait and dream of the sought after blue ribbon.

The judge took his time. "This is tough," he said.

My heart was racing. I am sure my face was flushed thinking if I could possibly win a ribbon—of any kind? And then the judge announced Number 72 was first and slapped a blue ribbon on my squash! I let out a muffled yell, very unprofessional, I might add, but I couldn't help it. If I had a garden full of squash to choose from I would not have been so excited about this win. First place brought in a grand total of $1.50!

ECKING ON THE CROPS — Mr. and Mrs. Fred enberg of near Calhan look over the organic gar... Paso County Fair in Calhan. This was the first orga ic gardening display in the history of the fair, whi has its final day today. (Gazette Telegraph Photos

Winning my blue ribbon.

After the judging in my department was over I went to the sheep judging area where Tommy was showing a ewe, a fat lamb, and a ram.

I got there just in time and several interested onlookers were leaning on the fence watching the judging including a young man of about twenty who stood next to me. He asked me if the only boy showing with all those girls was my son when Tommy handed me the trophy he had just won. We started to talk to each other and found out that Paul was a cadet at the Air Force Academy and that he came from a farm in the Mid-West where his parents raised sheep and a few cows.

He was so friendly that I asked him to come home with us to have dinner that night. In no time we became good friends. Paul often came out to the ranch and he and Tommy would go horseback riding. After we attended his graduation, he got married and soon thereafter we lost touch with him.

Our girls liked him, too, and spoke of him to their girlfriends in school. One of them said longingly to Bonnie: "I wished my mother would pick up a cadet like that for me!" Oh what a reputation I was getting!!

The fair lasted just a few days but they were filled with fun, disappointments, new friends, lots of junk food and a variety of ribbons plus one trophy.

This yearly event was a great learning opportunity for all of us. We loved the fair and were sad when Sunday, the final day, came and the show animals had to be loaded and brought home. This meant the end of summer and school was not far off. But being with all our friends, doing country things made us feel proud of our chance to live in the country like in John Denver's song, "It's Good to be a Country Boy!" 🐴

COLORADO   SPRINGS

GAZETTE TELEGRAPH

ANN TYNER BROOKS
Ranch, Farm and Garden Editor

SECTION C   COLORADO SPRINGS—WEDNESDAY, AUGUST 11, 1965   SECTION C

County Fair, Rodeo, Horse Show Set in Calhan

FAIR-MINDED FAMILY — Getting their Hereford heifers ready for the El Paso County Fair, Amateur Rodeo and Horse Show Friday through Sunday at the fair grounds in Calhan are Tom Vorenberg (left), 16; Jack Vorenberg (center), 7; and Susan Vorenberg, 11. Tom is grooming his Ketch-It-Keep-It calf, which he

caught in 1964. He has been active in five 4-H projects: beef breeding, range management, sheep breeding, soil conservation and junior leadership. Susan has participated in 4-H beef breeding and cooking projects. Their father, Fred Vorenberg, is one of the directors of the fair, and is assisted in this work by his wife. Not

pictured is Bonnie Vorenberg, who has also participated in the Ketch-It-Keep-It program and in 4-H beef breeding. The family's address is Star Route, Calhan. Judging will start at 1 p.m. Friday in the Home Economics Department and the Brown Swiss Canton Show, and at 2 p.m. Friday for 4-H Breeding

Beef. Slated to be judged at 9 a.m. Saturday are the Quarter Horse Show, the Agriculture and Poultry Departments, and the 4-H Dairy Department. The Open Livestock Department and the Open Dairy Department will be judged after the 4-H Show. The 4-H Horse Show

will be judged at 9 a.m. Sunday. The Livestock 4-H Parade will be held at 11:45 a.m., and the 4-H Market Steer Sale at noon. Admission to the fair grounds Saturday and Sunday is $1 for adults, 50c for children, and free for those under age 10. The County Fair Rodeo and Race Program is slated for 2

p.m. Saturday and Sunday. Rodeo events will include kids' calf riding, bareback bronc riding, calf roping, saddle bronc riding, girls' barrel race, bull dogging and bull riding. The race program will include five-eights mile, 220 and 440-yard free-for-all races and a 440-yard cow pony race.

— (Gazette Telegraph Photo)

The Beaudrys

We met Clayton and Jere Beaudry while they were building their home on Jones Rd., roughly five miles from our ranch. Their friendliness and openness inspired us to visit with them and soon we learned to love and respect them. Both Clay and Jere, were well-educated teachers in Colorado Springs who eventually moved into their new house. Being with these folks always seemed like inhaling a breath of fresh air. Indeed it was invigorating and stimulating.

We shared many meals with the Beaudrys and on one occasion, I was introduced to my first experience of tasting Schnapps. It did sting my throat a bit, but it was delicious!

The births of their two daughters, Emily and Lindsay, was as exciting as if they had been part of our own family. To our delight, their parents taught them to address us as Oma and Opa, the German equivalent of Grandma and Grandpa.

While her children were small, Jere stayed home with them and we visited frequently. One day I asked her, "Would you like to do some volunteering with me?"

"Of course, I would!" was her enthusiastic reply even before she knew what I had in mind.

Once a month we volunteered at the Health Department Branch in Calhan. The local Mormon Church had offered the use of several rooms where we could assist Public Health Nurses in the Well Baby and Well Senior Adult Clinic. Jere's speed of adjusting, her constant cheerfulness caused one of the nurses to ask me, "Where did you find her?"

To which I answered smart-alecky, "Oh, in the Sears Catalog." When I further explained that she was my friend and neighbor, the nurse merely said, "You are so lucky!" I agreed.

Both of us attended monthly gatherings of other neighbors in what was called the "Help Thy Neighbor Club." Here we would meet to share food, gossip and always do a craft project. It was something that we always looked forward to.

After Clay received his Ph. D., he was offered a fine job in Montrose on the Western slope of Colorado. They sold their place and moved away. We missed this lovely family greatly. A few years had passed when we visited them in their home. The girls had grown into well-mannered children, sweet and loveable. We promised each other to keep in touch.

To have friends is a true blessing. They are people who forgive you when, for which I am famous, would 'put my foot in my mouth.' Being real friends, they listened to my feelings, worries, and my silliness.

The day the Beaudrys moved onto their place on Jones Rd. was indeed a lucky day for us.

Clayton and Jere Beaudry, with baby Lindsay and Emily.

Chapter 10

THE ZOO!

A Snake in the Basement

One winter was especially snowy. Not a week went by without the heavy gray clouds releasing the white stuff making it difficult for the school busses to negotiate all the roads.

Jack missed many days of school. In the beginning, he was happy but soon realized that his dad expected him to work outdoors. The weather being so miserable made the boy wish, in a very short time, for a warm classroom.

When late spring arrived, Jack had missed a total of forty school days. Finally, the climate became mild; the buds on the trees and bushes opened and delighted every soul with a sea of pink and white blossoms. Bees were busy collecting nectar and birds were making nests. Spring had come and school days returned to normal.

The nights remained chilly. The process of snow melting in the root cellar, immediately north of the house, was very slow. The soil everywhere was saturated from all the moisture but after a few weeks the sun became stronger and melting began in earnest.

One afternoon, I descended the cement stairs leading to the basement with the intention of getting a jar of my homemade choke cherry jelly. Imagine my horror when I looked down and saw an empty Kerr jar, with the top on, floating aimlessly in a lake of water. The entire basement floor was covered about a foot deep from one end to the other. My frantic call to Fred, who was in the garage, made him hurry to the house.

"What's wrong now?" he asked, rather irritated and annoyed. He calmed down when he saw the flood but was not amused when I joked about Noah needing to build another ark.

At once, he got into the pickup, drove to Calhan and bought a sump pump. The apparatus worked beautifully and the water was gone from the basement. What a relief!

I praised my dear husband for accomplishing the job so quickly and so well. I didn't mention Noah anymore even though I thought it was funny.

A couple of days later more seepage from the melting snow began to trickle into the basement again. When I told Fred, his reassuring reply was "I'll take care of it." But he didn't. As the days progressed, the water continued to ooze in and Fred's answer always was the same, "I'll take care of it." But again, he never did.

A week after the basement was pumped out, the area where we kept coal for the furnace and whose floor was lower than the rest, had filled in again. Again, the water was close to a foot deep. I feared that the wooden posts supporting the first floor of the house would rot and disintegrate before long. It bothered me greatly that Fred didn't keep his idle promises. What could I do? Did I need to threaten him with something or just beg him sweetly on bended knee?

It was a Sunday and the children and I got ready to leave for Sunday School. A wonderful idea popped into my mind. After I dropped the kids off in Colorado Springs I drove to Woolworths on Tejon Street and bought a fake two-foot long snake, a life-like replica of a mature and mean rattler. I thought to myself, you got to do something desperate to get Fred into action. I knew I needed the children's cooperation.

On our way home I told them of my elaborate plan. We rehearsed the 'show' a couple of times until I was satisfied with that the 'actors' would do their part. Surely, we couldn't fail to achieve results—the plot was just too terrific.

The 'show' was to get underway after our one o'clock dinner. Never did the kids eat so fast, talk so little during the meal, and be so willing to help with the dishes.

Excitement was building by the minute as the curtain was about to be raised. Fred had just settled down to watch the Broncos play the Oakland Raiders. He had a satisfied and relaxed look on his face, anticipating three hours of sheer bliss. Now it was time. I tiptoed down the basement stairs with my important prop in my hand, walked over to the unsightly pool of water and partially submerged the snake into it. I curled the thing so that it looked like it was ready to strike. Back upstairs again, I asked Susan to go downstairs into the basement and get me a jar of applesauce from the basement, making sure that Fred heard me. The sequence went as follows: Bonnie was to stand on the bottom step and Jack would be on the upper one of the basement stairs. Susan, in the basement, was supposed to scream, "There's a snake!" The two actors on the stairs were to follow with realistic fear, very loud and clear.

The scene was set, the kids needed no more rehearsal and the production proceeded. Everything went right, the screams and commotion appeared genuine.

After the screams and the wild race up the basement stairs, Fred leaped from his comfortable easy chair as if a stick of nitro had exploded beneath him. He raced down the stairs while the kids continued to yell about that hideous snake in the water.

My brave husband yelled to Jack while he flew down the stairs. "Get me a hoe from the saddle room!" That snake really had him fooled and he kept telling everybody to step back. When Jack returned with the deadly weapon, Fred grabbed it, lifted it up. I swung at his arms, desperately trying to prevent him from 'killing' the toy snake. It was quite a struggle but eventually I yelled at him that this was not a REAL snake. He finally slowed down just before the hoe hit home. The slaughter of my innocent toy was prevented. I really did not want it decapitated; I might have to use it again!

Fred returned to his easy chair and his football game not in the best mood. He growled and muttered words I did not, nor want to, understand. He knew he had been had.

What a fantastic group of actors these kids were, I praised them loudly. Their enthusiasm was indestructible. Their joy of the ruse was delightful. The kids and I never laughed so hard! I retrieved my snake, washed it clean and let it dry, then placed it in my desk drawer for future use.

From that day on, the water 'miraculously' disappeared <u>every</u> <u>day</u>. Fred finally did what he'd promised to do so many times before—"He took care of it."

After a week, the seepage stopped altogether. But it took some time before the cement floor was completely dry.

My motto is: Sometimes you have to resort to trickery when nothing else works!

Months later, the floor of the living room buckled—a constant reminder of the snake episode. I am happy to proclaim that never again did I have to repeat the production.

Years later, I gave the snake to a boy who was delighted. "I'm going to scare my sisters with that!" he hollered. This proves that a $1.49 toy can bring not only joy, but also results. 🐴

The reason why Jack missed
40 days of school.

Hired Men

When the kids started leaving for college, the workload just became too much for the family. We decided to use hired men. It became a kaleidoscope of humanity—each more colorful than the next! They came from different parts of the country, one even from Mexico City.

We outfitted the Eis house for the hired man and his family. We fixed it up with dishes and cutlery, kitchen furniture, a bedroom set and linen and we brought over my old cook stove since I now had a new one with a larger oven.

We got proficient at interviewing the prospective hired help and tried to learn both the psychology and the art of making the right selection. Since money was always in short supply we had to spend the least amount possible. Fred took his time and casually chatted with them. Only on their first day did they see the 'real' Fred!

Unfortunately we became good at interviewing because the hired men did not stay very long. Other positions always presented themselves and they usually were easier and offered more money. We couldn't blame them for wanting to better themselves. But they did miss out on adventure!

Several of our hired men were fellows who had returned from Vietnam. One went berserk and shot four of our cows and then ran away never to be seen again. Another stole supplies from our saddle room and sold them at the weekly auction in Calhan. If he couldn't make it for the Friday event, he'd send his wife to do the honors!

Once we discovered that we had hired an ex-convict. He was a nice and willing person, probably on his way to becoming an upstanding citizen.

Then there was Charlie who confided to Fred that he made love to his wife before they were married. Fred told him that they should have waited to which he replied, "He couldn't, it was irresistible!"

One fellow came to work the first day, sat on the fence and fell off, spraining his ankle. He was out of commission a whole week. Guess who had to 'fill in' for that week?

Another ex-soldier from Vietnam frequently came to work wearing pink glasses. We later found out that he was so full of Hashish that he was too weak to work.

Don Fay was a fine worker who had a wonderful wife. He helped us through many a mean blizzard and stayed quite a while with us, teaching Jack sex education while they did their work!

One guy, during the interview, said he was good at riding horseback, an imperative skill. Yet, on his first day, I had to show him how to bridle a horse. Later he fell off but hung onto the saddle horn so firmly that he ended up sitting on the ground with the entire bridle off the horse and in his hand. I felt like saying, "I thought you could ride," but I didn't. His pride and his behind were hurt enough.

Once Fred hired an exceptionally big fellow. A few days afterward, a steer needed to be butchered and we had the new hired man help, after hours. We promised him a goodly amount of the meat, all cut-up, in return for his efforts. This guy remained on the job working for us until he proudly carried a large box of meat home. He never came back, neither for the job nor the money he had still coming. I hope he liked the meat!

Then, another man heard we had been looking for help. He drove up in a van with all his belongings, including a huge white Newfoundland dog. He was single. He worked that same day and promised to return the next day and move into the Eis house. He never came back for a week. When I asked him what happened he told me quite honestly, "I went to a bar, got into a fight with another guy and spent all last week in jail. Do you still want me to work for you?" I thanked him for being honest but we already had hired someone else, which was the truth. I think he would have been a good hired man. He was honest—and he loved dogs!

But the nicest fellow was Terry, our last hired man. He was young and handsome with straw-colored hair and a ready smile. Sensitive and thoughtful, Terry was a very hard worker who willingly took on the most difficult tasks. He was just simply a nice person and we became quite fond of both him and his wife. I wished we'd remained in contact.

As the hired men filed through the Eis House more and more things disappeared! One guy didn't like the metal kitchen cabinets on the wall, so he ripped them off. Dishes and linens vanished, even the bed linens, pillows, and, believe it or not, my old gas cook stove! Of course, not all the fellows stole, a lot of them were good men. Several even came back for a visit, after they stopped working for us.

The interesting characters that were our hired men proved to me, once again, how people are so very different. Here in the same environment and situation, they all responded in their own unique way. Even how they responded to us varied. But most of all, they were colorful! 🐎

Fred with Terry, my favorite, Carl, and George Bourbeau,
our friend and neighbor.

THE NEW MEXICO HEIFER

She come boiling down the alley, a rangy yearlin' heifer,
She was young and strong, lean and quick.
She was bawling an' blowin' an a' runnin' like the devil
It was damn sure that this sow wasn't sick.

When she got to the squeeze chute she caught us off guard,
She leaped, before anything could be done,
She flew right through the headgate and landed on her feet,
Still runnin' and now lookin for some fun.

The crew went out to the haze her, get her back into the pen,
See if we could get her in for another try,
But she come at us a' hookin' got us runnin for the fence,
And kicked Jesse in the groin as she ran by.

It seemed to last forever, we'd get down and here she come,
And we'd scramble to the top rail one more time,
She sure called the tune for this here dance, this I can't deny,
The way that critter used us was a crime.

We was holdin' a war council up there on the fence when she
Walked over to the pen all on her own.
Freddy slid across the fence, popped the gate and let it swing
An' she strolled on in like she's goin' home.

She went over to the corner an' took a big old drink,
Then went right into the alley like we'd hoped.
We closed the gate behind her, thought this time we'll get' er done,
She moved up, an' once again began to lope.

She wouldn't catch us napping this time, we'd seen this once before
We'll snag her in the headgate, do it right.
She's runnin' down the alley' till ten feet from the chute,
She set the brake, fell over an' wedged in tight.

She's layin' there a' pawin' at the air an' all of us,
She kept fightin's like it was all our fault.
We got ropes on her front feet an' also on her horns,
We pulled an' strained an' cussed, then called a halt.

It was obvious this labor was doing us no good,
That all this strain and heavin' was in vain.
Freddy got a bar an' hammer, we removed the bottom rails,
Got her upright and movin' once again.

She leaped into the chute, we caught her clean an' slick,
Couldn't do that good again if we tried.
Then that cantankerous young cow got the best of us somehow,
Laid down, had a heart attack, and died.

By George Bourbeau
(One of our colorful hired men who wrote this true story after working on the ranch.)

Homing Pigeon

"Mom, there's a big bird in the yard and it's not flying away," was Susan's anxious call to me. This sounded like another minor emergency. I stared at the pigeon which was obviously in trouble. It looked like it had a broken wing. I picked it up gently and saw that its left wing was hanging awkwardly by his leg. His little heart was beating furiously and his beak was partially open. It was a beautiful solid gray bird who didn't struggle while cuddled in my hand. Then I noticed a band around one leg. There was a number on it. Could it be a carrier pigeon?

We made a few calls around Calhan and found out that there was a Homing Pigeon Club in the Black Forest area, northeast of Colorado Springs and northwest from our ranch. We called the President of the club who told us that they had not lost any birds.

A bushel basket became the home of our wounded bird. We secured the broken wing next to the body with a bandage, filled a jar with water and a small can with chicken feed. Next, we placed some chicken wire over the top to keep the pigeon from jumping out. We left the basket on the enclosed porch.

By the second day, the bird was eating and drinking. It never was shy when we approached the basket which made us doubly sure that this was no average statue-loving pigeon.

We provided 'tender loving care' to Mathilde, the name we gave her and after three weeks Fred thought she was mended. She never gave us any trouble. She seemed relaxed, ate well and became used to us gawking at her!

We decided to release her and we all got together for the event, feeling nervous and worried for fear the wing had not healed properly. Could she fly, we wondered?

I picked her out of the basket, held her in one hand and had a "tete-à-tete" talk with her saying stupid things like, "Now fly away straight home. Don't stop anywhere and come back to visit us sometime."

Fred put Mathilde onto a low branch of a cottonwood tree by the house. All of us held our breath. Then with a rustling of feathers and a whoosh, she was flying around the house. Three times she circled before gaining altitude. Mathilda acted as if she knew where she was going—straight west. We were sad to see her go but happy that she could fly again: A true dichotomy! 🐎

Siamese Twins

On a ranch, checking cattle was a daily job. We kept all the springers, cows who were close to calving, in a nearby pasture so we could look at them several times a day. The first calf heifers concerned us most because we rarely had problems with cows who had calved before.

On a routine check, Fred noticed a cow in labor but he wasn't worried. However, when he returned a couple of hours later she had not progressed one iota. He then called for Carl, the hired man, who was fixing fence not far from the Old Place.

The men pushed the cow into the corral where they used a rope around her neck to firmly tie her to a post. Fred checked her and noticed that the calf's feet and head were coming right but he couldn't figure out why the birthing process was taking so long.

To help her out, Carl got another rope out of the pickup and placed it over the two front legs just behind the calf's hooves. Both started to pull. Finally, after struggling for at least 15 minutes, the head was delivered. But it seemed that something was just not right. Perhaps an obstruction was stopping everything. By now the cow's labor contractions had ceased so it was now up to the two tired cowboys to get busy! So far, the head and feet were out and the calf was alive. Its eyes were blinking and his tongue was moving.

"Let's try again, Carl. We got to get this calf out or we'll have trouble." Fred said. So, they pulled and pulled and all of a sudden another head appeared along with two more feet.

"Twins," someone shouted. "But why isn't one of them coming out first like twin calves usually do?"

By now the guys were perspiring profusely. This was proving to be a most difficult job and they needed to hurry. The poor cow bawled every time the guys pulled on those calves. Now, they worried about the cow. She was lying on her side, moaning, her breathing shallow and fast. Her eyelids were twitching and part of her tongue was touching the ground.

"We got to get these calves out of there or we'll lose the cow!" That's what the boss said, and again, they resumed the ordeal. "One—two—three—puuulllll!" and out came both calves at the same time.

"Siamese twins!" both said in unison. On closer inspection, the men noticed that their bodies were fused from the chest to the lower belly. They were alive and breathing, both even bawled a few times and then roughly ten minutes later, they died, almost simultaneously.

The cow didn't get up for several hours. Carl put some hay and a bucket of water in front of her and we happily noticed that she started to eat almost immediately.

Fred called the newspaper office in Colorado Springs and told them about our unusual birth. They sent out a reporter the same day who wrote the story and took a picture of the calves which ended up in the next morning's paper.

The cow recovered. We bought a Holstein bull calf and trained it to nurse on her. She took the calf willingly and raised a fine steer.

We had several twins born on our ranch but luckily this was our only set of Siamese. They are rare and, like ours, usually die soon after birth or are born dead. This was enough excitement to last us for a while and we hoped Mother Nature would not play any more tricks on us.

When animals suffered, so did I. They couldn't tell you what hurts and where. But by observing them closely, they will give you an idea of what's wrong. It was up to us to care for the animals to the best of our knowledge, be they domesticated or wild. That is why I am 100% against the inhumane form of trapping animals with snares, etc. It has been known that, on occasion, they actually chew their limbs off in order to get away. What a terrible price to pay! We need to be kind to all animals, all of the time.

Chapter 11

ACCOMPLISHMENTS & SETBACKS

Fire

It was a pleasant day, warm and sunny although the signs of an approaching fall were everywhere. The breeze loosened a few rusty leaves from the cottonwood trees scattering them around the driveway. This was Labor Day and we planned to take it easy.

We finished our noon dinner, cleaned up the kitchen and settled down in the living room to watch the yearly Muscular Dystrophy Telethon hosted by Jerry Lewis. It was funny as always but not enough to prevent Fred from going to sleep. My man can sleep at a moment's notice, even when standing up!

On television, Van Cliburn approached the piano as the telethon progressed and he, as somebody once said, "caressed the ivories" playing Chopin's Polonaise. I was completely absorbed in this music when someone in a pickup sped into our driveway honking furiously. "Wake up, Fred, someone's here. Something must be wrong," I hollered.

We both jumped up and ran to the door where we encountered a very upset neighbor. "Your barn is on fire. I saw it from the Calhan Highway. Call the Fire Department!"

Barely breathing and trying to comprehend what we just heard, our bodies felt like they were anchored in stone, our minds at a stand still. Nothing seemed to work; our world stopped turning. Luckily, we soon snapped out of our stupor, gave a quick look outdoors and stared at a sight we would never forget. The two-story barn to the north was completely engulfed by tongues of flame. Fred raced to the telephone and called the Fire Department, then both of us ran towards the frightful sight. One side of the barn, still untouched by fire, was the sheep corral. Squeezed into the farthest corner, away from the heat, all of our eight beautiful animals stood trembling from fright. Like lightning, Fred opened a gate so the animals could escape. I followed them with my eyes and saw that they never stopped running for at least a quarter of a mile.

Two fire trucks, one from Calhan and the other from Ellicott, arrived in minutes but were only able to control the fire and keep it from spreading. The barn, partially filled with bundles of feed, and built entirely of wood, was consumed in no time. The roaring noise of the fire stopped, but the heat remained. We could only stand and stare while the firemen doused the still-burning posts and patches of grass with gallons of water. The breeze was enough to send sparks into the air which could ignite areas quite a distance away.

By now, several folks from the neighborhood had come to see if they could help while others just watched. The smoke was so thick and dark that both the helpers and the onlookers started to leave.

We wondered, as did others, what had caused the fire. It finally dawned on us. On the south side of the barn was a spotlight, which when switched on manually, would illuminate several corrals. Fred had noticed some loose wires and had asked an electrician from the neighborhood to come to fix it a week before, but he never showed up. Wind from the south probably rubbed the wires together, causing sparks which started the blaze.

The frightened sheep never returned home before dark, as they always did. By morning, the next day, however, they reappeared. They approached the devastated area timidly not certain whether it was safe. We enticed them with their usual quota of tasty grain and turned them back out to pasture.

The day after the fire, Fred called our insurance company, the Farm Bureau, which for years had covered the house and all the buildings. The adjuster came out the following day, looked at the damage and immediately wrote a check. Now, that was service! We have sung the praises of the Farm Bureau ever since.

It took weeks to clear away all the debris, but eventually, with the help of our hired man and others, it was accomplished. Soon afterward, the men started rebuilding a new one-story barn.

The fright and tragedy of seeing your building burn down is immense. Yet, we were grateful for having lost only feed and no animals. Every year afterward when we watched Jerry Lewis' telethon, our thoughts returned to that fateful day which proved to be just another detour in the road of life. 🐴

Steve

Max, my elder brother, came for a visit and though it was always great to see him, we thought something was strange when he came alone, without his wife or children. Finally, he started to talk about the escapades of his son, Steve. Max mentioned the poor grades he was getting and the many days he skipped school. Steve was a junior in a parochial High School and obviously he was not happy there, to put it mildly.

And then it came, "Would you possibly consider taking Steve into your home and letting him go to Calhan School?" Actually, I kind of expected something like this. So, I was quick to answer that we would be happy to have him stay with us.

"Of course, he would have to do chores and go by the some routine and rules of the household like the other children," we warned him.

Max was relieved, especially when Fred said that he would teach the boy all about ranching. My brother, who was never at a loss for words, seemed to try to come up with something profound but all he could blurt out was, "That's just what the boy needs!"

We settled on a date for Steve to come and in a matter of a few weeks we picked him up at the bus station and brought him to the ranch. He was very pleasant, polite, downright sweet and appeared happy to be with us. We enrolled Steve in school, in the same grade as Jack, and after a week we realized that he was behind in his studies. It proved how the country schools are often ahead of the ones in the city, a fact I had often heard. Fred assured Steve that he would help him with Math and both of us would be there to guide him in all the other courses.

Every Friday, the boys had a spelling test and before long, because we made it a point to review the words every Thursday night, they both brought home top grades. We were especially proud of Steve because he really was trying to improve.

Steve did not like to dress up but he always looked nice when he went to school or when we went to town. He had a few habits, not bad ones, but I felt they needed to be eliminated. For instance, he ate everything with a teaspoon and his English was very poor. I have always been a stickler when it came to using proper English, both at home and away.

Steve's chores consisted of feeding and watering the chickens before school and collecting eggs in the evening. Every morning, as soon as he got up, he surprised me with a quick hug and wished me a "Good morning, Aunt Schlitza." Something like that would warm even the coldest person's heart!

Once, Fred had a problem with the John Deere tractor and Steve happened to hear his grumblings. Without ever having been near a tractor before, he went over and looked at the piece which was giving Fred the trouble. In no time at all, the city kid said, "Uncle Fred, I think if you push that bolt in here and string the wire through on the opposite side, it'll work." Fred did—and it worked! He later told me, "That kid is a 'natural' with machinery."

One weekend 'headquarters' announced that we had to butcher the chickens that were not laying eggs. Obviously, that meant the many roosters which we raised for meat and all the old hens had to go.

It turned out to be a chilly day. We talked it over and decided what everyone's job would be. Jack was busy at a 4-H meeting, so Fred, Steve, and I were left to do the work.

A less than enthusiastic eviscerator.

The butchering job had to be done fast and efficiently, according to Fred's orders. "Yes, of course, dear," I agreed, somewhat sarcastically.

The outside work was assigned to Steve and me while Fred considered himself the best eviscerater of the birds. I wondered why he chose that job for himself—was he really better than the rest of us or was a warm indoor job what he was looking for?

We soon assembled pans, dishes, lots of old newspapers, different knives, buckets, and a couple of kettles of boiling water. Steve and I ventured into the chicken house where the frightened birds flew in all directions, stirring up dust and feathers to block every conceivable orifice on one's face. "A haven for people with allergies," I joked. We each grabbed two chickens by the legs and carried them outdoors. I hate to chop the heads off, so I gave Steve the honors. He handed me one of his birds while I held an upside-down 'bouquet' of three in one hand.

With much gusto, down came the axe on the unsuspecting chicken's neck and it fluttered about headlessly, first in one direction and then in another. After all four were killed, we dumped them into a bucket, poured boiling water over them and pulled off the feathers, called dressing a chicken—perhaps it should be called 'undressing!'

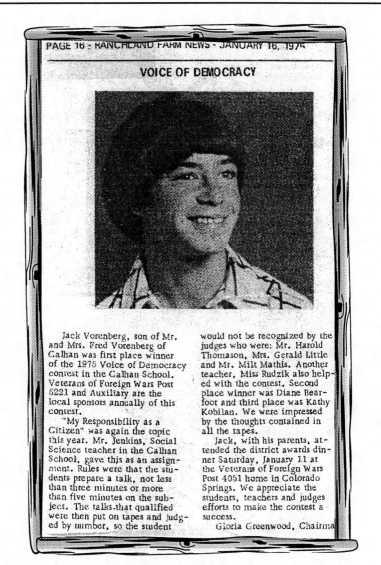

PAGE 16 - RANCHLAND FARM NEWS - JANUARY 16, 1975

VOICE OF DEMOCRACY

Jack Vorenberg, son of Mr. and Mrs. Fred Vorenberg of Calhan was first place winner of the 1975 Voice of Democracy contest in the Calhan School. Veterans of Foreign Wars Post 6221 and Auxiliary are the local sponsors annually of this contest.

"My Responsibility as a Citizen" was again the topic this year. Mr. Jenkins, Social Science teacher in the Calhan School, gave this as an assignment. Rules were that the students prepare a talk, not less than three minutes or more than five minutes on the subject. The talks that qualified were then put on tapes and judged by number, so the student would not be recognized by the judges who were: Mr. Harold Thomason, Mrs. Gerald Little and Mr. Milt Mathis. Another teacher, Miss Rudzik also helped with the contest. Second place winner was Diane Bearfoot and third place was Kathy Kobilan. We were impressed by the thoughts contained in all the tapes.

Jack, with his parents, attended the district awards dinner Saturday, January 11 at the Veterans of Foreign Wars Post 4051 home in Colorado Springs. We appreciate the students, teachers and judges efforts to make the contest a success.

Gloria Greenwood, Chairman

Jack wins another speech contest.

Our next job was to singe them over the flame of the gas stove in the house and pull off the pinfeathers. Then Fred took over and eviscerated the birds. He separated the livers, stomach, and gizzards to make several meals for future use.

We worked for hours. It was getting colder outdoors. The wind started blowing and our clothes were getting dirtier and wetter. Steve and I became quite proficient at our assignments and we got way ahead of Fred. The kitchen table was piled high with naked chickens, the smell of wet feathers saturated the entire house and some spilled water made the floor slippery.

After Fred got through with his chickens, we all helped stuff them into plastic bags and put them into our freezer. We did it! We butchered 38 chickens in one day. Quite an accomplishment! Needless to say, we went to bed early, thoroughly exhausted. Steve took all this extra-curricular activity in stride, but he mentioned later that he didn't really want to do this too often. Like with all the other facets of ranch life, he adjusted amazingly well.

Every year, the Mountain View Electric Association held a speech contest to high school students. Jack won the year before and was awarded a trip to Washington D.C. Now, Steve, who had never stood in front of a group and much less given a speech, was convinced to try. We worked with him and finally he was ready for the contest to be held in Limon, the headquarters for the association. To our joy and Steve's, he won and got to take a weeklong trip to Steamboat Springs, Colorado. This was the first time he ever won anything and he was so proud!

I hate to brag, but after being on the ranch, all Steve's grades improved and he was on the honor roll several times in addition to winning other speech contests. His many successes prove that with assistance you can take any child and guide them in the right direction. In Denver, Steve's parents were just too busy with their jobs and couldn't devote enough time to him.

When Steve returned for his senior year, we could immediately tell that he was not happy. He became moody and while he didn't refuse either advice or work, he was not the same. Once again, he struggled in school and became quite withdrawn. When other problems arose, I thought it was best if he returned to Denver. I was disappointed and I felt as if I had failed.

Not long afterward, we again became friends and no one was happier about it than I.

He married a lovely girl, Susan, and secured a job maintaining a police department helicopter fleet in Maryland. I am proud of him and I love him. 🐎

The Missing Thirty-Eight

April 26, 1972 was a date we always remembered. It had been one of the tougher winters and we knew that surely spring would be making its appearance soon. Early that day, Susan and Jack met the yellow school bus as usual while Fred and our hired man, Doug, left to mend fences. Though the meteorologist on the radio predicted cold and clear days, suddenly the Colorado weather changed and that morning he was proved wrong.

In no time at all, the world around us became white and angry. It soon was unsafe to be outside so Fred and Doug returned to the house. "This is probably a freak storm that will blow itself out pretty soon. After all, it is the end of April," these were Fred's now-famous words. How wrong he was! Before long the power went off, the wind rattled everything that wasn't tied down solidly and blew objects past the windows some not even touching the ground. Others simply rolled along, heading south in a big hurry.

This storm filled us with more worry than usual because we had just recently turned a herd of newly weaned Holstein steers out to pasture. We knew there was danger because their hide is thinner than other breeds making them less able to tolerate the cold. And now, an icy north wind mixed with snow was driving them south to the end of the pasture, leaving them unprotected and trapped by the barbed wire fence that divided our ranch from the neighbor's.

For about an hour in the afternoon the electricity returned, thank goodness, and a weather update told us about school closings. The Calhan School Principal called KOA radio to report that all the students were staying overnight in Calhan, all in different homes. We were glad to hear this, as busses often got stuck in the snow. Now we didn't have to worry about the kids.

The fury of the spring storm continued throughout the night making unbelievable loud noises. It lessened a little towards morning, much to the dismay of the hired man, who had hoped for a day off. He was stranded at our place, sleeping on our living room couch, blissfully and soundly when Fred roused him at 6:30 AM.

By the time we finished our usual enormous breakfast, the power which had been off all night, came back on. The morning sun climbed slowly upward, the sky lost its orange color and became blue. There was not a cloud in sight. Drifts of up to eight feet surrounded the buildings. It was bitter cold and the windows showed off their artistic ice flowers. Icicles, a foot long, decorated the bottom part of all the roofs. Fred and Doug now hoped to drive in the Jeep to where the Holsteins had drifted. They got dressed as if they were heading for Siberia. As they left the house, the snow crunched under their overshoes leaving deep footprints. Luckily, the jeep started and they were off.

Only 45 minutes later, Fred walked into the house. His face revealed the bad news, "All the steers in that pasture are dead. I couldn't count them, because they are lying on top of each other. It's a terrible sight."

Just then the phone rang. A neighbor told us that three of our Holstein steers were in his corral. Apparently, they had jumped over a tall fence to get shelter and safety. Lucky and smart. The guy then asked Fred to come and pick up the animals so he could go ahead and feed his own. Fred said, "I can't do that, the roads are all closed. I got to wait for the snowplow before I can get them. I'll pay you for the feed if you'll feed my steers too." The neighbor agreed.

Realizing that some of the herd was still missing, Fred decided to try and find them by riding horseback rather than using the Jeep because it was easier to get around and you didn't have to worry about getting stuck in a snow-covered hole! He added another layer of heavy clothes including a woolen scarf and a red fleece-lined cap with earflaps and was off again, hoping for better news this time.

Suddenly, the weather was getting worse again. The wind increased in velocity and the sun was unable to warm the countryside, making life even more miserable for man and beast. Yet, Fred did not complain. He worried and hoped the rest of the cattle would be all right. "Please, dear God, let me find them alive" was the silent prayer we both repeated many times.

He rode straight to the end of the south pasture, but found nothing. Where could they be? Snow whipped by the wind was reducing visibility and some of it stuck to Fred's eyelids and eyebrows. It was a gray and white world, unfriendly, and uncooperative! Eventually, the horse took him to another neighbor's ranch and there, next to the barbed wire fence, a dreadful image unfolded before his eyes once again. There he found the second bunch of missing cattle—all dead. He started to blame himself—he should have kept all the steers in the barns. And then, he thought, maybe he shouldn't have bought them in the first place. His mind was in turmoil, his stomach churned and he was afraid of being sick right there in the pasture. He continued riding home never noticing the cold nor the wet snow on his face while the horse trudged on steadily carrying a very distraught human being.

Late in the afternoon the school bus brought the children home and as they bounced out of the vehicle they sounded like a 'gaggle of giggling geese.' They had enjoyed their unscheduled slumber party, but now, they were about to enter the world of gloom, ranchers touched by sadness and depression.

The next day we picked up the three steers that saved themselves at the neighbors and paid him for the hay they ate. Dealing with the dead animals was a larger, more emotional task. We weren't the only ones suffering because all the neighbors had major losses. A dog food company heard about the disaster and offered to pick up the dead livestock for free. Within a few days the carcasses were gone and all we had left were the memories of some fine cattle.

We lost more animals in that spring storm than at any other time during all of our ranching years. All total, thirty-eight steers died in the span of a few hours. According to the veterinarians, it was not the cold that killed them, but instead the swirling snow that got into their nostrils and eventually into their lungs, causing them to drown.

Doug, the hired man, quit the next day saying how he "couldn't take this kind of abuse on the human mind and body." He told us how he had always hoped to have a ranch someday, but not anymore! He was serious yet we could understand his feelings. But now, on top of all this personal and financial disaster, the hired man was gone and we turned back to the family for help. Though we tried to put on a happy face for the sake of the children, it was not easy! In the cattle business and life, you learn to cope with adversities and go on from there. 🐂

Basketball Tournament

If there was a sports event on television, Fred wanted to watch it and would try to attend as many local games as possible. So it came as no surprise when he asked me, "My buddy, Clyde, and I want to drive to Denver next Thursday. You see, Calhan is going to play in the Colorado State Boys Basketball Tournament and since we are both on the School Board it would look good if we were there. Besides it should be fun. Can I go?" With the kids in college and only Fred and I at home, I had no qualms whatsoever of taking over for the day. In fact, I welcomed it.

"Why not!" was my immediate answer and I reveled at the thought of having a whole day to myself with no interruptions from you-know-who asking "Honey, give me a hand with..." and "What's for dinner? I'm starved." I decided this would be MY day, mine alone and I could either do something special or perhaps absolutely nothing at all. Though I now had a few days to formulate my plan, my decision came fast. I could write letters, one of my favorite pastimes. I'd go for a long walk with our three dogs, Pookie, Skipper, and Boy, and have a 'cold weather' picnic under the Cottonwood trees in the south pasture. Then another idea crossed my volatile mind. I could also go ice skating on the hard-frozen pond in the northwest pasture. Yes, that's what I'm going to do! I had not skated in a long time.

Thursday morning March 10, 1977 arrived. As all ranchers do, we listened to the weather report on the radio and were told that there might be a change in the weather but it was not predicted to arrive until much later in the day, perhaps at nightfall.

"I'll be home long before then. Calhan plays early and if it looks bad, we'll leave right after the game," Fred reassured me. Good enough for me! The only concern I had was that the bad weather might zoom in while the guys were on the lonely country roads. I tried not to think of it.

Fred finished the morning chores and then gorged himself on homegrown steak, our brown eggs, freshly baked bread, and all the trimmings. It was 6 AM and he was ready to leave. He gave me a loud and somewhat wet kiss, and marched off to our car on his way to meet Clyde at his home. Fred would leave the car there because Clyde volunteered to drive.

My chores were waiting for me but I didn't rush, it was still early. Another cup of coffee would do wonders for my psyche because getting up early was never one of my favorite things. It finally became light outdoors. The sky was overcast but there was no apparent breeze and it looked like a cloudy winter day.

My two baby lambs, which were still on the bottle, spent their time on the heated porch just outside the kitchen. During the day if the winter sun provided a few hours of warmth I would let the babies outdoors. How they enjoyed leaping around, jumping, moving their small bodies first to one side and then to the other, vaulting straight ahead with their front legs tucked tightly under their chest, always landing securely on all four feet. I loved watching them. The minute they got tired they would walk up the three steps to the house and ask to be let in. Today, however, was no day for outdoor recreation. Without the sun, it would be too chilly for them.

By the time all my chores were done, it was close to 9 AM. I waited until 9:15 when I could meet our ever-punctual mailman at the mailbox, 2/3 of a mile from the house on Calhan Highway. Leaving the garage door open, I slipped into the pickup and drove down the Vorenberg Road. Excited at receiving an armful of mail, I soon was disappointed when I realized the personal mail consisted of only one letter. I recognized the handwriting of Hedy Cleer's mother in Germany. Hedy had been such a good friend during our High School years and I missed her so much now that she was gone. The rest of the mail was an assortment of flyers, ads, and other junk mail. To my surprise, not a single bill.

While speeding uphill anxious to read the letter, a few soft and fluffy snowflakes clung to the windshield. "You are not supposed to be here until tonight!" I laughed, and immediately forgot about them.

But by the time I parked the pickup in the garage, it was snowing harder and the gray sky meant that it had no intention of stopping anytime soon. I thought I'd better close the garage door in case the storm materialized sooner than expected. Regardless of how much I pushed and pulled, the wooden door would not budge. The two sides seemed to be stuck against the other one. I gave up closing the door; it was just too difficult. All I could do was hope that Fred would return soon and that it would not snow too much.

Back in the house, I turned on the radio for news about the weather. It was not good. Denver's streets were slippery and the Mayor advised everyone to stay at home. This could mean trouble for us as it always snowed more on our hill. I worried about Fred and Clyde and wondered if they had left Denver or if they were stranded somewhere. I ached for a phone call, but none came.

I decided to quit worrying and instead tend to the cattle, horses, sheep, and chickens. The wind was picking up, howling around corners and spraying wet snow in my face. I quickly threw some bundles of feed to the cattle and horses and opened sheds for them so they could get relief from the cold and wet elements. The sheep and chickens were already settled in their houses. I fed all of them and closed the doors behind me. I didn't know how long the storm would last. This way, at least, they would be protected.

The three dogs who had been following me were as ready to be home as I was. The house was toasty warm. My outerwear was soaking wet. This was a typical wet spring snow, ones which are especially dangerous for livestock without decent shelter. They cause more pneumonia than winter storms and kill more animals than any others.

The day I had been looking forward to with so much anticipation was proving to be just another miserable workday. There would be no long walk, no picnic, no ice-skating. But I could write letters. I glanced out of the windows which by now were filling up with snow between the panes and the screens, causing darkness to infiltrate the rooms.

I was thankful for the electricity for without it, the water pump would not work and not much heat would be pushed into the rooms. To sum it up, no power meant no water, no heat, no light, no radio or television, no Mixmaster, no iron, no...! I would be alone and without the help of all the wonderful conveniences we had come to depend on.

Towards evening the telephone rang twice. The first caller was Charlie Warren. He and his brother, Hal, owned the gas station and mechanic repair shop in Calhan. Both were always extremely helpful to us and whenever we needed any repairs on our vehicles they always found time to take care of us right away.

Fred and Clyde had stopped at Warren's Garage and had told Charlie they would be gone all day. "I don't think Fred and Clyde can make it back. The weather looks bad and the forecast sounds dangerous. Do you need anything like food or medication? Someone can bring it to you before the storm gets worse." I assured him everything was under control and I thanked him. What a dear person he was and how I appreciated his concern.

The second call was from Fred. He told me that he and Clyde left Denver as soon as the game was over. They drove cross-country and when they arrived in Elizabeth, a small town about 35 miles Southeast of Denver, they had an accident. The visibility was poor causing a chain reaction that damaged four cars as they slid and zigzagged into each other eventually ending in ditches on both sides of the road. Fred remembered that Sophie, the daughter of Miguel, the foreman on the Uncles' ranch, lived in Elizabeth. He and Clyde stomped through miles of snow and eventually arrived at her house. She was more than willing to let the men stay overnight. Then Fred ended our conversation with, "Do the best you can. I'll be home as soon as I can. I'll call tomorrow. I love you, Schlitza." It wasn't until I hung up the phone that I realized I never asked about the ball game. Who won, what was the score? I guess the storm had pushed those thoughts into the furthest background.

What a relief, Fred was safe! I could relax. The wind howled ever stronger. I tried hard to open the front door so the dogs could do their 'thing' but they looked at all the cold and wet outside and turned right around. Next, I spread newspapers on the porch for them to relieve themselves there, but they refused to use them even though they had been trained on paper when they were puppies. So I told them, "O.K., have it your way, guys, but you better hold it!"

The night proceeded slowly because I couldn't sleep. Off and on I heard things hitting the side of the house. Since all the windows were completely covered with snow I couldn't see whether it was still snowing or what was going on outside.

The next morning, Friday, showed no change in the weather. The wind had not lessened and the blizzard's howling sounded like some wild beast ready to devour anything and everything in its way. By now I became accustomed to the eerie noise. Whenever things got a bit depressing, I kept reminding myself that I was thankful I had electricity. The dogs were thirsty but I rationed their water because they had not used the paper on the porch. Hopefully their bladders would not burst.

The lambs were happy, now, that I had placed them in the North bathroom, along with several layers of newspaper which, incidentally, they had used, not being as finicky as the dogs! The small folding gate we used with the children many years ago now kept the lambs in their new 'corral.'

I could not open any doors to the outside as snow had blocked all of them. There was over two feet of snow piled onto the south door and a bit less on the main, east-facing door. I was homebound and in need of being dug out. I had annoying visions of a fire breaking out or the roof blowing off. But — I had electricity!

Fred called again. He was surprised that the phone was still working. He told me that Clyde's brother was coming to pick them up and bring them home but he didn't know when.

The papers on the porch remained dry. Poor things, the dogs must have felt terrible — and meantime the wind continued its mournful song, or was it anger?

Charlie called a second time and was pleased that I was fine. He asked me again if I had enough food. My day was spent watching television and listening to weather reports which did not improve. So far, I had not written a single letter!

I proceeded to bake a cake in preparation for whoever might be able to help me out because it was customary to invite those wonderful souls for a cup of coffee and a slice of cake. It always added an extra measure of appreciation.

Friday went by just as it began, noisy and unfriendly. I was slowly becoming accustomed to the storm's frantic behavior. In fact, the steady racket seemed to lull me to sleep that night. The dogs still refused to use the newspaper. They must have been miserable by now.

Around 4 AM on Saturday, something woke me up. I could not figure out what it was. The dogs and the lambs were quiet. And then the sudden stillness penetrated my sleepy brain and made me realize that the wind had stopped. I leaped from my cozy bed, ran to the south door and tried in vain to open it. Now, the entire door was solidly closed by snow. I ran to the porch door on the east side of the house and after rattling around — low and behold — I was able to open it. An icy breeze greeted me. Snow sprayed from the overhang of the roof into my face as if to say, "Wake up kid, the storm is over."

I didn't have to encourage the dogs to go outside and do their business. And they did! I swear, they stood in their different areas doing their thing for what seemed like five minutes. I had to laugh!

Because it was still dark and quite early, I returned to bed hoping for perhaps another hour of dozing. Instead of relaxing, I became restless and got up. I stepped into my long handled underwear, a sweater I had knitted sometime ago, and a rather worn pair of jeans which had been patched over the knees. Then I put on my warmest pair of socks, shoes, and overshoes followed by my navy blue parka, a wool cap, and a scarf. I was ready to face the cold outdoors. Armed with a flashlight, I braved a dark and silent world. The stars in the darkness winked at me as if to say, "It's all over, the sun will be up soon!" The pale full moon provided me with some degree of light.

But for now, there in front of me, behind me, and as far as I could see were snowdrifts at least twelve feet deep, everywhere. The barns, barely able to peep over the snow heaped against their walls, were all still standing. The road which divided our ranch was solidly blocked with drifts the size I never saw before. The garage appeared as if solidly filled with snow and there was no sight of the pickup parked inside. If I had had the strength to close the doors this would not have happened. Oh well!

Feeding the calves after being 'saved!'

It was so quiet. No sounds from the animals. Nothing stirred. It seemed as if the world stood still. And it was bitter cold.

After a while, a pink color appeared on the Eastern horizon announcing the sun's arrival. It soon spread over the snow-covered pastures and, within moments invaded the Rocky Mountain range to the west. I feasted my eyes on this display of dazzling splendor for some time. How long I stood there I don't know. To this day, while I am recalling this moment, the imprint of this glorious event has neither left nor dimmed. Despite the hardships, this state, Colorado, is and always will be my favorite place on earth. Its beauty is indescribable and unforgettable.

It was remarkable how fast it became daytime and I knew this would be a long and busy day. I wondered how the horses survived. I started to climb up the first snowdrift. Halfway up my feet began to slip and I zoomed back down to the bottom. The wet snow had frozen and it was difficult to ascend. "I'll never become a mountain climber," I thought. Eventually, after 'attacking' several more drifts, I stopped breathlessly on the top of the last one from where I could see our three horses standing on completely bare ground. The wind had whipped the snow forming a perfectly round corral. The open shed was only partially filled with snow but it blocked the entrance so the horses could not enter it.

Instead of trying to descend the slippery mountains like a lady, I opted for the tomboy effect and slid down on my behind with much gusto. Returning with a goodly amount of hay, I retraced my steps and dumped the feed into the horse's fancy ice corral.

This took a lot of energy and I felt the need to rest a moment. The air was thin and quite cold. The sun now shone hard in the sapphire blue sky. Before checking the other animals, I climbed one of the drifts which crossed the road and I laid there 'spread eagle' soaking in the golden rays of sunshine. I needed rejuvenation. Just at the moment of deepest relaxation, I heard the humming of an engine. Looking in the direction of the sound, I spied—of all things—a helicopter, going at high speed and heading not only to the area where I was enjoying a quick R & R, but zooming down on me. Embarrassed, I jumped up just as the pilot yelled to me, "Are you all right? Do you need anything?" After I assured him that everything was fine, he took off probably looking for more 'look-alike-dead-people'.

The inspection tour took me next to the cattle corrals. They seemed fine but were thin. They needed food and water but they would have to wait until I got help.

Next I went to the sheep shed where I had locked in the thirty-five woolies last Thursday. The building was completely covered with snow and the only door on the building's south side was unpenetrable. I worried about the animals' health. Frantically, I called to them and everything was quiet. Could they have suffocated? My only idea was to climb up on the roof. I took a shovel and made some foot holes in the snow that now was a solid sheet of vertical ice. When I reached the roof I tore off a couple of long sheets of tin with my ever-ready pair of pliers and peeked down into the bowels of the shed. A draft of warm and smelly air hit my face and suddenly all the sheep crowded into one spot and looked up at me, making their usual sounds of welcome. They seemed to say, "Look what the wind blew in!" I retreated to the haystack, gathered an armload of hay and scrambled again up the snowy wall of the sheep shed towards the hole I had just made in the roof.

Next, I threw a small amount of hay through the opening, squeezing and dropping the rest into several areas. The hungry animals sauntered on top of each pile and on top of one another in order to at least get a mouthful. It was not enough for them, I had to think of a way to get them out of the shed and feed them properly. They needed water and I had to have time to think!

By now, total and complete exhaustion had set in. I was overheated from all the climbing, sliding, and the carrying of feed. I needed to get back to the house after having already spent several hours outdoors. No sooner did I enter the very warm kitchen when I tore off all the heavy clothes and sat down at the table with a tall glass of water. It was then that I noticed the electric clock on the wall had stopped. Well, it finally happened! The power was off. I didn't really care. The blizzard was over, the livestock at home seemed OK, and the marvelous, warm sun was out. All I needed was for Fred to return.

Minutes later, I was back at the sheep pen only wearing a jean jacket instead of the parka and the many layers underneath it. I had an idea of how to get water down to the animals. I would use a bucket filled to the brim and anchored by a long rope. Quickly, I got an axe, chopped the ice in the water tank and filled the battered old bucket. I slipped and slid as I ascended the snowdrift again, spilling part of the precious water onto my overshoes. Finally, I carefully lowered it into the shed holding on tightly to the rope. The sheep pounced onto it spilling the entire good will offering. What to do next?

I sat there on top of the roof, next to the hole and felt like 'The Fiddler on the Roof' but I was neither singing nor playing a fiddle. Suddenly, I heard the sound of an engine. Standing on the roof, I could see for miles around and I noticed a tractor in the north pasture. It was coming towards our place, slowly but steadily.

At last, I again slid down the roof, letting the bucket tumble down ahead of me, as I landed hard on my bottom. Who said ranch life was fun, romantic, and healthy?

The chugging of the tractor got louder as it approached and I strained to see who might be coming. Perhaps it was the 'friendly helicopter guy' again. Or maybe he sent someone to check on me. Just then the tractor turned the corner of the open sheds which had been obstructing my view.

Joy and relief spread over me as Fred and our closest neighbor, Bob Wilson, rushed towards me. I never was so happy to see anyone and my love for Fred, while it was never dead, was rekindled a thousand times. Here he was, grinning, laughing, and healthy. We hugged and kissed while Bob watched intently as if he didn't want to miss a thing.

Then in a loud voice, Hubby announced, "I'll never leave you again!" After which he turned and headed for the house. "I'm going to change my clothes and Bob and I are going to ride horseback to the Old Place to check on the cattle there."

I had to grin as I said to Bob, "Didn't he just say that he would never leave me again?" Bob laughed, "Thems just words!"

Fred later explained how Clyde's brother had picked them up in Elizabeth, Colorado and Fred called Bob from Calhan to meet him at the corner of Judge Orr Road. Only a tractor could navigate, so they drove through the pasture, since huge drifts blocked all the roads, especially the east/west ones.

The guys left while I tackled the job of watering the sheep again. It was a thankless effort, for as soon as the bucket 'landed', the animals fought and pushed in order to get there first. One or two drank and then the bucket tipped over and all the water spilled once more. After another attempt, the same thing happened and I gave up.

Fred and Bob were gone for several hours. They found one of the bulls in a corner inside a barn standing on a snowdrift that was so tall that he almost touched the roof. The snow had blown in where he stood and he just kept stepping up on top of the ever-increasing snowbank until he couldn't go any farther. Other cattle actually died standing up. The snow was too deep for them to pull their legs out if it and they suffered a heart attack.

After both men returned, Bob suggested that they make an emergency door to the east of the sheep shed. "Let's do it tomorrow, I'm bushed," was Fred's reply. But later, around five o'clock, Fred decided to knock out the east side of the barn. You never saw a happier bunch of animals as they leaped out and danced around the corral.

After a very long Saturday and a simple evening meal, two weary bodies dragged themselves to bed. Almost asleep, I finally asked about the ball game. "We lost," was all Fred could mutter.

"What was the score?" I asked and instead of an answer, the sound of a contented grunt emanated from the other side of the bed.

The next day, the newspaper headline read, "Storm Worst Since the 1920's." Eleven people lost their lives including three children from Ramah, East of Calhan. Thirty-five motorists stayed in Calhan churches. The basketball students remained in Denver until

Sunday in a Red Cross Shelter. One man was stranded for 39 hours in his jeep on a country road near Ramah, as were many more all over the eastern plains of Colorado. Both highways 24 and 94 had huge drifts and the snowplows worked day and night to open these important thoroughfares. The Army was called in to help dig out peoples' houses and barns. The helicopters dropped food for stranded families and feed for the cattle. The Electric Company never stopped trying to get power restored.

The stories of hardship went on and on. The report from El Paso County was that more than 5,000 head of cattle died, not surprising to us, while the loss of sheep, hogs, and chickens mounted. Barns and trailers were toppled by the ferocious wind and roofs were blown off houses.

Several days after the storm was over, late in the day, we heard engines and looked outside expecting the snowplows. Instead, a vehicle similar to a tank lumbered up our road and easily climbed over all the huge drifts. The 'weasel,' chauffeured by a soldier from Fort Carson, was transporting workers from the Electric Company to all the areas still without power. Ours was the last job of the day and after the four fellows restored our electricity, they were rewarded with all of the cake I made on Friday, along with many cups of hot coffee.

The next Thursday, a whole week after the storm began, a stray dog appeared at our house. We quickly put food out for the hungry Irish Setter and began searching for its master. We found out that he belonged to the son of the former owner of our ranch. We called the relieved young man to come and pick up his dog, while the animal not only ate a second dish of dog food but also found the kitchen counter where half of a two layer cake was standing. He devoured the whole dessert meant for that night's dinner.

The young man came, overjoyed to see his dog again. "Can I do something for you, anything at all?" he begged.

Yes indeed, there was something. "Would you check our attic for snow?" He climbed through the narrow access opening in the bathroom ceiling which led to the unfinished attic. We told him to be sure and only walk on the 2 x 6 boards.

"Give me a bucket, there's a lot of snow up here," he called down to us.

"Here you are," I said as I handed one to him. He filled it up and we emptied it, at least four times. He was getting ready to leave the attic when he suddenly crashed through the ceiling, his two long legs dangling in mid-air in the bathroom while his torso remained in the attic. Ouch! Another casualty! What's next, we thought!

The following week the ceiling was fixed, none of those letters I had intended to write were written, and I didn't go ice skating until the following year. The picnic was postponed until summer. While we suffered financial losses from that blizzard it was not as severe as it was for other ranchers and our family was still intact and healthy. We were thankful for good neighbors, concerned citizens, the Electric Company and its workers who worked in all kinds of weather, and the crews who were busy day and night trying to keep the roads open. And especially the 'friendly helicopter guy' who probably thought that he had found a 'dead one', only to laugh when I suddenly stood up! And, of course, we were thankful for a strong, helpful marriage that got us through another crisis. 🐴

Having been raised in a German household is quite different from the American way. Both my parents were strict and expected respect. Foolishness was not allowed. Politeness and honesty were stressed. At the same time there was love and watchful concern. Both my parents never missed an opportunity to teach us about the sudden spectacle of a shooting star, how a kernel of wheat growing in the field found its way into the housewife's flour bin, and many other lessons.

Back row: Tom, Fred, front row: myself, Jack, Bonnie and Susan - country kids?

When the time came for Fred and me to raise our family, I felt that the above qualities had much merit and so I embraced the same ideas. While the children were still small I expected them to take care of their toys at the end of the day. Later on, I stressed that they used proper and polite language. We insisted on thoughtfulness towards family and strangers and honesty and love for everyone in the home. These were considered important necessities.

"Be on time," and "Finish one thing before you start another" were important qualities which I continually stressed because they were essential to organizing your life. I always have tried to live by these rules and encouraged the children to do the same.

We were blessed with four children: Thomas Joseph, born 1949; Bonnie Louise 1951, Susan Ruth 1954 and Jack Allan 1958. All their different temperaments and characters emerged long before the babies reached their first year.

I always thought that raising children in the country is super. The early years are character building with copious learning opportunities that arise when you are close to the land. In our case, most of the rancher/farmer families were intact so both parents contributed to their children's upbringing. I can't imagine the difficulty it must be to be a single parent on a ranch.

But children also like to mimic their parents, be it physically or psychologically. Raising a family is not an easy job, but it is enjoyable. As they grow up you realize you did a fine job when you see a person displaying empathy and compassion for others, appreciating one's surroundings whether animal or plant life, and accepting things which can't be changed. And above all, respect for honesty and truthfulness.

The children were well behaved, most of the time, and when we felt it was needed, a pat on the behind plus a few strong words straightened things out in a hurry. By the time they reached the age of four none of them ever needed to be paddled again. They knew just how far they could push us.

There were moments when the kids used wonderful expressions. Children are inquisitive, often asking "Why?" One time I remember Tommy asking me in a concerned tone, while watching a plane in the sky, "Will he run into God?" Another time he asked for a "naked" slice of bread, meaning one without butter or jam.

Children growing up on a ranch learn the facts of life early. So it was not much of a surprise when Tommy overheard Fred and me talking about Cindy, our German Shepherd, who was in heat. Suddenly, he suggested, "We'd better get a 'bull-dog' for her." This made sense to him because he knew when a cow is in heat you need to get the bull! Responding to their unusual comments was not always easy!

On a ranch, most kids did not have many toys but somehow they always managed to make their own fun. When they were young they entertained themselves with a complete line of mud pies and cookies. In warmer weather we found them playing among the choke cherry bushes, north of the house. They would build make-believe houses, using dolls as their children and furniture from their dollhouses. Of course, Tommy always was the father of the family and everybody thought he was too tough on the 'kids,' the dolls.

Other times they used the saddle room to create a store and sell items like nails, staples, and other stuff from the ranch, complete with a cash register and play money. The children were full of ideas and it was easy for them to stay busy and happy with very little.

Chore time started early in life for our children. Everybody helped whenever needed, especially with the outdoor chores. Each one began by learning how to move aggressive chickens off their nests, so the eggs could be gathered. Often problems arose when the youngster carrying a can filled with eggs stumbled and all the contents broke into a pile of yellow goop. On the ranch, one of the first lessons they learned was not to 'cry over spilled milk!'

All the kids were willing workers even though the things asked of them were often unpleasant. There were many chores to do, both before and after school. Every day, one or two kids would ride horseback to gather cattle and bring them into the corral to protect them from the cold weather. Sometimes it was so frigid that they had to be helped off their horse because their feet were almost frozen to the stirrups.

When our children were nine years old we taught them to drive the jeep and the pickup. Every day, one of them drove in the pasture at a slow pace while Fred threw bales of hay and sacks of feed to the ever-hungry cattle from the back of the vehicle. All the country kids learned how to drive at a very early age. It was no big deal. The jeep was perfect for that purpose and soon afterwards they graduated to the pickup, and later, to the car. Of course, the kids didn't have a drivers license but none of the ranch kids around Calhan did and most drove cars, tractors, and pickups, and usually without mishap.

The children learned how to work closely with different kinds of animals from the largest to the smallest. Susan was a whiz with horses, even at a very young age. Once in a while, a horse scampered away trying to escape the bridle and the upcoming work. All tiny Susan had to do was to approach him, stand on tiptoes, and hold onto the leather of his halter. Then she proudly walked the huge horse to us while the animal no doubt thought, "Foiled by the littlest kid!"

Jack was the most orderly. His room and chest of drawers were always tidy and well organized. We could always leave the door to his room open; not so with the girls' room.

Amateur theatrics, ranch style.

Though it was their duty to keep things picked up, this usually was not the case when Susan lived in it! It didn't bother me as long as I didn't have to see it.

In addition to chores and school, the children were busy with other activities. Early on, Bonnie showed an interest in ballet, so for years she took lessons for which we paid in eggs, two dozen per lesson! She was in many recitals and loved them. When Bonnie was about seven years old she wrote her first play and the 'performance' was held in honor of Aunt Blanche and Uncle Herman's visit. It took her no time at all to think about a story with a plot and assign parts to the 'actors' (her siblings), select the stage manager, and make programs. Tommy always played the leading man!

As the time went by, the performances became better and more artistic. The plays were usually held in the basement. The stage curtain was an orange bedspread attached to wires with large safety pins. Additional lights in the form of strong flashlights and even an occasional candle was used for 'special effects'. As the audience entered, we were handed a very cleverly printed program and ushered to our seats. Just before the show began Bonnie would step in front of the curtain to welcome the 'public,' stress that the performance was free, and that there would be a five-minute intermission during which treats would be served.

Then from behind the curtain we heard lots of giggling, things falling, and then somebody would say, "Sh, sh sh!" and so the show began. The costumes were colorful and it seemed everybody wore something on his or her head. They danced, sang, and spoke beautifully.

Whenever we had visitors they were asked to come to the 'show' by you-know-who. When Aunt Blanche was in the audience she usually was touched to tears and we always enjoyed and were proud of the childrens' efforts.

The daily routine was changed on Sunday morning when we took the children to Sunday School in Colorado Springs.

They did not like the two hours spent in the classrooms at the Temple. I, however, enjoyed doing some grocery shopping and, visiting our friends, Is and Bert Simons. Relaxing over a cup of coffee and exchanging ideas and thoughts was strengthening and invigorating. It helped me continue the whirlwind life we were leading.

As with all children, holidays were special times. Of course, Christmas was a heightened time for we also celebrated Hanukkah while putting up the Christmas socks, baking cookies, and sending presents. We always made a big deal out of Easter. Once, I remember little Susan asking, "How come rabbits lay colored chicken eggs on Easter?" You needed to be a professor or a child psychologist to answer that one!

The day before Easter, we all colored hard boiled eggs and early Easter Sunday either Fred or I would sneak outdoors to hide them in strategic places. After breakfast, I would suddenly shout excitedly, "I think I just saw a rabbit!" All hell broke loose and the kids were off to the big treasure hunt. Without our help, they continued the game all day long with one of them pretending to be the elusive rabbit while the others searched desperately to retrieve the same eggs over and over again. Before long, the shells were so badly cracked that they were not safe for human consumption and the dogs got an unexpected feast.

4-H was an activity which consumed the children beginning when they were nine years old and accelerating until they were eighteen. The club was originally for youngsters on farms and ranches but it later spread to the cities. The children had a wide array of diverse subjects from which to choose and it was exciting to watch their enthusiasm as they finally selected the topics for the year. They attended monthly club meetings and periodic study groups such as cooking clubs, livestock judging, square dancing, gun safety classes and others.

All the children had cattle projects where they selected an animal and trained it to show during the following months. During the 4-H years, they were involved in caring and showing all sorts of livestock including horses, cattle, sheep, chickens, and geese. The girls also focused on cooking projects and later expanded into sewing, home nursing, gun safety, and others. For each topic, record books had to be kept. It was quite a job and one of us usually had to help them. The work culminated on Exhibit Day for cooking and the other 'inside' projects while the livestock was exhibited at the El Paso County fair, in Calhan.

A proud Susan with her 4-H calf.

Bonnie's Banana Bread was not only the County winner but advanced to win a blue ribbon at the State Fair. There was, however, one problem. She practiced baking it so often that the family's former love of banana bread was completely extinguished. Even now, whenever any of us ever eats a slice of it, the memory of that summer comes back in full force — actually, none of us consider banana bread a favorite, anymore!

In addition to the meetings, there were special contests in livestock judging where they evaluated cattle, sheep and hogs, public speaking contests, square dancing contests, demonstration contests, and dog training competitions. All four kids entered speech contests and won. I don't know who was more anxious during these times, the children or their parents.

Fred was a 4-H leader for many years and I helped out teaching home nursing and other topics. It was an especially busy time during the summer months but well worth it because the kids learned a lot about competition, teamwork, and how to complete a project.

Most importantly, 4-H gave opportunities for all four of our children to excel. They went on trips to Gunnison and Fort Collins for livestock judging. They won many ribbons, trophies, plus higher honors of exchange trips and scholarships. As each child left home, we packed up their trophies and an array of their colorful ribbons. They happily took them, and once they were in their room in the dorm, proudly placed them on shelves for all to admire. We really enjoyed being involved and, most certainly, were extremely proud of each of them for their many accomplishments.

We cannot say enough about the 4-H program. The learning opportunity is immensely profitable. It helped mold our children's character and thus their future.

In high school, Susan turned her interests from 4-H to cheerleading. After winning, all five of the students were sent for four days to Colorado State University to learn proper technique and new routines. Susan was an energetic and dramatic cheerleader but she often experienced shinsplints, a severe pain in the lower part of her legs. It was a handy excuse for not doing chores, much to the chagrin of her brother. In her senior year, Susan was selected as Homecoming Queen, a special honor.

In those days, jeans were not allowed in school. So both Bonnie and Susan learned to sew dresses to wear along with their required nylon hose. We always thought this was a stupid rule considering the kids had to wait outdoors for the school bus. And as one knows, Colorado winters are mighty cold.

Assigning chores became a work of art as the kids got older. While the two girls became proficient at cooking, it was no secret that my love for being in the kitchen was almost nil. Gardening, however, was something else. I enjoyed sinking my knees into the soil, so that the whole garden almost looked like a picture out of "Home and Garden Magazine." What a delightful sight! My dad would have been proud of me, as he was a perfectionist when it came to gardening. I had one-foot wide paths between each bed and everybody including the dogs, knew to stay within them.

Often I would be in the garden close to dinnertime. It was my way for me to procrastinate the meal preparation as long as possible. I remember asking the girls if they would like to finish my job in the garden or to start dinner? Knowing what their choice would be, they dashed off to the house while I continued weeding. They always appreciated me giving them options of chores, but sometimes I believe they laughed behind my back, knowing it was plain trickery.

Though the kids worked closely with large animals, machinery and, in essence, learned to operate a ranch, we luckily had few major accidents. Riding horseback brought on most of the problems. When Jack was seven years old, he was bringing in the milk cows when suddenly a rabbit jumped up in front of the horse scaring it into a bucking frenzy and he was thrown off. He landed, unluckily, on his right elbow. Meanwhile, the horse continued to push the cows home straight into the corral while poor Jack walked home with his elbow cradled in his left hand. It was his first trip to the Emergency Room and soon afterward, he proudly showed off his cast.

Years later another horse accident occurred when Fred, Bonnie, and Susan were moving cattle to a rented pasture. It happened right after Bonnie's second year in college and a day after securing a job in the ticket office at the Broadmoor Hotel's International Theatre in Colorado Springs. She was to start working the following week. All three horseback riders had been moving cattle for three hours and were nine miles into the drive. It was getting hot and the animals slowed down when suddenly Bonnie's young horse, Daisy, reared up and started bucking until she fell off. She landed on her left hand.

I was busy preparing dinner when the gang arrived home. Bonnie, showed me her, by now, quite swollen hand. So, it was off to the Emergency Room again where a cast was applied to the fractured hand and arm.

Imagine the shock when a few days later Bonnie appeared at her new job, sporting the cast and facing her boss. "I'm afraid I won't be able to type," was all she was able to express. Despite her disability, Bonnie managed to retain her job.

Tom loved to operate machinery, especially the manure spreader and other farming equipment. One time he was one-waying, a procedure where the farmland is being plowed very shallow to conserve the deep lying moisture. I happened to be outdoors when I noticed him coming home on what looked like a run-away tractor. Within minutes he arrived in the driveway, leaped off the seat, and ran screaming towards the front door, "I got a bee in my ear!" I rushed behind him into the kitchen, grabbed a bottle of salad oil, and poured a small amount into his ear canal. At once, a soggy and apparently helpless insect swam to the surface, probably wondering what all the fuss was about. This time a trip to the Emergency Room was not necessary!

Of course, the weather made ranch work even more hazardous for the children. One afternoon I was at the hired man's house warming my almost frozen toes after gathering the cattle on horseback, when Fred called to tell me that he was organizing neighbors to search for Susan. "What happened?" I half screamed.

"Well," he calmly explained, "I sent her out in the jeep to get the milkcows. I did not want her to ride her horse because it's too cold and snowy and besides, she has a cold. She's been gone for over an hour and I can't find her. I looked everywhere. That's why I am phoning the neighbors." And with this he hung up.

Hurriedly, the hired man and I put on our soggy boots and all the other winter gear and plowed through several drifts as we drove home. We stopped by the front door, rushed into the kitchen, and found Susan sitting there relishing the thought of being the center of attraction. "You want to hear what happened to me?" she asked innocently. "Well, I found the milk cows but suddenly it was snowing so hard I didn't know where I was. I kept driving until I found the fence and followed it. We were going steadily until suddenly the engine quit. I tried and tried to restart it, but it wouldn't turn over. I got out and started to walk behind the cattle, remembering how Dad had told me to stay next to the fence if we ever got lost. It surely was a long walk and the wind kept blowing snow all around me so I couldn't see anything but the fence. It saved me."

I hugged her and said, "You took Dad's advice about the fence and you didn't need help. I'm proud of you." I had read this saying somewhere, "The gap between advice and help is very wide." How true this was in Susan's case. As it turned out a very cold Susan walked into the house even before any neighbors arrived for the search.

For us, raising children in the country was better than in the city. Our routine was centered around the needs of the animals so most children did chores and then stayed home during the evenings. There were no friends dropping by, no corner drug stores. Instead they did homework which we supervised. The schools, while not as wealthy as the ones in the cities, were excellent. They did a fine job of teaching the basics and most of the students continued onto college. The rural location insulated the children from city problems like crime and other forces which could influence them. They stayed innocent, but safe.

Raising kids 'country style' is a special genre. Theirs was a youth spent with plants and animals in a simplicity that helped their young minds grow creatively. They were our strongest asset, a family working together in a team, sharing an interest and love of land and animals while developing a deep appreciation of the environment.

These years were extremely busy, exciting, and fulfilling and after the children departed for college we were left with an emptiness as deep as the ocean. It was hard for me to fully understand that now their futures were in their hands. We hoped we did a good job of raising them. Would they become good citizens, considerate and kind? Would they be able to have a fulfilling life? We hoped so with all our hearts.

Ballerina Bonnie at home—a dress
rehearsal on a make-believe stage.

Chapter 12

DIFFICULT TIMES

Heart Bypass

It was middle of May and still dark in the mornings with a chill in the house that made getting up rather unpleasant. We became 'speed-dressers' long before the coal furnace would deliver, somewhat reluctantly, the much sought after warmth. It seemed we were facing another one of those cold and dreary days and I was getting tired of them. These days, the cold seemed to penetrate your very soul. During the past week we had experienced snow, rain, fog, thunder, lightning, and at intervals, sunshine.

I was tired of trudging through the mud mixed with manure and having everyone bring their good-sized samples into the house. I had placed a big cardboard box on the enclosed warm porch to receive dirty manure-laden boots and shoes, along with a second one that was filled with slippers to be worn in the house, obviously. Obviously? My family, the hired man, and I were clearly on different wavelengths! What must I do short of committing mayhem, for them to do this one small favor for me?

"I'm coming in only for a few minutes. It takes too long to take off my shoes before I need to put them back on again," was the excuse I got from 'Friend Husband,' or was it 'Enemy Husband'?

"Say nothing, it won't do any good to lose your temper," I muttered as I somehow quelled the idea of cheerfully murdering everyone who went against my wishes. But it proved to be a long, lengthy and, I might add, losing battle!

To take my mind off of the newly deposited 'treats' awaiting me on the floors, I decided to feed my sheep. I loved those animals and being surrounded by them made me forget the evil thoughts that had pestered me only minutes before.

Feeding the sheep took only about thirty minutes and when I was on my way back home, I noticed that Fred was heading for the house from the opposite direction. I sensed something was not quite right. His walk was different as he shuffled his feet with a dragging gait.

Fred was not a complainer and when he said quietly, "I don't feel good," I believed him. I helped him into the kitchen, loosened his clothes and removed his heavy and soiled overshoes. He collapsed onto the floor. His color was white with blue circles around the eyes and his lips trembled as he complained of the pressure over his chest. He had no pain but experienced shortness of breath and beads of perspiration were rolling off his forehead. Except for the absence of pain these were textbook-like symptoms of a coronary occlusion, a heart attack.

While waiting for Calhan's ambulance to arrive, I called our doctor's office. The nurse didn't think it was serious and she argued with me. I got really upset and told her that

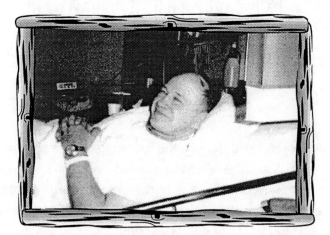

Fred in the hospital.

Fred was lying on the floor and we were coming in by ambulance. "OK," she agreed, "I'll call the doctor."

At Memorial Hospital, two physicians were waiting for us. They performed an angiogram that showed two blocked coronary arteries. A few days later a cardiac surgeon did a double bypass operation. Very few of these procedures had been done in those days and it was the first one at Memorial Hospital. Naturally, this worried the whole family, but Fred was tough and a week later he was ready to be dismissed.

Early that day, before I left for the hospital to pick up Fred, I got a telephone call from Jack Evers, Fred's Platoon Commander during World War II. He and his wife, Mal, were in Colorado Springs asking if they could come out to the ranch to see us—today. I told them about Fred.

We both liked the Evers. They had visited us before and we always had a good time. Several weeks before we had invited them to come, but now, they hesitated to accept the offer. We persuaded them and once again, we enjoyed their presence immensely. Their pleasant ways helped Fred who was doing nicely and his strength was gradually returning. They only were with us a couple of days and I appreciated that they cut their visit short.

On Fred's third day home from the Hospital we were having breakfast when our neighbor, Bob Wilson, knocked on the porch door. I motioned for him to come in but he did not see me. I rushed towards the kitchen door that led to the porch and tripped on the step, crashing to the floor. Sharp pains surged up from my ankle and through my legs. Bob helped me up and led me to the easy chair in the living room where I scolded myself for being so careless. It probably was just a sprain but the pain would not lessen. Bob, bless his heart, fed the cattle for us, something he had done while Fred was hospitalized.

Patient #1, Fred, called another neighbor, Bill Bogner who came over with his wife, Nancy. He was big and strong so he easily picked me up and carried me to our car. Then

Nancy drove me to the emergency room in Colorado Springs. The x-ray showed that I had a fractured ankle. So now, I was the proud owner of a cast that immobilized my leg from my toes to my knee. This was a terrible time for me to pull such a stunt, now when Fred and the animals needed me more than ever. I was an embarrassed Patient #2.

Bill, the wonderful person that he was, helped with the chores for days. We couldn't have managed without those kind folks in our immediate neighborhood. Soon, Jack came home from college to help, promising to stay for an extended period of time.

On the following Sunday Fred's operation and now, my calamity was announced at a church service in Calhan. Apparently, they joked that I was jealous of all the attention that Fred was getting. My cast was still moist and I had to stay lying down. Imagine our surprise when over a dozen people came by that afternoon bringing plenty of food and gifts. Fred 'entertained' in the living room while I did the same in the bedroom. As it so often happens, the men stayed with the men, and the women with the women. Why is this?

Later, Fred had a couple more incidents with his heart but luckily the angioplasty and medication did the trick.

Now we are aware of how stress, tension, and most of all, cholesterol contributes to heart problems. Ranchers are prime targets because they eat plenty of homegrown meat, eggs and butter. Hopefully, future generations will be educated so that they can live healthier and longer lives. 🐎

Vorenberg Family Says "Thanks"

We would like to thank everybody for all the generous deeds our friends, neighbors and relatives did for us while Elizabeth broke her ankle and Fred had a heart attack and heart surgery.

The Calhan ambulance was most helpful in its prompt and efficient action, and many thanks to Lawrence Brase and David Woolsey.

Equally attentive were the doctors, nurses and staff of Memorial Hospital.

Many thanks for the flowers, cards, gifts, food, phone calls, and visits. A special thanks to the Bob Wilson, Bill Bogner and Dr. Werner Heim families.

Thank you so much for all the prayers in the churches and temples, and a special thanks for the visits of Rev. Strohmeyer, Rev. Robert Fortenbaugh and Rabbi David Kline.

Thanks to all the U.S.A. is a great country!

Fred & Elizabeth Vorenberg
& Family   R16-1X

Money-Money-Money

972 turned out to be a good year making everyone in the ranching community enthusiastic and optimistic. Still we needed the help of the Cattlemen's Credit Association. Fred often told me, "If we didn't have to borrow all that money we would be doing quite well financially." And how we had to "work for months just to pay the interest on our loan."

Once again, it was time for the annual trip to Colorado Springs to apply for money for the next year. Fred dressed up in extra special duds, almost looking elegant in his six-year-old Western suit.

"Cross your fingers," he whispered as he gave me a quick kiss, barely touching my cheek, before he was out the door. The car left a cloud of dust as he drove towards the big city. I didn't worry, but I was always concerned when it came to banks—they were so unpredictable. It was made worse because Fred set his hopes very high and he was easily disappointed.

The house was peaceful but I needed to stay busy. Of all things, I decided to wash the kitchen curtains! Much too soon they were clean, starched, ironed and back on the curtain rods. Now what? It didn't take a rocket scientist to figure out that I was a nervous wreck. I started making an apple pie, thinking that regardless of the outcome of the meeting, it would make Fred happy when he returned.

It was late afternoon, supper was ready and most of the chores were done when I noticed Fred driving into the garage.

"Well?" was all I could squeeze out of my tight, somewhat shaky voice. "Are we going to get the money?"

"Don't know yet. I told them exactly what I needed. They'll tell me next Friday." Then he explained how he asked CCA for $150,000 to buy 750 head of cattle. At $200 each, they should bring $225,000 in the fall of '74, at least that's what my mathematician husband figured out. He thought it shouldn't be a problem since we cleared $40,000 in profits the prior year, 1972.

'Let's eat, I am starved." And so we did.

Friday came and both of us were in a cautious mood. This time I went with Fred to the bank because both of us had to sign the new loan. On our way to Springs, I half-heartedly asked, "Are you sure we can make that much money and finally pay off all the debt?"

"Of course, quit worrying so much," he reassured me.

Fred always told me that I worry too much. I know that I do, but I can't seem to help it.

At the CCA, we were greeted pleasantly as always and led into a neat office with big, red upholstered armchairs. "Would you like some coffee?"

"No, thanks," was Fred's immediate reply. He just wanted to get down to business.

"Folks," the man began, "we can't give you all the money you asked for. It says here that you want to borrow $150,000. It's impossible! The best we can do is $6,000 and we can't give you any money to buy yearlings. That's all, I'm sorry."

"Why," Fred questioned, "we made a profit of $40,000 last year?"

"We can't help it, Fred, money is tight," he replied.

That's all that was said and Fred stormed out of the building followed by the manager, but my very upset husband had no intention of sharing the time of day with the smooth talking 'official.'

"I can't stand how they are treating me. I'm going to write some letters that the Association won't forget!" By now, Fred was at least twelve feet ahead of me and already in the car while I ran behind, trying to catch up with him.

The following day the 'Master Letter Writer' was at his desk composing several volumes to people in all levels of government and to all the upper management of the Lending Agency. He took the rejection as a personal attack, especially after having been with the bank for over 14 years. If it wasn't a personal affront, then what was it?

We waited for an answer from the Association but none came. During this difficult time Fred finally decided that you catch more flies with honey than with vinegar. So, he planned his next trip to the CCA using his best manners and behavior. He asked the manager if anything had changed.

"No nothing. But please, no more letters. I found out you wrote a lot of them. So please," and he repeated again, "no more letters!"

Dejected, Fred left the office. He felt defeated. A week later we both returned to sign up for our measly $6,000. The future of our ranch hung in the balance.

With less money, we were forced to give up some of the rental pastures we had used in the past few years. We simply had no cattle to place there. It was a shame since they had been difficult to locate and they helped us grow and meet our goal of having 'a good sized spread.'

A year later we found out that the letter writing did indeed have an affect. The local CCA had been reprimanded for how they handled our loan. According to the President of the company, the loan committee should have at least given us money for 300 calves worth $60,000.

Unfortunately, it was too late for us. Our income from the yearling cattle operation, which had been our mainstay, was nil for that entire year. We were severely affected by the modern ranching motto: "You need money to make money." 🐎

Squeezed Into A Corner

We continued pressing on. In 1985, we purchased 1,541 yearlings, steers and heifers. The yearlings cost us between $516,000 and $517,000. We were able to re-rent the pastures that we had given up many years before. The summer was wet and the cattle grew fat and happy. We were working hard, seven days a week, and we anticipated a future while not overly prosperous, yet comfortable and satisfying.

What we didn't plan on were factors beyond our control. In an effort to help the dairy farmers, the United States Congress voted to buy out thousands of cows to reduce the milk production in the nation and increase profits. This caused the market to be flooded with cheap dairy meat. As a result, the price for beef cattle plummeted. Later, Ross Perot said, "The dairy buy out was one of the dumbest wastes of Federal money in history." This policy affected our very way of life.

In 1985, we lost $48,571. The only solution was to sell our entire herd that fall. Our fine line of Hereford cows headed to the market, taking our hearts with them.

We didn't know what to do. Eventually, we decided to lease our land to several different ranchers. We stayed in the house while other peoples' cattle enjoyed the lush grama grass over the rolling hills of our dear pastures.

The following winter brought more problems with Fred's heart. He was unable to shovel snow and do the many other strenuous activities required on a ranch. Actually, I believe that the bleak financial situation and his lack of activity combined to exacerbate his ill health. Now, depression became a frequent and unwelcome guest in our house making it difficult to regain the cheery disposition that had sustained us for years.

The thought of selling the ranch surfaced more and more frequently. Though our relationship with the CCA was back to being pleasant, our difficulty in borrowing the money we needed aggravated the situation. In the end, they won.

We decided to put our ranch up for sale. Our neighbors and friends were both shocked and surprised. They couldn't believe we were joining the ranks of so many family ranchers who suffered because of the banks and couldn't recover from their squeeze.

Still, it hurt. We loved ranching and knew we were good at it. All the hard work, long hours, and frugality were simply not enough.

We were introduced to a steady stream of Real Estate salesmen and women who brought out prospective buyers, most who turned out to be 'lookers.' Some wanted us to carry their loans, rather than a bank—not an idea we thought prudent! A few developers wanted to buy several small parcels. None of the deals were acceptable to us.

Finally, in 1987 we sold 2,900 acres and in 1988 we liquidated the remaining 800 acres of the Eis place. All of our equipment including the tractors, trucks, horse trailers, cattle chutes, and household goods were sold at a farm sale held on July 18, 1987. It brought in $8,432. Our gross income from the 3,700 acres was $482,000 and our debts to several lending agencies were $300,000. From the remaining $182,000, we had to pay $36,000 in

Federal and Colorado Income Tax.

For the first time in years we found ourselves completely out of debt. We didn't owe

A large crowd gives us support at the farm sale.

anyone a single dime and I must admit it was a good feeling! Slowly our state of constant tension lessened. Relief replaced uncertainty and we felt free for the first time in decades.

But we were sad to realize that we would be leaving the world of agriculture, a science that was dear to our hearts. We had studied it, applied it daily, and, I might add, even prospered by it. Suddenly, there was a vacuum.

We received down payments for several different parcels and thought that the closings would happen soon thereafter. But, once again, we were mistaken. It seemed to take forever to finalize each sale. The waiting was exasperating as we endured one postponement after another.

It was during those days that my outlook on life in general deteriorated. There were days when depression set in and it seemed like nothing went right. Fred had explained to me that each day the ranch sale was postponed we lost more money. I could see the 'Poorhouse' looming at the end of the road. It seemed as if the symphony of my world only played heavy music like that of Wagner while my psyche ached to hear strains by Mozart and Vivaldi.

One afternoon I felt so bad that I walked the mile to the cottonwood grove in the South pasture. I wanted to be alone, I didn't want to have Fred see me so depressed—he was upset enough. I sat under one of the huge trees and broke down. I could not stop crying. I did not hear the yellow Datsun pickup drive up. Nor did I see Fred jump out of it and run towards me. Suddenly, I felt his strong arms around me and I sobbed. After a while, I calmed down and Fred explained how he had been looking for me and figured I had gone to my favorite 'thinking place.'

My melt down released tension and I immediately began to feel better. I was amazed that I almost felt encouraged, even hopeful, that things would work out all right in the very near future.

Two weeks afterward, the entire sale was finalized. Much too soon, we had to give up possession of the ranch house and all the buildings. We made a quick trip to Colorado Springs to rent an apartment. There, we easily found one in a fairly new complex on Pikes Peak Avenue, across from Montgomery Ward and Doctor's Hospital.

Fred arranged to have our furniture moved and it was my turn, naturally, to clean the house. Susan, bless her heart, came from her home in Los Alamos, New Mexico, to help with the job, which took several hours. The gas stove and the oven shined like new, the cabinets glistened inside and out and the floors hadn't been this clean in a long time. We had done a good job and we hoped the unmarried, hired man of the new owner would appreciate our efforts, though we rather doubted it. The main thing, however, was that I felt good about myself and that we had made the right decision.

I was looking at the clean house and the gleaming white barns when suddenly, in a single moment, the reality 'hit me.' I thought of the many years we had lived in this house, of all the fun times along with only a few sad ones. I couldn't take my mind off the many good people we had come to know, depend on, and to love. There were all the many new things we learned and everything we had endured, all those many exciting experiences. What a wealth of memories!

Looking towards the out buildings, especially the barns, now empty and quiet, all were so cold and so very stark. They seemed more depressing to me than the empty house. My eyes did not search out the big garage, neither the chicken house, nor the milk barn, but they seemed to be glued to the corrals and the sheep pen. That was where I spent my fondest times.

I struggled for composure while tears streamed down my cheeks. Embarrassed, I tried to wipe them away, but to no avail. I cried because hard times had interfered with our plans and dreams. I cried for the gentle horses, my beautiful sheep, and all the dogs we so enjoyed. It all was no more.

I thought I had plenty of time to get used to the idea that this moment would come. I also thought I was too tough, but true feelings do show up regardless how hard you try to hide them. And so I allowed myself to wallow in self-pity for a few moments longer.

Just as storm clouds glide away over the horizon, soon my mood lightened and I suddenly realized my true fortune: We had four healthy and good-hearted children and I had a very devoted and relatively healthy, husband.

It was time to leave. There was one more labor of love that Susan and I wanted to do. We hopped into the car with Pookie in the lead and drove towards Peyton where Lew and Laura Eis lived. We parked in front of a big doublewide mobile home and were at once greeted by a friendly yellow puppy.

We had a wonderful rapport with Lew and Laura who both loved our children, especially Bonnie and Susan. The girls had spent time during summer vacation working in

Lew's office while they were in college.

But now, Lew was a very sick man. He sat in an armchair supported by several pillows. A tube delivering oxygen from a huge tank in the back room was attached to a green plastic hose draped across his nose. The life giving, life aiding, gas was supposed to help Lew breathe easier but it took quite an effort especially when he wanted to talk. He was thrilled to see us and gave Susan a warm hug. He always loved girls!! While I stood there he grinned at me and said, "Come here, kid, you deserve a hug, too, for having such beautiful daughters." And so I bent down to collect 'my' reward.

The thinness of his body shocked me. Lew was emaciated, his bones lining out their locations under his blue silk shirt. His breathing became somewhat labored and I realized he was talking too much, causing a strain on his system.

The three of us, Laura, Susan, and I stood there trying to find words of encouragement, when, for the second time within an hour, the tears came. And Lew, the usual brave soldier, broke down, too. We all knew that his days on earth were numbered. And as we said our good-byes, I honestly hoped that they would happen soon and be gentle.

Susan and I stumbled into the car and drove in silence to the new apartment in Colorado Springs.

We never saw Lew alive, again. He died in his sleep just three days after our visit, and he was buried in his hometown in Oklahoma, a dear friend had gone home for good. Laura gave us a painting that Lew had done of a rural scene, a constant reminder of someone we would always remember.

"Time marches on," a country-western artist sings about the fleeting years. At this moment it seemed to be directed towards me and me alone. Alas, thirty-six years of ranching were behind us and we were leaving a great lifestyle. What vivid memories we accumulated, good and bad. While our ranching experience ended on a pessimistic note, we still felt blessed that we were able to fulfill our hopes, at least, for a while. We were grateful. Yes, after all, we counted our blessings. Life was good. 🐎

VORENBERG RANCH AT AUCTION

SATURDAY — **JUNE 13, 1987** — 1:00 P.M.

CALHAN, COLORADO

3900±ACRE EL PASO COUNTY RANCH

TRACT 1

TRACT 23

29 Parcels . . . Will be offered in tracts-combinations-total. 40-acre ranchettes, 80s-160s & 320s-up. Mobile homes-O.K. Something for everyone! Excellent terms.

Auction Site & Headquarters . . . Colorado Springs Holiday Inn North at I25 & Fillmore (Exit 145).

Ranch Location . . . Calhan - go 6 Mi South, 2 East, 3 South on Calhan Highway and ½ East to Ranch Headquarters. From Ellicott - go 7 Mi East and 5 North. Presently "WORKING RANCH-DEVELOPMENT POTENTIAL!" Unlimited front range view; 17 miles NE of Space Center! 30 Mi to Colorado Springs-40 miles to Air Force Academy - 2 sets of improvements & 2½ Mi Calhan Hwy frontage - Minerals (purchaser will receive ½ of Vorenberg interest), currently leased to EXXON.

Terms . . . Cash OR 25% down and OWNER finance balance (15% earnest money payment required auction day), payments amortized over 10 years at 10% interest -monthly payments.

Note . . . All information is from sources deemed reliable, but not guaranteed. Prospective buyers are urged to inspect all properties PRIOR to auction date and satisfy themselves as to acreages, boundaries, roads, water, phone & electric lines, representation, etc. Purchaser will have to provide own water, septic systems, electric & phone service, road improvements — other than that which is now installed and in use. Property sells "where-is, as-is, subject to restrictions, reservations, easements, community contracts and zoning order, if any, now existing against said property. Acreages shall be considered approximate. All warranties are between buyer and seller. What you see is what you get! Come prepared to buy. All sales subject to owner confirmation. Announcements made auction day shall have precedence.

Showing . . . Anytime (Fred Vorenberg Phone 347-2580). Drive out!

Open House . . . Sunday, May 31 and June 7 at Ranch Headquarters (1 to 6 P.M.) Illness forces sale - after open heart surgery, and 2 recent heart attacks, Fred says "SELL"!

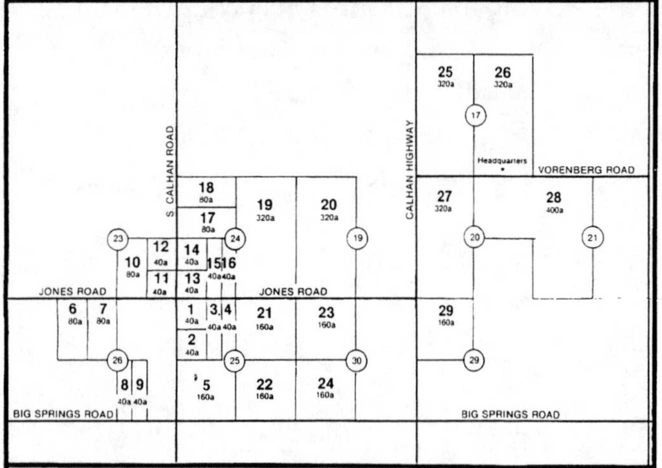

TRACT26

TRACT 28

Tract #1: 40 Acres, NW¼NW¼ of Sec. 25-T13S-R62W, pastureland, home, barns, corrals, well, Miami School District, El Paso telephone, electricity (garage may encroach upon Tract #3).

Tract #2: 40 Acres, SW¼NW¼ of Sec. 25-T13S-R62W, pastureland, Miami School District, El Paso telephone, electricity on road.

Tract #3: 40 Acres, W½E½NW¼ of Sec. 25-T13S-R62W, pastureland, Miami School District, El Paso telephone, electricity on road.

Tract #4: 40 Acres, E½E½NW¼ of Sec 25-T13S-R62W, pastureland, Miami School District, electricity, El Paso telephone 1/8 mile away.

Tract #5: 160 Acres, SW¼ of Sec 25-T13S-R62W, pastureland, Miami School District, El Paso telephone, electricity on road.

Tract #6: 80 Acres, W½NW¼ of Sec 26-T13S-R62W, pastureland, Miami School District, El Paso telephone, 1/10 Mi to electricity.

Tract #7: 80 Acres, E½NW¼ of Sec 26-T13S-R62W, pastureland, Miami School District, El Paso Telephone, 1/10 mi to electricity.

Tract #8: 40 Acres, W½W½SE¼ of Sec 26-T13S-R62W, pastureland, Miami School District, El Paso Telephone & electricity on road.

Tract #9: 40 Acres, E½W½SE¼ of Sec 26-T13S-R62W, pastureland, Miami School District, El Paso telephone & electricity on road.

Tract #10: 80 Acres, W½SE¼ of Sec 28-T13S-R62W, pastureland, well (plastic lining), Miami School Dist, El Paso Telephone & electricity on road.

Tract #11: 40 Acres, SE¼SE¼ of Sec 23-T13S-R62W, pastureland, pond, Miami School Dist, El Paso telephone & electricity on road.

Tract #12: 40 Acres, NE¼SE¼ of Sec. 23-T13S-R62W, pastureland, pond, Miami School District, El Paso telephone & electricity ¼ Mi. away.

Tract #13: 40 Acres, SW¼SW¼ of Sec 24-T13S-R62W, pastureland, tank & partial pond, Miami School Dist, El Paso telephone & electricity on road.

Tract #14: 40 Acres, NW¼SW¼ of Sec 24-T13S-R62W, pastureland, partial pond, Miami School District, El Paso telephone & electricity ¼ mile away.

Tract #15: 40 Acres, W½E½SW¼ of Sec 24-T13S-R62W, pastureland, Miami School District, El Paso Telephone & electricity on road.

Tract #16: 40 Acres, E½E½SW¼ of Sec 24-T13S-R62W, pastureland, Miami School District, El Paso Telephone, 1/8 Mi away, electricity on road.

Tract #17: 80 Acres, S½NW¼ of Sec 24-T13S-R62W, pastureland, well (plastic lining), Miami School District, El Paso telephone & electricity ½ Mi. away.

Tract #18: 80 Acres, N½NW¼ of Sec 24-T13S-R62W, pastureland, pond, Miami School District, El Paso telephone & electricity ¾ mile away.

Tract #19: 320 Acres, E½ Sec 24-T13S-R62W, pastureland, pond, Miami School District, El Paso Telephone ¼ Mi away, electricity on road.

Tract #20: 320 Acres, W½ Sec 19-T13S-R61W, pastureland (some subirrigated) 2 ponds-one with spring, well (plastic lining), terraced field planted to permanent grass, Miami School District, El Paso Telephone ¾ Mi away, electricity on road.

Tract #21: 160 Acres, NE¼ Sec 25-T13S-R62W, pastureland, well (430 ft-submersible pump-steel casing), tank shared with Tract #23, Miami School District, El Paso Telephone ¼ Mi away, electricity on road.

Tract #22: 160 Acres, SW¼ of Sec 25-T13S-R62W, pastureland, Miami School District, El Paso Telephone & electricity ½ Mi away.

Tract #23: 160 Acres, NW¼ Sec 30-T13S-R61W, pastureland, barns & corrals, pond, Miami School District, El Paso Telephone ¾ Mi away, electricity on road.

Tract #24: 160 Acres, SW¼ Sec 30-T13S-R61W, pastureland, Miami School District, El Paso Telephone & electricity ½ Mi away.

Tract #25: 320 Acres, W½ Sec 17-T13S-R61W, pastureland, well (600 ft-submersible pump), pond, Calhan School District, Calhan telephone & electricity on road.

Tract #26-Ranch Headquarters: 320 Acres, E½ Sec 17-T13S-R61W, pastureland, 3 bedroom home, 2-car garage w/shop, divided granary, hopper bottom bin, dairy barn, horse barn, loafing shed, corrals, sheep shed, chicken coup, 3 ponds, well (steel casing), 56 acre field planted to permanent grass, Calhan School District, Calhan Telephone & electricity.

Tract #27: 320 Acres, W½ Sec 20-T13S-R61W, pastureland, one tank shared w/Tract #28, 2 dams, Miami School District, El Paso Telephone & electricity on road.

Tract #28: 480 Acres, NE¼ of Sec 20 & W½ Sec 21-T13S-R61W, pastureland, 2 dams, shared tank with Tract #27, barn, corrals, 3 open sheds, 2 car garage, Miami School District, El Paso Telephone & electricity on road.

Tract #29: 160 Acres, NW¼ Sec 29-T13S-R61W, pastureland (seeded farm ground), 5 dams, well 800 ft (submersible-steel casing), Miami School District, El Paso Telephone ½ Mi away, electricity on road.

• EVERY TRACT HAS ROAD FRONTAGE! •

FRED & ELIZABETH VORENBERG - OWNERS

Odle Cumberlin
AUCTIONEERS
P.O. Box 248 Brush, Colorado 80723
(303) 842-2822

Performance Builds our Business

EVENINGS CALL:
SHANE WILSON AUCTIONEER
GRAND JUNCTION . . . 245-2205
C.E. CUMBERLIN
BRUSH 842-2302

PRE-SORTED FIRST CLASS PERMIT Brush, CO 80723 Permit No. 3

Pookie

My favorite little dog was like my shadow. Although we picked him up at the Humane Society and hoped to train him to be a housedog, he had other ideas. He loved to be outdoors. His heavy white and black coat kept him comfortable in the winter and insulated from the heat in the summer. Pookie would walk or wallow through the deepest puddle while all our collies would tiptoe around the muddy water being careful not to soil their white paws. Often I took Pookie to the pond in the south pasture. He would swim the full length of it, then turn around and swim back again. He also loved riding in the pickup propping his head on somebody's thigh. Nothing could move him until he was back home again.

But he was the best pal when I was sick with a migraine. I'd have to go to bed in a darkened room and Pookie then would always jump onto the bed, something he never did at any other time. If any of the other dogs wanted to only look into the bedroom that little rascal would growl and show his teeth. Those two other dogs, three times as large as my protector, immediately retreated, pretending that they never meant to enter the bedroom anyway!

Unfortunately, our apartment in Colorado Springs did not allow dogs. I was terribly upset but Susan offered to take him with her to New Mexico. Her dogs knew Pookie and they got along very well.

A week later Susan called, saying that she had to take my sweet dog to the veterinarian who diagnosed an advanced case of cancer. He was put to sleep. I felt sad and guilty that I couldn't have kept him with me for that one week. I had no idea he was so sick. Fortunately, I know dogs go to Heaven!

My favorite dog, Pookie.

Who liked to sled more—Pookie or me?

267

Chapter 13

RECOVERY

Back to City Life

It was 1987 and we had moved to one of Colorado's most beautiful cities, Colorado Springs. Our second floor apartment had two bedrooms, a small living room and a kitchen, hidden in back. The carpet was soft beige and the walls were painted off-white.

It was a quiet place with lawns and trees meandering throughout the complex. In one area was a small swimming pool. Everything was beautifully manicured.

We had decided to stay in the apartment until the sale of the ranch finally closed. Only then could we figure out where to retire. Meanwhile, this was a good area and we were pleased to have found it.

It had come full circle for me. I started out living in large cities and here I was again enjoying, or at least trying to enjoy, my return to city life. But something was different. Was it 'culture shock?' What was I missing? Though I am lucky because I can adapt easily to changes and new situations, now that I was 67 years old and Fred 65, we wondered what we wanted for the rest of our lives. Could we both be searching for a more sedate, peaceful existence? We wondered whether our adjustment would be difficult. Time would tell!

We needn't have worried. Having been active all our lives we soon became restless and began looking for employment. Fred found a job in a flower shop and in his free time, he learned to bake bread, usually whole wheat. He was so good at this new endeavor that most of our friends and family ordered theirs on a regular basis. Meanwhile, each week I worked three days in a Health Clinic and a couple volunteering at Doctor's Hospital across the street from our apartment complex.

Early that summer, we decided to search for a place in which to retire. Fred's doctor told us that a lower altitude and milder climate would be best for his health. But we also wanted good hospitals, a temple, a city where living expenses were moderate, and a place that had a good college. From our well-meaning family we received a couple of books on the topic and we began making a plan. Our preferences quickly became clear. We wanted to stay in the west and perhaps in the southwest. We compiled a list of several towns to visit, and off we went!

First we headed south from Colorado Springs on I-25 to Las Cruces, New Mexico. After a brief visit we decided to visit our friends, the Masons, who lived in El Paso, Texas. Lee and Fred both grew up in Meimbressen, Germany and had been life-long friends. Though they had visited us on the ranch twice, now it was our turn. Lee and his wife, Hilde, who hailed from Frankfurt, showed us El Paso and we liked what we saw. But we kept an open mind because there were a lot of other places to investigate.

Back in our Chevrolet Caprice we drove through Arizona and on to San Diego

California. We stopped briefly to visit my cousin, Manfred Kulp, to make a condolence call since his wife, Olly, had recently succumbed to a massive coronary.

Afterward, we had planned to stop in San Francisco to visit our relatives, but my brother, Max, was sick at the time so we by-passed the Bay Area. We continued, stopping only in places 'the book' had mentioned.

One of the towns that especially interested us was Chico, in Northern California. A college town in the moderate price range, at low altitude and supposedly, with good weather. As we arrived, we found a delightful, small town dotted with walnut and pecan groves, trees everywhere, clean streets and new homes sprouting in every direction, shown to us by an anxious real estate salesman who wanted to make a deal on the spot.

That same evening while we were having dinner at a Denny's restaurant, I started a conversation with a family seated next to us. "How do you like living in Chico?" I asked.

The mother took her attention off of her two unruly kids to answer, "I've lived here all my life and it's a nice town. But the winters are cold and very rainy, so if you've never had arthritis, this is where you get it!" Though I never told the lady my reason for asking the question, my years of living with arthritis immediately eliminated Chico. It was a most welcome piece of information.

After Fred left a negative message for 'Mr. Anxious Real Estate Man,' we were off driving towards Portland, Oregon, where Bonnie was directing senior citizens in a 'delightful play' that she wanted us to see. She was right—it was delightful!

We travelled next to Utah to see some of its beauty and we were rewarded with a $15 parking ticket received while we were going through a guided tour of the Mormon Temple in Salt Lake City. We took that hint as a message and immediately left for the breath-taking beauty of Canyonland and Arches. A day later, we were in the car heading back towards Colorado Springs.

As we drove home, it became clear that El Paso, Texas was the best place for us. It had everything we wanted in addition to the Masons, who became our best friends.

Immediately after finally closing the ranch sale, in November 1988, we set out for El Paso. In two days we arrived to sunshine and balmy weather instead of snowstorms. We rented a house and moved in with what we had brought along in the car. Thinking ahead, we had sleeping bags where we spent two restless nights awaiting our furniture. I never knew a floor could be so hard!

Just days after we arrived in El Paso, "Tex", a Schnauzer puppy became a family member. He learned fast and within a few months he had learned to not only do stupid tricks, but also to do smart and helpful ones, like bringing in the newspaper from outdoors, picking up articles I dropped, and almost anything else I tried to teach him. He continued to thrill us for the next 11 years.

El Paso was completely different from any other city I had ever lived in. The population of 650,000 was growing and was comprised of 75% Hispanic and 5% African Americans. The city, in the shape of a horseshoe, hugs the sides of the end of the Rocky

Tex, what a clever little dog!

Mountains in North America and the Rio Grande separates the U.S. from Juarez, Mexico. Like in Colorado Springs, we immediately got involved. We joined a Senior Center and took courses in Spanish and Bridge.

A year later, we bought a house and Fred got a job as a substitute teacher, specializing in math and bilingual education. I attended classes at the University of Texas at El Paso in a program especially for Senior Citizens and volunteered at the Alzheimer's Association office.

Our many neighbors are great and decent people, especially our friends, Roger and Delia Ingram. We spent many pleasant times and delicious meals together. Roger, tall and handsome, is a gifted man who is an accomplished pilot and flies his own Cessna 182. He has taken me flying often and even let me handle the controls as we zoomed across the Texas sky. Such a thrill for me! You feel "free as a bird and light as a feather," as the saying goes. How I envy those who have ready access to such a pleasurable diversion.

Though both Fred and I are very happy in El Paso, we miss the Colorado mountains and the spruce trees. But instead we find the surrounding desert beautiful and even, aesthetically pleasing. Fred's health — excuse me while I cross my fingers — has improved, now that we live in a much lower altitude and with much less stress. I praise our Colorado doctor for his advice.

Many years have passed since we left the world of ranching, yet our thoughts are never far away from those busy years. Almost every night Freds' dreams seem to overpower him. He leaps around in bed, occasionally crashing to the floor, while he yells out orders or tells his bed partner that a mean cow is after him and he is on his way to climb a fence. Obviously, this ex-rancher has never retired completely.

The walls in our house are covered with paintings done by my gifted brother, Martin, depicting ranch scenes and animals so lifelike, you almost feel as if you were back on the old homestead. Is it then a wonder why our thoughts so often travel north to our beloved Colorado?

A rancher is a person who has unlimited optimism, is fearless and courageous, is stubborn, takes unbelievable chances and appreciates life. He or she also complains, eats too much, and cusses. This is my Fred, my ex-rancher and my husband of many years, many colorful years!

Retirement, according to *The American College Dictionary* means, "withdrawal into privacy or seclusion." Our lives are nothing like that, possibly just the opposite. City life seems to agree with us. 🐄

Volunteering for the Alzheimer's Association.

Roger Ingram and myself with his Cessna 182.

Chapter 14

Reflections

n The Running Of A Ranch

n Colorado State University in Fort Collins in 1948 we were
es and dreams were to own and operate a good sized spread,
ful state of Colorado. We were determined to reach our goals.
ed a lot at his Uncle Herman's ranch and from the four years he
y studying Animal Husbandry.

t perception was! Very soon we learned that MONEY is the most
d money—we didn't have. You need money for the land, money for
nery, tools and you certainly need money to live on.

follow our dream, Fred got an income from a teaching job. A banker who
had fa. us loaned us the money and we were fortunate to find a very primitive and
stark looking ranch. We didn't mind. Occasionally, Uncle Herman loaned or even gave us
financial help and once he gave us a badly needed car. How we appreciated that!

We were always extremely careful about how and where we spent our money. The only
place we did not scrimp was on the grocery bill. We always ate well.

Our independence and willingness to learn new things helped us scrape by. I cut Fred's
hair and he gave me kinky Toni Home Permanents. I knitted sweaters and socks, and
sewed simple clothing. I also did my most distasteful task, mending all the holes and tears
in everyone's jeans! Our garden provided us with all sorts of vegetables and Fred helped
me with canning and a lot of other tasks so we could save money.

A lot of our operation was done by hand rather than by machine. This included
milking cows and sacking feed.

We also learned a lot about veterinary work and did most of it ourselves including
delivering calves, giving medication, and diagnosing illnesses. We administered calcium
gluconate to cows with milk fever and watched them come out of a completely debilitated
state to a bright-eyed and healthy animal in minutes. We lanced 'lumpy jaws,' applied
casts to broken legs, and did the usual things like branding, castrating, dehorning, and
treating scours. Only occasionally did we call the vet or take animals to his hospital for
bladder stones, caesarian births, cancer of the eye, or other severe problems.

Our lives were quite similar to many of our neighbors who would drop what they
were doing to help a person in need. It wasn't only branding season when you would
enjoy a party-like attitude with everybody doing their thing. Many times were considered
social events where people had more fun than a mosquito in a blood bank! The women
always cooked for hours and fed the hungry ranchers meals fit for a king. They say, "One

hand washes the other." This is certainly true in any ranching community and ours was no exception. It was the best.

Being a ranch family brings with it obligations to the community including volunteering, running for office, and the hardest one, asking for contributions for worthy causes. Fred did well in the volunteering department. He was on the Fair Board for 20 years; on the Farm Bureau for 5 and he helped with the Fair Queen Contest. He also was a charter member of the Calhan Co-op and in charge of the Agricultural Department at the County Fair. He was elected to the School Board and served for 18 years.

I organized and then volunteered at an Adult & Baby Clinic that I set up in Calhan, judged speech contests and grew to love the country women who joined me in the Help Thy Neighbor Club. Our monthly meetings taught me how to do quilting and other crafts. But most importantly, it was a way for the neighborhood women to share our common experiences.

One time I was asked to collect money for a charity. After knocking on the door of a two-story house, a woman came out and greeted me as if she knew me. Perhaps she did, I don't remember faces too well. I looked at her and started to laugh because she reminded me of what I had read in "The Egg & I" years ago, "White breasts bobbing like dumplings in a hot stew." Suddenly I was embarrassed to look her in the face though she was pretty and had a lovely smile and fiery red cheeks. I didn't get a donation and I hurried back to my car as fast as I could. I was not good at this and I decided that for me, raising money was like raising the Titanic with tweezers!

Fred convinced us that we were a team. But when I offered advice on how to make things run more efficiently, Fred never received it well, misinterpreting my intentions. Years passed before he would finally listen to me, admitting that my ideas made sense to him. I was not always right but it bothered me when he answered my suggestions with, "Uncle Herman always did it this way" or "I've always done it that way." I considered it a major victory when, as Frank Sinatra sang: "I did it my way." Or how I would sing it, "He did it my way!"

Profits in the ranching business are never guaranteed no matter how diligently you manage your place. Success depends on so many factors. But most ranchers have a determined sense of stubbornness and optimism. They always think, "Next year will be better"

Fred deserves a lot of credit for having accomplished so much. Not only was he torn away from his family during the madness of the Nazi years, but at 14 he entered a new country with an extremely limited amount of English. When it came to physical things, nobody was more thorough than Fred. He welded, roped and doctored livestock exactly by the book—and he is honest. Fred couldn't tell a lie if he was forced to. After all these years, I have yet to catch him even in a 'little white' lie. Most importantly, he has a strong drive to be successful. He sought advice from many people and read every periodical and textbook he could find on a topic of concern. He is quite a guy even though he never fulfilled all of my husband pre-requisites: the appreciation for classical music, love of dogs, and beautiful penmanship. Happily, in our retirement, he finally has clean fingernails!

I often am reminded of my Colorado ranching years when I would leave my warm and cozy bed and it was still dark outside and the temperatures were just above freezing. After a cup of hot coffee, daylight replaced the gloomy darkness. Chunks of fog drifted aimlessly hiding the red barn that stood only 100 feet from the house. Minutes later the building reappeared while the breezes dictated the fog's next route. Suddenly glorious sunshine burst through the kitchen window igniting every corner in the house. The dark blue sky, accentuated by white lacework of thin clouds, came alive, illuminating all of our many animals.

My happiest times.

The mind is a wonderful gift. It must be constantly nurtured, encouraged and inspired even if it is only by something as insignificant as a ray of sunshine and a blue sky with white lacy clouds. Ranching taught me this and so much more.

Afterword

$\mathbb{F}$red and I returned to the ranch ten years after we left to rekindle our love for the place where so many memories were created. As we were nearing the Jones Road and the Old Place, newly built houses and many trailers and modular homes appeared everywhere. There was no livestock except an occasional horse standing by a crudely built shed. The same picture continued along the mile long stretch of Calhan Highway and up Vorenberg Road. Subdivisions had taken over completely. We were told that now roughly 50 families live in the space where our one family of six had raised hundreds of cattle. It was an extremely depressing sight—roadkill beneath the wheels of progress!

But what greeted us next was a most devastating experience. The house we loved was gone. According to its new owner, whom we met just down the road, the place had been torched just two weeks prior to our visit. There were our memories, lying in ashes covered by blackened cinder blocks and partially burned timbers.

I bent down to pick up an object about 3" x 4", hoping to touch something familiar. It turned out to be just a jagged chunk of burned wood that I immediately returned to its black grave. I stared at my now empty and dirty hand when a wave of intense sadness

The remains.

slowly crept over me like a wet blanket. I thought of how we sold the cattle, then the ranch, and how it was such a comfortable and happy home. And now, everything was gone. This indeed was the last straw! My body started to shake—and I cried.

...but not for long. I soon realized that the pain and distress I felt caused by a fire of a former home was not enough to destroy or daunt my inner peace. Life had been good and had given me strength when I needed it.

The body of work, the success we encountered during our ranch years was the catalyst responsible in building a solid foundation and in no time, my confidence returned. Sometimes it takes a lifetime to form character, to form the kind of attitude one has admired in others—and as I smiled a butterfly with wings like stained glass windows flitted by.

It reminded me of my early childhood in Germany and how my father explained the metamorphosis of what he called "the perfect insect" and how because of their brief lifetime, they could only rest a short time with each flower. Butterflies have to make each moment count. Since that day, I have felt a kinship with that lovely creature. Likewise, I also thrived by trying to live fully and by continually striving for excellence. I relished the many experiences that carried me from one situation to another—always learning new things, always buoyed by a sense of wonder, and always amazed at the strength of rebounding optimism.

ORDER FORM

A CALF IN THE KITCHEN: Echoes from a Ranch Women

Yes! Please send me _____ copy(ies) of *A Calf in the Kitchen: Echoes from a Ranch Woman* for $20.00 each plus $5.00 shipping and handling. I understand it will take 2 to 4 weeks for delivery.

Name: _____

Address: _____

City: _____ State: _____ Zip: _____

Phone: _____ Email: _____

Pay with Visa ___ or MC ___ Card No.: _____ Expiration Date: _____

Signature: _____

Please send checks or money order payable in U.S. dollars only. Mail to:
ArtAge Publications, P.O. Box 12271, Portland, Oregon 97212-0271.
Phone: (503) 249-1137 (800) 858-4998

Thank you for your order.

ORDER FORM

A CALF IN THE KITCHEN: Echoes from a Ranch Women

Yes! Please send me _____ copy(ies) of *A Calf in the Kitchen: Echoes from a Ranch Woman* for $20.00 each plus $5.00 shipping and handling. I understand it will take 2 to 4 weeks for delivery.

Name: _____

Address: _____

City: _____ State: _____ Zip: _____

Phone: _____ Email: _____

Pay with Visa ___ or MC ___ Card No.: _____ Expiration Date: _____

Signature: _____

Please send checks or money order payable in U.S. dollars only. Mail to:
ArtAge Publications, P.O. Box 12271, Portland, Oregon 97212-0271.
Phone: (503) 249-1137 (800) 858-4998

Thank you for your order.

15 food garden
19 chicks
23 calf feed
24 oatmeal for scone
27 cold water
29 items on a ranch
33 milking cows
34 good grass
47 Heifer calf
51 Dry Kelly
52 Kelly a cow
59 Milk to chicks
62 Vegetable
63 planting trees
71 Cacti
72 general auction
74 Description of a man
76 weaning calves
80 Law of the Ranch
88 Guse
100 Canned food
272 Rancher
139 Cattle prices
144 Calf puller
156 Root cellar
157 Windmill pump
167 Turkey
170 Baby sheep
188 Cattle auction
192 Breakfast a day from chicks chicken
223 springer cow
275 treaty animals
276 community duties